# TRANSFORMING THE LATIN AMERICAN AUTOMOBILE INDUSTRY

# Perspectives on Latin America and the Caribbean

**THE CHAINS OF INTERDEPENDENCE**
U.S. POLICY TOWARD CENTRAL AMERICA, 1945–1954
*Michael L. Krenn*

**A HOLY ALLIANCE?**
THE CHURCH AND THE LEFT IN COSTA RICA, 1934–1948
*Eugene D. Miller*

**QUISQUEYA LA BELLA**
THE DOMINICAN REPUBLIC IN HISTORICAL AND
CULTURAL PERSPECTIVE
*Alan Cambeira*

**BRAZILIAN LEGACIES**
*Robert M. Levine*

**THE HAUNTING PAST**
POLITICS, ECONOMICS AND RACE IN CARIBBEAN LIFE
*Alvin O. Thompson*

**TRANSFORMING THE LATIN AMERICAN AUTOMOBILE INDUSTRY**
UNIONS, WORKERS, AND THE POLITICS OF RESTRUCTURING
*Edited by John P. Tuman and John T. Morris*

**PUERTO RICAN WOMEN'S HISTORY**
NEW PERSPECTIVES
*Edited by Félix V. Matos Rodríguez and Linda C. Delgado*

# TRANSFORMING THE LATIN AMERICAN AUTOMOBILE INDUSTRY

## UNIONS, WORKERS, AND THE POLITICS OF RESTRUCTURING

Editors | John P. Tuman and John T. Morris

### M.E. Sharpe
Armonk, New York
London, England

**Library of Congress Cataloging-in-Publication Data**

Transforming the Latin American automobile industry : unions, workers, and the politics
of restructuring / John P. Tuman and John T. Morris [editors].
p. cm. — (Perspectives on Latin America and the Caribbean)
Includes bibliographical references (p. ) and indexes.
ISBN 0–7656–0199–0 (hardcover : alk. paper)
1. Automobile industry and trade—Latin America.  2. Trade unions—Automobile
industry workers—Latin America.  3. Automobile industry workers—Latin America.
4. Industrial relations—Latin America.
I. Tuman, John Peter, 1964–  .  II. Morris, John T., 1961–  .
III. Series.
HD9710.L32T7 1998
338.4'76292'098—dc21
97–30598
CIP

Printed in the United States of America

The paper used in this publication meets the minimum requirements of
American National Standard for Information Sciences—
Permanence of Paper for Printed Library Materials,
ANSI Z 39.48-1984.

MV (c)   10   9   8   7   6   5   4   3   2   1

# Contents

# List of Tables

# Acknowledgments

This project would never have been completed without the assistance and support of many colleagues and friends. We would like to begin by acknowledging the financial support for the translations given by the Office of the Provost, Texas Tech University; the Center for Latin American and Iberian Studies, Texas Tech University; and the Department of Political Science, Texas Tech University. We also thank John Burns (Provost, Texas Tech), Philip Dennis (Director, Center for Latin American and Iberian Studies), and Nelson Dometrius (Chair, Political Science) for helping us to secure funding for the translations.

Several organizations provided us with financial assistance for field research in Mexico. John Tuman's work was supported by a fellowship from the Center for International Business and Education Research (CIBER), UCLA, and a research travel grant from the University of California Institute for Mexico and the United States (UC MEXUS). John Morris received a grant from the University of Connecticut's Teaching Foundation, and a fellowship from the Center for the Comparative Study of Development, Watson Institute, Brown University. While we were completing our field research, we also benefited from the help and advice given us by workers, union leaders, and company and government officials; unfortunately, the names of these individuals must remain confidential.

We are also grateful to Stephen Dalphin, executive editor at M.E. Sharpe, for helping to bring this project to fruition, and to Esther Clark for assistance in preparation and production of the manuscript. In addition, Jorge Bracero provided expert research assistance.

Finally, we thank Danielle Roth-Johnson, Elizabeth McQuerry, and Greg Greenway for reading drafts of the manuscript, and for their patience, good humor, and emotional support.

# TRANSFORMING THE LATIN AMERICAN AUTOMOBILE INDUSTRY

John P. Tuman and John T. Morris

# 1 | The Transformation of the Latin American Automobile Industry

## Introduction

In the early 1980s, many analysts remained optimistic about the possibilities for growth in the Latin American automobile industry. Producing more than one million vehicles in 1980, Brazil became the eighth-largest automobile manufacturer in the world. In that same year, Mexico manufactured more than 500,000 cars and trucks, establishing new records in production and domestic sales; Argentina posted strong gains in sales as well. Against the backdrop of market saturation in Western Europe and the United States, Latin America appeared to be emerging as a large, dynamic market for automobiles.

The emergence of the debt crisis in 1982, however, dramatically altered the course of growth and development in the industry. The spread of the crisis generated a severe recession throughout Latin America, causing sales and production of finished vehicles to plunge to very low levels. The implementation of governmental austerity measures in the wake of the debt crisis only served to reinforce the stagnation of the industry. Faced with recession and uncertainty about the future, transnational firms responded by imposing layoffs, wage restraint, and other policies designed to reduce costs and boost productivity. By the close of the decade, however, companies in selected countries were increasingly shifting toward production for export markets, a project that enjoyed strong support from their host governments, the IMF, and the World Bank. More recently, governments throughout Latin America have liberalized trade in automobiles and parts, reshaping the industry in the process.

The trend toward restructuring and export promotion has produced significant challenges for workers in the Latin American automobile industry. Layoffs and reductions in real wages and benefits have threatened the traditionally privileged position of many automobile workers. Beyond this, however, workers have been confronted with demands for sweeping changes in the preexisting framework of industrial and labor relations. Company managers have argued that quality standards and productivity must be increased to globally competitive levels in order to meet the challenges posed by liberalization. As a result, firms and state elites have sought reforms in labor laws and work rules that would permit the introduction of team concepts, pay-by-knowledge compensation, and other practices associated with the Japanese, or "lean," model of production.[1] Nevertheless, since flexible production systems have directly challenged the power of unions to mediate conflicts and power relationships on the shopfloor, workers and union leaders have faced difficult choices about how to respond to these changes. In some cases, unions have attempted to adapt, create a new role for themselves, and negotiate concessions in exchange for restructuring. In other cases, however, unions and workers have resisted change and sought to preserve work rules and gains made during previous periods of development.

This book focuses on the transformation of the Latin American automobile industry. It discusses the factors compelling firms to introduce reforms and export production in the sector, and it explores the variation in responses that unions and workers have adopted to such changes. The case studies were drawn from Argentina, Brazil, Colombia, Mexico, and Venezuela. These countries were selected because of the size of their automobile industries, and because of their potential to illustrate meaningful contrasts in workers' responses to liberalization and industrial restructuring. The overall goal of the project is to assess recent changes in the industry, and to do so in a way that facilitates comparisons with other sectors that are experiencing industrial transformations.

The transformation of the Latin American automobile industry has important public policy implications for the region's new democracies and liberalizing regimes. Given the size of the industry and its links to other sectors, the performance of the automobile industry often affects industrial employment and growth in the manufacturing sector as a whole (Arbix 1995, 141; Novick and Catalano, this volume; Table 1.1). Moreover, there are strong reasons to suppose that the types of strategies that unions and workers have adopted in response to restructuring have affected the performance of the industry. Indeed, an emerging body of literature has suggested that the degree of union resistance or accommodation to restructuring partially influences the overall success (or failure) of economic reform efforts, both in the automobile industry and in other sectors (Nelson 1992, 245–49; Humphrey 1992, 328–9; Tuman 1994a; Towers 1996, 5).

Table 1.1

**Economic Impact of the Automobile Industry in National Economies: 1980s and 1990s**

|  | Industrial Employment (%) | Industrial Investment (%) | Balance of Trade (%) | Industrial Robots (%) |
|---|---|---|---|---|
| France | 9.6 | 8.1 | n.a. | 50 |
| Germany | 11.0 | 16.0 | n.a. | n.a. |
| Italy | n.a. | n.a. | n.a. | 63 |
| Sweden | 7.8* | n.a. | n.a. | 30 |
| United Kingdom | 5.0 | 9.2 | n.a. | 40 |
| Japan | 7.0 | 25.0 | 50 (of surplus) | 26 |
| United States | 3.6** | n.a. | 30 (of deficit) | n.a. |
| Mexico | 7.3*** | n.a. | n.a. | n.a. |

*Estimated using OECD total employment figures for 1994, with data provided by Ruigkrok et al. (1991).

**Estimated using 1994 sectoral data from the American Automobile Manufacturer's Association, *Motor Vehicle Facts and Figures, 1996*, and OECD figures for 1994.

***Data for Mexico are preliminary figures for 1993, and were obtained in INEGI, *La Industria Automotriz en México, Edición 1995.*

While analysts have recognized the importance of the changes occurring in the Latin American automobile industry, most studies have not explored the roles of workers in the processes of adjustment and restructuring (e.g., Lee and Cason 1994). Indeed, the last surveys of labor in the Latin American automobile industry were completed in the mid-1980s, prior to the reforms that transformed the industry's structure and its systems of labor relations (Kronish and Mericle 1984a; Jenkins 1987). Moreover, much of the recent literature has tended to focus only on single cases, neglecting the contrasts in development outcomes across different Latin American countries (Mortimore 1995; Deyo 1996). As one step in filling this gap in the literature, this volume includes several comparative studies of labor in the Latin American automobile industry, with a focus on the period of 1980 to 1995.

In the remaining sections of this chapter, we provide an overview of changes in the Latin American automobile industry. The chapter begins with a discussion of the development of the industry during the period of import-substitution industrialization (hereafter, ISI), and then analyzes the trend toward restructuring. We then compare selected countries in Latin America to one another, and the industry in Latin America to other regions in the world, exploring the contrasts in patterns of investment, production, and compensation. The final section provides a brief summary of the findings of the country-studies, and attempts to connect those findings with some of the current themes in the literature of comparative industrial relations and political economy.

## Historical Overview

The Latin American automobile industry has gone through three clear phases of development and performance since the 1920s: (1) import-substitution industrialization (ISI, 1930–1960); (2) a transitional phase that sought to deepen industrialization while maintaining the protectionist policies characteristic of ISI (1960–1982); and (3) economic crisis and liberalization after 1982. In what follows, we briefly analyze the main tendencies in each of these periods, giving particular emphasis to the structure of the industry and its systems of labor relations.

### *The Early and Mature Phases of ISI*

Transnational automobile firms entered the Latin American market in the beginning of the twentieth century. At first, most companies exported finished vehicles to countries exhibiting strong market potential. However, by the late 1920s, changes in trade and industrial policies in Latin America quickly forced the major producers to establish assembly operations throughout the region.[2]

Automobile production was initiated in Argentina, Brazil, and Mexico between 1916 and 1935, when the major firms, based primarily in the United States, starting exporting completely knocked-down kits (CKDs) for assembly by domestic workers. Ford began operations in Latin American prior to its competitors, establishing assembly facilities in Argentina in 1916, Brazil in 1924, and in Mexico in 1925 (Meza 1984, 25; Jenkins 1987, 18). By the 1930s, General Motors had initiated production in Mexico City and other areas as well. In large part, the decision to import "kits" for assembly had been prompted by new tariffs that made domestically assembled vehicles far cheaper than imported ones (Jenkins 1987, 19). However, since most Latin American countries lacked the technology and infrastructure required to produce automobile parts, firms found it necessary to import kits for assembly instead of manufacturing vehicles in these countries. Throughout much of the early phase of ISI, the initiation of assembly generated a modest growth in industrial employment, but failed to stimulate the development of a domestic automobile parts sector. Indeed, between 1940 and 1947, a high percentage of spare parts and materials used in assembly continued to be imported from abroad (Jenkins 1977; Hinojosa-Ojeda and Morales 1992, 403–4).

The second period (1960–1982) was characterized by governmental efforts to "deepen" the ISI model throughout the region. A much smaller number of transnational producers emerged in the post–World War II era, and competition in foreign markets intensified among the American and European producers. At the same time, state regulators moved to impose new trade and industrial policies on the sector as a result of ongoing concerns regarding the absence of a domestic parts industry and chronic balance-of-payments problems (generated by automo-

tive parts imports). In many cases, these regulations created domestic parts industries by imposing restrictions on imported inputs, and by implementing domestic content requirements and new investment rules (Bennett and Sharpe
1985, 94–6, 129–51; Jenkins 1987, 22–3; Shapiro 1991, 878–89).

The basic framework of labor relations was also consolidated in the automobile industry during this period. Transnational firms operating in Latin American
introduced industrial relations systems that partly conformed to the norms established in advanced countries. Often termed "Taylor-Fordism" (or "peripheral-
Fordism"), this system was characterized by highly elaborated systems of job
and skill hierarchies, combined with multiple categories and grades, a strict
respect for seniority, and relatively high wages (Lipietz 1987, 70–9; Jenkins
1987, 78–9; Jessop 1990). In the context of the Latin American, however, Fordism aimed at securing the discipline of workers, and was not, strictly speaking,
linked to productivity growth. In Argentina, Brazil, and Mexico, Fordist systems
were implemented and reproduced through the medium of state-corporatist[3]
unions that had direct ties to a hegemonic political party or the state bureaucracy.

For a variety of different reasons, governments were confronted with the
exhaustion of the ISI model by the beginning of the 1970s. In the first place, the
perpetuation of income inequality throughout Latin America limited domestic
demand for automobiles. In addition, the combination of many producers, and
the proliferation of large numbers of product lines, limited the potential growth
of the industry. As a result, most producers were unable to achieve economies of
scale (Kronish and Mericle 1984b, 276–7). These problems were compounded
by the continuation of balance-of-payments problems generated by automotive
imports. In response, transnational producers began to pressure policy makers for
greater market access and for reduced trade restrictions on capital goods and
parts imports. However, national components manufacturers—which had been
nurtured (and even created and owned) by national governments—opposed these
measures. In Mexico, the compromises reached in the 1970s specified that capital goods imports could be increased, but that their value had to be offset in
exports of vehicles. Restrictions on the number of models were eliminated, but
domestic content requirements were maintained (Bennett and Sharpe 1985).[4]

Latin American countries generally resolved the dilemmas posed by ISI by
borrowing abroad, particularly after 1973, when international banks sought out-
lets for the massive deposits of petro-dollars made by oil-producing countries
(Frieden 1991). Nevertheless, by resorting to more debt, policy makers only
postponed difficult choices involving the resolution of the structural problems of
the ISI model. After a decade of accelerated borrowing, rising international
interest rates, combined with a fall in world oil and commodity prices, undermined the capacity of Mexico (and several other heavily indebted countries) to
meet their debt service obligations. Mexico informed its lenders in New York in
August 1982 that it would not be able to pay interest on its debt. This caused
panic throughout the financial sector as it became evident that other regional

borrowers, like Argentina, Brazil, and Peru, were in similar danger. The response by private financial institutions of temporarily denying further lending plunged the region into crisis and initiated the so-called década perdida (lost decade). Faced with the complete collapse of a long-standing model of growth, with little hope for restoration, Latin American countries abandoned state-led development and ISI, and began the process of structural adjustment and economic liberalization.

### The Impact of the Debt Crisis

In the aftermath of the debt crisis, the cessation of lending and the introduction of austerity measures provoked a strong recession throughout Latin America. As a result, sales and production of automobiles fell in Argentina, Brazil, Mexico, and several other countries. Despite some improvements by mid-decade, production in Brazil and Argentina contracted by 5.5 and 28 percent, respectively, between 1985 and 1990. Mexico was one of the few cases to post gains in this period. In any case, growth in the region was restored definitively only in the early 1990s (see Table 1.2).

As noted previously, changes in domestic market conditions in the 1980s forced transnational firms to take drastic measures to shore up the profitability and competitiveness of the industry. Some firms reconsidered their participation in the region. For example, by 1986 Renault had decided to stop producing automobiles in Mexico, and also to reorganize its operations throughout Latin America. However, most of the other companies—including Chrysler, Ford, General Motors, Nissan, and Volkswagen—responded to the crisis by introducing a variety of different restructuring measures. For the most part, these policies involved reducing employment and growth in wages and benefits; introducing changes in the labor process to boost productivity and product quality; relocating production to new greenfield sites; selectively adopting just-in-time (JIT) production methods to reduce shipping costs and inventory; and, in some cases, the introduction of export production.

By the decade's end, the emerging consensus around neoliberalism in Latin America led to the elimination of many of the trade and investment rules associated with ISI. Most governments privatized state owned vehicle and parts companies and abandoned investment laws that promoted domestic ownership in the sector. During this period, governments also embraced trade liberalization, lifting tariffs and quantitative restrictions on imported vehicles and automobile parts. In the aftermath of liberalization, many transnational producers in the terminal sector began importing parts from abroad, often with devastating effects for domestically owned parts producers. In addition, imports of new vehicles stimulated intense competition for market share in certain Latin American countries. The formation of new regional trade blocs (e.g., NAFTA and MERCOSUR) during the 1990s has also given transnational firms even greater

Table 1.2

## Latin American Automobile Production by Country, 1985–1994

| | 1985 | 1986 | 1987 | 1988 | 1989 | 1990 | 1991 | 1992 | 1993 | 1994 |
|---|---|---|---|---|---|---|---|---|---|---|
| *Thousands of Units* | | | | | | | | | | |
| **Latin America** | **1,736** | **1,772** | **1,695** | **1,938** | **1,884** | **1,942** | **2,221** | **2,578** | **3,004** | **3,279** |
| Argentina | 138 | 170 | 193 | 164 | 128 | 99 | 139 | 262 | 342 | 409 |
| Brazil | 967 | 1,056 | 920 | 164 | 1,013 | 914 | 960 | 1,074 | 1,391 | 1,581 |
| Chile* | 8 | 5 | 7 | 10 | 16 | 11 | 13 | 18 | 21 | 20 |
| Colombia* | 39 | 44 | 52 | 61 | 54 | 49 | 44 | 50 | 75 | 74 |
| Mexico | 459 | 341 | 395 | 513 | 641 | 821 | 989 | 1,081 | 1,081 | 1,122 |
| Peru* | 9 | 13 | 13 | 7 | 4 | 4 | 2 | 1 | 1 | 1 |
| Venezuela* | 116 | 144 | 115 | 114 | 28 | 43 | 74 | 92 | 93 | 72 |
| *Percentage of Regional Total* | | | | | | | | | | |
| **Latin America** | **1.00** | **1.00** | **1.00** | **1.00** | **1.00** | **1.00** | **1.00** | **1.00** | **1.00** | **1.00** |
| Argentina | 0.08 | 0.10 | 0.11 | 0.08 | 0.07 | 0.05 | 0.06 | 0.10 | 0.11 | 0.12 |
| Brazil | 0.56 | 0.60 | 0.54 | 0.55 | 0.54 | 0.47 | 0.43 | 0.42 | 0.46 | 0.48 |
| Chile | 0.00 | 0.00 | 0.00 | 0.01 | 0.01 | 0.01 | 0.01 | 0.01 | 0.01 | 0.01 |
| Colombia | 0.02 | 0.02 | 0.03 | 0.03 | 0.03 | 0.03 | 0.02 | 0.02 | 0.03 | 0.02 |
| Mexico | 0.26 | 0.19 | 0.23 | 0.26 | 0.34 | 0.42 | 0.45 | 0.42 | 0.36 | 0.34 |
| Peru | 0.01 | 0.01 | 0.01 | 0.00 | 0.00 | 0.00 | 0.00 | 0.00 | 0.00 | 0.00 |
| Venezuela | 0.07 | 0.08 | 0.07 | 0.06 | 0.01 | 0.02 | 0.03 | 0.04 | 0.03 | 0.02 |

*Assembly only.
Source: American Automobile Manufacturers Association, *World Motor Vehicle Data*, 1995.

flexibility in deciding where to produce certain product lines, and in what quantity. Collectively, these changes in trade, industrial, and labor policy represent a complete break with the ISI model, and have initiated a new phase of development and transformation in the Latin American automobile industry.

## The Transformation of the Latin American Automobile Industry: Regional and International Comparisons

### Production and Export Promotion

The economic recovery in the early part of the 1990s has had a favorable impact on the industry. Production in the region as a whole grew by approximately 48 percent between 1991 and 1994. The regional leaders posted strong gains as well. In Mexico and Brazil, the cumulative change in production between 1991 and 1994 was 13.5 and 65 percent, respectively. In absolute terms, both countries began producing more than one million units annually, establishing new production records. In Argentina, production grew by 194 percent during the same period, although the absolute number of vehicles produced was far smaller than in Mexico or Brazil (see Table 1.2). By 1994, 7 percent of the world's finished vehicles were produced in Latin America, with Brazil and Mexico ranking as the world's ninth and thirteenth largest producers, respectively (see Table 1.3; Shapiro 1996, 33).

The efforts to promote export production throughout the region have not, however, been uniformly successful. While the growth in investment has led to an increase in the volume of production, it would appear that most production has continued to be aimed at domestic markets, and only secondarily at other markets of the region. This is not an insignificant point, since many national policy makers throughout Latin America view exports as central to their plans for economic development.

Thus in Brazil, for example, total exports of finished vehicles actually fell by 10 percent between 1985 and 1990, with an average of 25 percent of production being exported. Although vehicle exports from Brazil increased 95.5 percent between 1991 and 1994, exports continued to represent an average of only 25 percent of production (Table 1.4). Vehicle exports from Argentina increased by 45.5 percent between 1985 and 1990, although they represented an average of less than one percent of total production. Moreover, the data in Table 1.4 show that the absolute number of exports from Argentina remained at very low levels during this period. Despite strong growth in Argentine car and truck exports between 1991 and 1994, exports have increased to an average of only 7 percent of production.

Mexico has had the best performance in export production. Mexico's exports of automobiles are greater in absolute terms, and far greater as a proportion of production, than any country of the region. Exports grew by 374 percent between

Table 1.3

**World Automobile Production by Region, 1985–1994**

|  | 1985 | 1986 | 1987 | 1988 | 1989 | 1990 | 1991 | 1992 | 1993 | 1994 |
|---|---|---|---|---|---|---|---|---|---|---|
| *Thousands of Units* | | | | | | | | | | |
| **World** | 44,909 | 45,410 | 46,042 | 48,359 | 49,248 | 48,554 | 43,928 | 48,088 | 46,785 | 49,440 |
| | | | | | | | | | | |
| **Sum** | **43,577** | **44,110** | **44,498** | **46,513** | **47,707** | **47,725** | **46,694** | **47,821** | **46,358** | **49,209** |
| U.S. and Canada | 13,586 | 13,189 | 12,560 | 13,136 | 12,876 | 11,704 | 10,699 | 11,690 | 13,145 | 14,585 |
| Western Europe* | 12,242 | 12,904 | 13,646 | 14,340 | 15,310 | 15,067 | 14,534 | 14,814 | 12,278 | 13,884 |
| Eastern Bloc | 2,728 | 2,753 | 2,757 | 2,695 | 2,647 | 3,007 | 2,682 | 2,183 | 2,118 | 1,667 |
| Asia | 12,880 | 13,101 | 13,517 | 14,066 | 14,635 | 15,592 | 16,225 | 16,260 | 15,512 | 15,456 |
| Oceania | 405 | 391 | 323 | 338 | 355 | 413 | 333 | 296 | 301 | 338 |
| Latin America | 1,736 | 1,772 | 1,695 | 1,938 | 1,884 | 1,942 | 2,221 | 2,578 | 3,004 | 3,279 |
| | | | | | | | | | | |
| *Percentage* | | | | | | | | | | |
| **Total**** | **1.00** | **1.00** | **1.00** | **1.00** | **1.00** | **1.00** | **1.00** | **1.00** | **1.00** | **1.00** |
| U.S. and Canada | 0.31 | 0.30 | 0.28 | 0.28 | 0.27 | 0.25 | 0.23 | 0.24 | 0.28 | 0.30 |
| Western Europe | 0.28 | 0.29 | 0.31 | 0.31 | 0.32 | 0.32 | 0.31 | 0.31 | 0.26 | 0.28 |
| Eastern Bloc | 0.06 | 0.06 | 0.06 | 0.06 | 0.06 | 0.06 | 0.06 | 0.05 | 0.05 | 0.03 |
| Asia | 0.30 | 0.30 | 0.30 | 0.30 | 0.31 | 0.33 | 0.35 | 0.34 | 0.33 | 0.31 |
| Oceania | 0.01 | 0.01 | 0.01 | 0.01 | 0.01 | 0.01 | 0.01 | 0.01 | 0.01 | 0.01 |
| Latin America | 0.04 | 0.04 | 0.04 | 0.04 | 0.04 | 0.04 | 0.05 | 0.05 | 0.06 | 0.07 |

*Western Europe includes: Austria, France, Germany, Italy, Netherlands, Spain, Sweden, United Kingdom; Eastern Bloc: Czech Republic, Poland, Russia, Yugoslavia; Asia: China, India, Indonesia, Japan, South Korea, Malaysia. Oceania: Australia.

**Percentages do not always sum to 1.00 because of rounding.

*Source:* American Automobile Manufacturers Association, *World Motor Vehicle Data, 1996.*

Table 1.4

**Automobile Production and Exports: Argentina, Brazil, and Mexico, 1985–1994: Units Produced, Units Exported, and Percentage of National Production Exported**

| | 1985 | 1986 | 1987 | 1988 | 1989 | 1990 | 1991 | 1992 | 1993 | 1994 |
|---|---|---|---|---|---|---|---|---|---|---|
| Argentina | 137,675 | 170,490 | 193,315 | 164,160 | 127,823 | 99,639 | 138,958 | 262,022 | 342,344 | 408,777 |
| Brazil | 966,708 | 1,056,332 | 920,071 | 1,068,756 | 1,013,252 | 914,466 | 960,044 | 1,073,761 | 1,391,376 | 1,581,389 |
| Mexico | 458,680 | 341,052 | 395,258 | 512,776 | 641,275 | 820,558 | 989,373 | 1,080,863 | 1,080,572 | 1,122,109 |
| Argentina | 774 | 357 | 430 | 1,634 | 1,841 | 1,126 | 5,205 | 16,353 | 29,976 | 38,657 |
| % | 0.01 | 0.00 | 0.00 | 0.01 | 0.01 | 0.01 | 0.04 | 0.06 | 0.09 | 0.09 |
| Brazil | 207,640 | 183,279 | 345,555 | 320,476 | 253,720 | 187,311 | 193,148 | 341,900 | 331,522 | 377,627 |
| % | 0.21 | 0.17 | 0.38 | 0.30 | 0.25 | 0.20 | 0.20 | 0.32 | 0.24 | 0.24 |
| Mexico | 58,423 | 72,42 | 163,073 | 173,147 | 195,999 | 276,869 | 358,666 | 383,374 | 493,194 | 575,552 |
| % | 0.13 | 0.21 | 0.41 | 0.34 | 0.31 | 0.34 | 0.36 | 0.35 | 0.46 | 0.51 |

*Source:* American Automobile Manufacturers Association, *World Motor Vehicle Data, 1996*. Export data for 1988 through 1992 obtained from the Government of Mexico, Instituto Nacional de Estadística, Geografía, e Informática.

Table 1.5

**Foreign Direct Investment Flows, by Country of Origin, 1990–1994**
(millions of dollars)

|  | 1990 | 1991 | 1992 | 1993 | 1994 |
|---|---|---|---|---|---|
| Argentina | n.a. | n.a. | n.a. | 4724 | n.a. |
| Brazil | 944 | 1,402 | 2,522 | 1,989 | n.a. |
| Chile | 1,321 | 980 | 995 | 1,714 | 2,532 |
| Colombia | 230 | 101 | 350 | 436 | n.a. |
| Mexico | 3,722 | 3,565 | 3,599 | 4,900 | 4,431 |
| Paraguay | 39 | 73 | 117 | n.a. | n.a. |
| Peru | 43 | 39 | 160 | 146 | 2,695 |
| Venezuela | 778 | 231 | n.a. | n.a. | n.a. |

*Source: La Inversión Extranjera en América Latina y el Caribe.* Santiago: CEPAL, 1995.

1985 and 1990, and represented an average of 29 percent of production. Between 1991 and 1994, Mexico continued to show improvement, with exports growing by 60.5 percent, reaching an annual level of approximately 1,200,000 units in 1994. During this same period, vehicle exports averaged 42 percent of production. In 1994—the year that NAFTA took effect—vehicle exports climbed to 51 percent of production. The automotive sector undoubtedly helped cushion the impact of the peso crisis that began in December 1994. As the peso lost more than half its value in the first few months of 1995, exports of automobiles and other finished productions continued to rise (AMIA 1995, 1).

Trade in automobile parts and finished vehicles has been influenced by the formation of new trade regimes throughout the region. Before NAFTA was ratified, an increasing share of Mexico's exports were already destined for Canada and the United States. Indeed, the percentage of Mexican cars and trucks exported to North America increased from 4 percent of all exports in 1982 to 86 percent in 1989 (INEGI 1990, Table 4.2, parts 1–7; INEGI 1992, Table 3.19, part 4).[5] Since 1990, between 85 and 90 percent of Mexico's vehicles and engine exports have been shipped to North America (INEGI 1992, Table 3.19, part 4; AMIA 1994, 1–3). Similar changes have been initiated in the MERCOSUR countries. In Brazil and Argentina, transnational firms' investment projects in the 1990s were designed to ensure that Brazilian and Argentine auto exports would be sent primarily to each other and their two additional MERCOSUR partners, Paraguay and Uruguay, while Venezuelan and Colombian exports remained concentrated on Andean Group countries (Gonçalves and Veiga 1995, 1–7, Table 1.6; Catalano and Novick, and Cárdenas, this volume). Such trade concentration demonstrates the impact of regional free-trade agreements, but it also reflects the strategy of the automotive multinationals to consolidate regional production and distribution "car complexes," at least as an intermediate stage before true internationalization.

### Foreign Direct Investment

The geographical distribution of investment in automotive plant and equipment in Latin America has conformed to the overall pattern of foreign direct investment (FDI) in the region since 1982 (Table 1.5). Investment in the industry increased appreciably over the course of the 1980s. Although complete data on investment are unavailable, it would appear that Brazil and Mexico, in particular, have received considerable sums of FDI. Arbix (1996, 145) reports that in Brazil, the average annual investment in the automobile sector was about US $900 million between 1990 through 1994, and this figure is expected to increase throughout the decade. The resulting contribution to GDP in Brazil rose steadily from an impressive 8 percent in 1990 to 10.8 percent in 1993 (Arbix 1996, 141). Investment in the automobile industry has been strong in Mexico as well. Between 1990 and 1994, Ford, General Motors, Nissan, and Volkswagen invested approximately US $3.25 billion in order to construct new plants and increase the installed capacity of some older ones (Berry, Grilli, and López de Silanes 1992, Table 2). Terminal and automobile parts companies in Brazil have announced an additional US $2.7 billion of investment in the 1995–1997 period alone, while in Mexico the corresponding figure was US $2.24 billion (El Financiero, 13 March 1996, 21). These two countries, along with Argentina, have experienced strong growth of installed capacity, and, as noted previously, they represent the cornerstones in an evolving regional production and distribution structure that is fundamental to the search for production efficiencies and high growth markets.

### The Spatial Dispersion of Production

Recently, Tagliabue has argued that as the automobile industry moves toward the greater production of small cars globally, the pressure to reduce costs has transformed the industry's space, the economic geography of production (Tagliabue 1997; see also Storper and Walker 1989). The lower retail prices of small cars require that profits must be enhanced by cutting costs. Making parts adjacent to the assembly plant virtually eliminates packing and shipping costs, eases just-in-time inventory control, and permits quick identification and correction of production defects. These decisions are often coordinated by assemblers and suppliers (Lima 1989, 16–17; Marx 1993, 68; Ramirez 1993, 61–63).

Thus, as the transformation of the Latin American automotive industry has proceeded, ownership concentration has been accompanied by spatial dispersion of production. In both Mexico and Brazil, the automobile multinationals have largely avoided the old industrial cores in and around Mexico City and São Paulo when establishing new production sites. Indeed, Morris's and Tuman's chapters demonstrate the rapid abandonment of Mexico City, generally for greenfield locations in the states of Aguascaleintes, Guanajuato, Chihuahua, and Coahuila. Volkswagen's new state-of-the-art truck assembly plant in Brazil is located in Resende, in the state of Minas Gerais. Typically, the establishment of a new assembly or engine plant has been accompanied by the arrival of transnational parts makers, such as Bosch, AC-Delco, Nippondenso, and others.

The spatial relocation of the industry into remote local production complexes has been undertaken partly to contain wage growth. Tagliabue reports that workers in the components companies at Ford's new assembly complex in Valencia, Spain, earn about 40 percent less than those who work directly for Ford. In Mexico, workers in the auto parts industry earn 35 percent less than those in the assembly industry (INEGI 1995). Moreover, when Ford, General Motors, and Chrysler constructed new export plants in greenfield sites in northern Mexico during the 1980s, they established contract wage scales that were far below those prevailing in the older plants situated close to Mexico City (Carrillo V. 1990b; Middlebrook 1991a, Table 1).[6]

These factors explain the search for greenfield sites, where this is ample space for numerous plants that constitute a localized production complex. From Valencia, Spain (Ford), to Melfi, Italy (Fiat), to Guanajuato, Mexico (General Motors), transnational firms have created entirely new local car complexes. However, relocation to greenfield sites and the creation of new automobile complexes has not involved substantial participation of local capital. The high costs of constructing new facilities, developing new products, and coordinating with the major assemblers has implied that only large, multinational companies can direct this process.

### Changes in Work Organization

Trade liberalization and the partial shift toward export production have also increased competitive pressures on transnational producers. From the point of view of company managers, meeting the challenges posed by liberalization could only be achieved if work norms were altered in the terminal industry. As one step in raising productivity and product quality to internationally competitive levels, managers have made significant changes in work organization. Although the content of these reforms has differed somewhat in different countries, a majority of producers have embraced team working, continuous training and improvement practices, job rotation, skills-based compensation, reduced job hierarchies, and flexible work hours. In addition, some companies have experimented with quality circles.

While managers and state officials have endorsed these changes, unions have been less forthcoming in their approval of lean production. The fragmentary evidence suggests that workers in older plants have resisted team concepts on the grounds that they represent a strategy intended to undermine union power and worker solidarity (Navarro Delgado 1989; Middlebrook 1991a; Humphrey 1992, 341; Tuman 1994b). Nevertheless, some studies have identified modest support for programs that increase participation, although even here workers voice concern that team working creates an excess of group discipline in the workplace (Humphrey 1992, 329; 341–3; Covarrubias 1995). One point of agreement in the literature is that the effects of Japanese production methods have been mediated (or limited) when they are introduced into plants that have strong unions (Graham 1992, 141–51; Humphrey 1992, 343–4; Rinehart et al. 1992; Ortiz 1996). Certainly, more research needs to be completed to assess the impact of these new systems in the industry.

Finally, the mode of change has varied considerably across firms and countries. As the case studies in this volume demonstrate, some firms in Argentina and Brazil have introduced change through sector-wide agreements negotiated by representatives of management, unions, and the state. In these cases, unions have supported negotiated change partly because firms have guaranteed employment, offered to increase real wages in the future, and have safeguarded the existence of union organizations at the plant level. Yet in other cases, managers have transformed labor relations through more unilateral measures. With the tacit support of state actors, some companies have implemented changes after eliminating union resistance, or by offering selective inducements to union elites in exchange for their acquiescence to reform. Plants in Mexico and Colombia, in particular, have followed the latter trajectory. In sum, then, one can observe stark contrasts between negotiated change and concertation, on the one side, and unilateral company action on the other.

### Wages and Compensation

Wage disputes became particularly contentious in the Latin American automobile industry during the 1980s, when managers and state elites sought to control real wage growth in order to increase competitiveness. For their part, workers often responded to these initiatives by insisting that changes in work organization should be linked to real wage gains. While the outcomes of wage disputes varied, the evidence suggests that firms have been winning the struggle in many cases.

The contraction of wages has been significant in some countries in the region. As noted previously, workers in Mexico's new export plants work longer hours and are paid less (in nominal wages) than those in the older plants in and around Mexico City, even among those working for the same company (Carrillo V. 1990b). Moreover, the available evidence suggests that real wages in the Mexican automobile industry fell during the 1980s. In his study of six older plants in the terminal sector, for example, Tuman found that average wages in most plants failed to keep up with inflation between 1985 and 1993 (Tuman, this volume, Table 6.6). For the industry as a whole, chronic inflation resulted in a contraction in real wages between 1982 to 1987; real wages surpassed their 1982 level (in real terms) only in 1992. The limited data on Brazil, which cover the period between 1982 and 1985, indicate that real wages declined from 1982 to 1983, and remained stagnant for the rest of the period.

Average wages in Latin America also lag behind those of other industrializing countries. In 1992, average compensation of workers in the Mexican automobile industry was US $4.35 per day, which represented only 66 and 62 percent of what their Taiwanese and South Korean counterparts earned, respectively, during the same period. In 1985, Brazilian automobile workers earned about the same as workers in South Korea, but only 89 percent of workers in Taiwan.

A comparison of Mexican and Brazilian industries to those of the developed countries shows even greater disparities. In Japan, the United States, and Germany, automobile workers received on average hourly rates of US $19.97, $25.12, and $32.61, respectively, in 1992. In that same year, Mexican workers received only 17 percent of the average of workers in those three countries, and only 25 percent of the remuneration earned by workers in Spain, a country with a growing industry well suited for participation in the European market. Moreover, differences in productivity and product quality do not always account for the wage differentials cross-nationally or across plants in a given country (Shaiken 1994; Tuman, in this volume).

The low pay received by Latin American automotive workers is also clearly demonstrated in the survey of purchasing power conducted by the International Metalworkers' Federation (1996). Table 1.6 presents some of their comparative data on the number of hours workers must complete to purchase of a variety of goods in different countries. Among the three major auto-producing countries of Latin America, Argentine workers exhibit the greatest earning power. A liter of gasoline costs only 6.5 minutes of work in Argentina, versus 8.5 in Brazil and 26 in Mexico, despite the fact that gasoline prices in Mexico are among the lowest in the world. In addition, rent and consumer durables (including refrigerators, color televisions, and automobiles) all cost least in Argentina. These data are illustrative, given that Brazil and Mexico have significantly larger auto complexes. Even more suggestive is that Mexican auto workers earn far less than workers in either Argentina or Brazil, despite the fact that Mexico exports more vehicles (to advanced markets in North America) than the other two.

## Workers, Unions, and the Politics of Industrial Restructuring: Contrasting Responses

### Argentina

Since 1990, the structure of the Argentine automobile industry has been profoundly influenced by trade liberalization and the country's integration into MERCOSUR, a regional market involving Argentina, Brazil, Paraguay, and

Table 1.6

## Cost in Hours Labored for Selected Purchases by Automotive Industry Workers in Selected Countries, 1993

| | Argentina | | Brazil | | Colombia | | Mexico | | Venezuela | | Japan | | Republic of Korea | | Spain | | United States | |
|---|---|---|---|---|---|---|---|---|---|---|---|---|---|---|---|---|---|---|
| | hrs | min | hrs | min | hrs | min | hrs | min | hrs | min | hrs | min | hrs | min | hrs | min | hrs | min |
| **Food** | | | | | | | | | | | | | | | | | | |
| Bread | 0 | 17 | 0 | 26 | 0 | 55 | 0 | 7 | 0 | 34 | 0 | 13 | 0 | 18 | 0 | 8 | 0 | 4 |
| Beef | 0 | 42 | 1 | 58 | 3 | 38 | 6 | 37 | 6 | 51 | 2 | 2 | 2 | 42 | 0 | 42 | 0 | 22 |
| **Clothing** | | | | | | | | | | | | | | | | | | |
| Shirt | 4 | 33 | 6 | 31 | 23 | 26 | 14 | 9 | 32 | 13 | 2 | 10 | 7 | 50 | 2 | 13 | 1 | 39 |
| Coat | 9 | 17 | 4 | 37 | 70 | 22 | 58 | 59 | n.a. | n.a. | 17 | 11 | 70 | 56 | 15 | 48 | 4 | 24 |
| Shoes | 14 | 34 | 19 | 7 | 31 | 30 | 35 | 23 | 56 | 23 | 6 | 0 | 10 | 8 | 3 | 48 | 4 | 57 |
| **Gasoline** (1 liter) | 0 | 7 | 0 | 9 | 0 | 14 | 0 | 26 | 0 | 2 | 0 | 4 | 0 | 4 | 0 | 4 | 0 | 1 |
| **Rent** (4 rooms) | 80 | 6 | 133 | 37 | 223 | 21 | 471 | 46 | 201 | 21 | 78 | 42 | n.a. | n.a. | n.a. | n.a. | 54 | 57 |
| **Durables** | | | | | | | | | | | | | | | | | | |
| Refrigerator | 67 | 21 | 106 | 2 | 201 | 57 | 707 | 39 | 402 | 43 | 42 | 23 | 97 | 17 | 37 | 54 | 43 | 57 |
| Color Television | 78 | 17 | 130 | 46 | 315 | 2 | 589 | 43 | 241 | 38 | 32 | 49 | 101 | 20 | 37 | 54 | 16 | 29 |
| Automobile | 2,402 | 48 | 3,119 | 3 | 8,885 | 30 | 8,255 | 56 | 20,135 | 19 | 894 | 12 | 2,432 | 4 | 1,136 | 60 | 879 | 1 |

*Source:* International Metalworkers Federation, *The Purchasing Power of Working Time, An International Comparison: 1994–1995.* Geneva: 1996.

Uruguay. As Catalano and Novick observe in Chapter 2, although the industry is not yet competitive on international levels, regional integration has spurred reforms that have resulted in strong gains in productivity and product quality.

Catalano and Novick focus attention on changes occurring at the firm level, and within the political institutions shaping industrial relations in the sector. They note that integration has pushed firms to specialize and concentrate their efforts on the production of certain product lines. In addition, subcontracting in the terminal plants has increased, creating new relations between terminal firms and local and regional suppliers. With regard to work organization and labor relations, managers have implemented new systems based upon total quality management, team concepts, and JIT production. However, automobile unions in Argentina used their corporatist ties with state actors to pressure the government into promoting change through negotiations and concerted action. Thus, beginning in 1991, representatives from the state, management, and unions signed sectoral and plant-level agreements[7] covering a wide array of issues, including wages, employment, strikes, automobile taxes and tariffs, and so forth. Importantly, unions won employment guarantees and real wage increases in exchange for accepting "labor peace clauses" (i.e., clauses committing the union to negotiation instead of strikes) and other changes in labor relations. For its part, the government attempted to forge compromise by agreeing to implement policies that would spur growth in the industry. In general, these included policies that cut automotive taxes, and ones linking trade liberalization to the introduction of new production technology in the terminal sector.

### Brazil

Over the course of the 1990s, growth was restored in the Brazilian automotive industry following a strong recession and a long period of restructuring. Transnational firms invested in plants in order to maximize participation in MERCOSUR and in the domestic market. In addition, firms have introduced the core elements associated with the lean model of production. These changes have affected workers on two levels. At the plant level, lean production has generated strong growth in productivity, combined with a reduction in employment and an intensification of the pace of work. In addition, lean production has required greater training and worker involvement in production, although worker participation often has been limited and initiated from an inferior and defensive position.

The responses of workers and unions to such changes have varied. As Arbix and Rodrigues observe in Chapter 3, automobile unions perpetuated militant bargaining styles in the post-transition period (1985–1988), when long-standing worker demands were given expression through the formation (and proliferation) of "internal commissions," legally unrecognized, plant-level organizations that pressed local demands independently of the national union, the Central Única dos Trabalahadores (CUT). During the years of severe economic crisis (1988–1992), the government promoted negotiated agreements through a national "sectoral chamber," a tripartite organization involving labor, the government, and management. Grounded in wage restraint, employment protections, and other financial incentives for consumers, the sectoral agreements implemented between 1991 and 1994 revived sales and growth in the industry. When the crisis subsided in 1992, the government withdrew its support for the sectoral chamber. Consequently, labor–management relations have devolved back to the firm level in the sector, a trend that, paradoxically, has been strongly supported by the Social Democratic administration of Fernando Henrique Cardoso.[8]

### Colombia

The Colombian automobile industry developed within the context of a highly protected market and limited integration with other Andean Pact countries. Despite the small size of the domestic market, production and sales increased in the 1970s, in particular for Renault, the dominant firm in the terminal sector. However, the economic recession of the 1980s resulted in a steep decline in sales, and triggered restructuring throughout the industry.

In Chapter 4, Cárdenas examines labor conflict in Renault-Colombia. He notes that as the economic crisis worsened in the 1980s, Renault's workers protested layoffs and restructuring by engaging in strikes, protests, and sabotage of vehicles and equipment. Workers were also radicalized by the company's use of ex-military officers in supervisory positions, and the presence of army units in the plant during periods of labor unrest. In retaliation, some union members allegedly coordinated guerrilla attacks on managers. In an effort to defuse tensions in the firm, Renault implemented total quality management programs in the late 1980s and early 1990s. While these were partially successful, the continuation of layoffs and restructuring forced union leaders to maintain a fairly militant bargaining stance with the company. The conflict was finally resolved when workers became convinced that they could better advance their short-term, immediate interests without a union. Indeed, in late 1993, Renault successfully eliminated the union by offering to pay workers a higher wage settlement if they gave up their union membership. In the aftermath, a small number of union members remained, but their numbers fell short of the legally required number to call a strike or act as a collective bargaining representative.

### Mexico

In Chapter 5, Morris looks at recent changes in the structure of the Mexican automobile industry. He suggests that much of the foundation for an export-oriented automotive sector in Mexico was in place well before the 1982 debt crisis and the recession of the 1980s. After 1988, the industry experienced growth once again, although its rapid development produced a dualistic structure with new plants oriented toward export production for the United States, and an old industrial "nucleus" producing for the domestic market.

The adoption of lean production practices reflects the dualistic structure of the industry. In the new export plants, located in greenfield sites in northern Mexico, managers integrated lean production systems into their planning before construction of the plants had even commenced. Despite impressive productivity gains and enhanced opportunities for training, workers have suffered from low wages, an erosion of seniority-related rights, and control by authoritarian union leaders affiliated with the *Confederación de Trabajadores de México* (Confederation of Mexican Workers, CTM).

Organized labor's responses in the export sector were generally limited. With some notable exceptions (e.g., strikes in Ford's Hermosillo and Chihuahua plants), the new plants experienced relatively little conflict. The CTM has organized all of the new plants opened since 1980, and it has guaranteed labor peace in exchange for obtaining a monopoly on union representation in the export plants. In addition, the workforce in the export plants was relatively young, and many lacked experience with union activism. Moreover, government intervention and union repression dampened resistance in the few conflicts that did emerge.

Nevertheless, union resistance to flexible production developed in some of Mexico's older plants. In Chapter 6, Tuman argues that militancy in the ISI plants was related to the outcomes and legacies of union democratization movements in the 1970s. In those cases where these movements were successful, workers severed (or weakened) their ties to the CTM, increased participation, and institutionalized union democracy. In the absence of corporatist controls over the bargaining process, democratic unions pushed for stronger work rules, controls over the production process, and higher wages and benefits. Democratic unions perpetuated militant stands once restructuring emerged. In particular, workers often struck because neither employers, nor the Mexican state, would agree to provide employment guarantees, retraining, or wage gains in exchange for union concessions over work rules.

In contrast, where union democracy movements in the ISI plants were defeated, labor elites linked to the CTM increased their control over bargaining, and also took measures to remove dissident workers. As a result, workers lacked the autonomy and institutional capacity to act against employers and the CTM. Moreover, since elites in these unions were linked to the regime, they came under strong pressures from state actors to facilitate the processes of adjustment and restructuring at the plant level.

### Venezuela

Venezuela is primarily an assembly platform for a relatively small regional market encompassing the Andean Pact countries. As such, it was powerfully impacted by domestic economic turmoil and the subsequent trade liberalization of the late 1980s and early 1990s. In particular, liberalization became the impetus for the introduction of some aspects of lean production. In his chapter, Héctor Lucena shows that the terminal assembly firms have reduced the number of job categories while moving to subcontract work and also introducing contingent compensation to increase productivity and quality levels.

Lucena argues that Venezuela's workers have been notably quiescent in the face of these changes. First, the majority of workers are concentrated in a small number of multinational and national assembly firms, and organized through "traditional" corporatist unions linked to Venezuela's two major political parties (AD and COPEI). As labor organizations based upon conciliation and control, corporatist unions have lacked the capacity to develop alternatives to the changes in labor relations. The absence of sufficient financial and economic resources in most unions has also undermined the capacity of most automobile unions to mount struggles against firms. Finally, despite the hardships caused by adjustment, automotive workers are still relatively well paid, enjoying favorable working conditions and a measure of employment security. The conservative bargaining style of union leaders, combined with the weak capacity of unions, has reinforced the tendency for conflict to be expressed through individual struggles and disputes on the shopfloor.

## Conclusion: Comparative Implications

In this chapter, we have argued that the Latin American automobile industry is being transformed in at least two ways. First, the structure of the industry has changed as policy makers have dismantled ISI in favor of market liberalization, regional integration, and export production. Second, the models of work organization and labor relations in the industry have been reformed significantly through the introduction of practices associated with flexible production. Although the degree of change has varied somewhat, there is little doubt that the structure and orientation of the automobile industry has been altered in all of the major producing countries (e.g., Argentina, Brazil, and Mexico), and in a majority of the smaller markets as well.

The political and economic implications of restructuring in the industry remain open to debate. In this book, we have attempted to clarify one aspect of the politics of restructuring by focusing on the role that workers and unions have played in the adjustment process. Certainly, the studies presented in this volume offer contrasting assessments of union responses to the transformation of the automobile industry. Nevertheless, despite the theoretical diversity of the explanations advanced in each chapter, the results of the research would appear to support several observations about the politics of restructuring in the developing world.

One conclusion that emerges from the research is that the effects of restructuring policies, and the mode(s) through which they are implemented, have been mediated by state actors and unions in each country. In other words, the diffusion of lean production and other restructuring initiatives has been shaped and influenced by the variations in union organization, industrial relations practice, and political institutions in each of the countries under review (Elger and Smith 1992, 55). This observation underscores the utility (and necessity) of comparative research that remains sensitive to differences in national context.

A somewhat broader issue has to do with the underlying basis of negotiated compromise between labor and capital in the sector. The evidence from Argentina, Brazil, and Mexico suggests that workers have been willing to commit themselves to compromises only under certain circumstances. In particular, union acceptance of work rule changes was often linked to company guarantees that employment levels would be maintained, or that real wages would increase in the future.[9] Moreover, the inclusion of state actors in negotiations helped to secure labor's consent since the government's presence reassured workers that firms would be required to comply with their end of the bargain. When state elites and employers have been unwilling to make these sorts of guarantees, or have failed to implement policies negotiated previously, workers have shortened their time horizons, rejecting concessions in favor of immediate gains.

Finally, the studies suggest that corporatist relations between unions and the state continue to have relevance in the Latin American context. However, the exact form that corporatist relations have assumed, and their effects on union bargaining strategies, have varied significantly from one case to another. In Argentina, for example, automobile unions used corporatist ties with the Partido Justicialista and Peronist leaders in order to pressure the state into pursuing social concertation with unions and firms. As a result, Argentine automobile unions were able to negotiate the terms of trade liberalization and preempt unilateral change at the firm level. This outcome may be a reflection of changes in Argentine corporatism in the post-transition era, where the party has remained linked to trade unions, but the state's capacity to control union demand making has diminished.

By contrast, the Mexican regime relied heavily upon corporatist controls over union bargaining to limit worker resistance to restructuring. Corporatism in Mexico therefore reinforced the capacity of managers to implement changes unilaterally. Given the differing effects of corporatism in these two cases, it is clear that the institutional forms of corporatism in Latin America vary and are evolving in different directions from one another. In examining the influence of corporatism on economic restructuring, then, we join others in calling for more finely shaded distinctions of the institutions that link organized labor and the state.

## Notes

1. Lean production practices refer to "the minimization of stocks and work in progress through 'just-in-time production' and by an emphasis on the continuous improvement of

production procedures. . . . [It is claimed] that these methods are only successful with a skilled and committed workforce attuned to problem solving under pressure, providing a basis for a convergence of interests between management and workers" (Elger and Smith 1992, 3). In many cases, lean production relies upon the use of work teams, multi-skilled workers, and other organizational changes designed to boost productivity and to increase self-discipline among workers. For a critical discussion of the results of this model, see Elger and Smith (1992).

2. In the early ISI phase, a favorable combination of factors (i.e., the prevalence of many producers, and small markets in Latin America) allowed national policy makers to impose modest regulations on producers, creating the foundation of import-substitution industrialization. The extraordinary international contexts of global depression, followed by the post-war economic boom in Western Europe and the United States, probably reduced the urgency for transnational automobile firms to construct more favorable economic regimes in Latin America.

3. Following Collier and Collier (1991, 51; emphasis in original text), unions can be characterized as *state-corporatist* to the degree that there is: "(1) state *structuring* of groups that produces a system of officially sanctioned, noncompetitive, compulsory interest associations; (2) state *subsidy* of these groups; and (3) state-imposed constraints on demand-making, leadership, and internal governance. Corporatism is thus a *non-pluralist* system of *group* representation. . . . [I]n the case of corporatism the state encourages the formation of a limited number of officially recognized, non-competing, state-supervised groups." Importantly, in many Latin American cases, the leaders and members of corporatist unions received state benefits and subsidies in exchange for supporting the regime and for making demands that were consistent with the regime's economic policies.

4. Government attempts to increase export production found support among American producers toward the end of the 1970s. In particular, the oil price revolution and the penetration of Japanese imports had compelled Chrysler, Ford, and General Motors to invest heavily in the development of smaller and more efficient vehicles. In addition, plants had to be re-tooled for the new product lines. As a result, the "Big Three" hoped to begin cutting costs by exporting labor-intensive parts from export platforms in Mexico and Brazil. By 1981, General Motors had also initiated export operations for small cars from Mexico. As Bennett and Sharpe (1985) have noted, the growth of export-oriented production in Mexico reflected a convergence of interests on the part of Mexican regulators and transnational producers, made possible through changes in the international political economy.

5. During this period, Nissan and Volkswagen exported vehicles primarily to other countries in South America and the Caribbean. By the early 1990s, however, Volkswagen had started exporting significant numbers of vehicles to Canada.

6. Indeed, in Mexico, nominal and real wages in the export plants have continued to lag behind wages in the ISI plants. In August 1996, for example, average daily wages in Chrysler-Saltillo and Ford-Chihuahua (two export plants) were 71.07 and 84.83 new pesos, respectively. During that same month, average daily wages in Chrysler-Toluca and Ford-Cuautitlán (two older plants) were 86.9 and 96.11 new pesos, respectively. Moreover, as Tuman shows in his chapter (see Table 6.6), between 1985 and 1994, the average annual change of real wages in Chrysler-Toluca was better than in Chrysler-Saltillo. For additional evidence, see wage revision agreements and collective contracts, in Junta Federal de Conciliación (JFCA) Archive, Mexico City, Files CC–6-XII and CC–8-XII; and Secretar'a del Trabajo y Previsión Social, Coordinación General del Cuerpo de Funcionarios Conciliadoras (STPS-CGCFC) Archive, Mexico City, Files 2.1/(6)"82"/3311, and 2.1/(12)"83"/3504.

7. Since the policies also promoted firm-level agreements negotiated at lower levels of

organization, they departed partially from the traditional mode of concertation, which was based upon centralized negotiations and decision making. For an instructive discussion of the parallels here with the Brazilian case, see Martin (1997, 64–5).

8. For contrasting assessments of the impact (and implications) of the sectoral agreements in Brazil, see also Shapiro (1996) and Martin (1997).

9. These agreements share certain similarities to corporatist pacts that have been negotiated historically by Western European unions and social democratic actors. On this point, see Przeworksi (1985; 1987).

Ana María Catalano and Marta S. Novick

# 2 | The Argentine Automotive Industry: Redefining Production Strategies, Markets, and Labor Relations

## Introduction

Throughout its four decades of development, the Argentine automotive sector has served as an important point of reference in the areas of work organization, industrial employment, new modalities of labor relations, and for collective bargaining. In 1974 the industry reached its highest historical level of employment with 57,400 workers, while in 1983, when the military dictatorship came to an end, it employed 23,260 workers producing 150,000 units. A decade later, in 1994, based on a Framework Agreement signed between management chambers, unions, and the government, with a spectacular increase in production and productivity, it employed the same number of workers, who produced 400,000 vehicles. While it is true that the falloff of demand in 1995—produced by the internal and external crisis—lowered the level of industry sales, activity did continue in the area of investment projects and the installation of new plants, particularly those oriented to the manufacture of utility vehicles. The total production[1] of vehicles dropped by 15.2 percent if we compare the first half of 1995 with 1996. In turn, 78 percent of the product of the first half of 1995 entered the internal market, showing a drop of around 21 percent in comparison with the

---

Translated by Ludwig Tuman. Some sections in this chapter are reprinted with permission from *Los efectos laborales de la reestructuración productiva*, ed. Héctor Lucena (Venezuela: Universidad de Carabobo and Asociación de Relaciones de Trabajo, 1996).

same period of the previous year. The year 1995 closed with a drop in automotive production of 30.2 percent with respect to the previous year.

In effect, while the automotive industry had contributed the most to the economic reactivation in the first parts of the 1990s, the recent fall in internal demand forced the principal terminal assembly firms to suspend production activities. According to information gathered from Argentine newspapers and other primary sources, temporary shutdowns have taken place in almost all the terminal plants. The metallurgic workers union (UOM) and automotive industry mechanics union (SMATA) have stated that these suspensions of activity affected more than 8,000 workers.[2] In some terminals this recourse was not sufficient. Sevel laid off approximately 1,500 workers in 1995.

The automotive industry in Argentina is one of the economic sectors most heavily influenced by public policy. The state has played a major role in it even during periods of deregulation and economic liberalization. The sector is presently undergoing a profound structural transformation that involves not only its models of work organization but also the shape and behavior of the sector as a whole and the regulative and institutional framework in which it operates. The process of opening up to external markets, together with the processes of regional integration, have given rise to a new model of industrial organization unlike the one that prevailed during the stage of import substitution industrialization (ISI). The model of the automotive industry associated with this most recent stage is moving toward a reorganization of labor processes, a new kind of establishment, and new models of market behavior.

The forty-year history of the Argentine automotive industry can be divided into three main stages. The first, which developed between 1959 and 1975, was characterized by the establishment of transnational terminal assembly companies and by the installation of the "Ford model" in Argentina. In this stage two subperiods can be distinguished, one linked to the implantation and development of the industry, and the other associated with a process of promotion and affirmation of a sectorial model of productive organization.

The second broad stage, covering the period 1976 to 1990, played itself out in a setting that involved the breakup of the "import substitution" model, concentration of capital, crisis with the Ford system of production, free market policies, the introduction of technological changes, and the rupture of the "Ford agreement" in labor relations. The second part of this period corresponded to the massive introduction of organizational innovations and the beginning of a strategy, on the part of the companies, to specialize in auto parts. The context of this subperiod, above all in its final phase, was a heavy recession and a pronounced decrease in consumption.

The regional integration of markets presently being carried forward by MERCOSUR (an integrated market involving Argentina, Brazil, Paraguay, and Uruguay) and the signing in 1991[3] of a sectoral agreement between the government, the unions, and the management chambers have given rise to a new stage.

In the present setting, we have an industry that has tripled its annual production since 1990 (though sectoral employment has not grown in the same proportion), that has substantially renewed its equipment, and that has implemented, in many of its firms, new work and production methods.

In December of 1994 the automotive industry employed 59,830 people if we combine the terminal industry and the auto parts sector, with 25,734 workers corresponding to the terminals and 34,096 to the auto parts sector. In 1993, it represented 3.2 percent of the GNP with 2.4 percent corresponding to the terminal sector and 0.8 percent to auto parts (Nofal 1994).

Along these lines, we observe in the past decade a clear evolution in the terminals' strategies, a process that has consequently involved their networks of suppliers, given the latter's lack of independence. The terminals, then, are attempting to find a market niche where they can compete and, simultaneously, finance part of the reconversion of their productive apparatus, in the context of the globalization of the automotive market. It is clear that the Argentine automotive industry has not yet reached a level of development that will allow it to compete on an international level. It is also clear, however, that with effort it has gone beyond being limited to a highly protected internal market. Evidently its projection into globalized automotive production is not yet defined. To achieve this it needs to develop its relations with a network of local, regional, and international suppliers that would allow it to compete in quality and price. The subject of productivity, reduction of manufacturing costs, and the ability to operate on the basis of new sources of profitability is central to the redesigning of this industry and its international projection. In view of this, the local terminals have designed development strategies at two levels (Morales and Katz 1995):

(a) At the level of the individual firm:

- Redefining its lines of "business" and trying out various options (specialization in components, parts or subassemblies, development of new models geared toward market strata having greater purchasing power, development of models intended for export within a regional market as assigned by company headquarters, development of utility models, etc.);
- Redesigning the organization of production and its work processes by incorporating new management technologies in more or less generalized form (Total Quality Programs, Quality Circles, JIT forms "Argentine" style, stock reduction programs, etc.); and, in some sectors, promptly installing microelectronics and information technology (robots for soldering and painting and various forms of automation);
- Redefining a particular form of production linkage with the sector's suppliers. The strategy points to the breakdown of the vertical integration model and to substantial changes both in the manner of subcontracting and in the relationship with its network of local, regional, and international

suppliers. This redefinition of the links of production requires a change in operational procedures not only on the level of the network of suppliers but even in the interior of the suppliers' and subcontractors' plants. This situation requires providers to be able to develop their businesses maintaining certain autonomy with respect to the terminals' agile, responsive, and changing strategies. This relative autonomy in the chain of suppliers presents serious difficulties for their development, partly because they lack a knowledge of market dynamics, and partly because they lack the flexibility needed to find items they can market in a counter-cyclical way.

(b) At the institutional level:

- Redefining forms of bargaining between government, companies in the sector, and unions to carry out the sector's reconversion within a framework of globalization. These new forms of concertation, in our case, are expressed in the Framework Agreement signed in 1991, and renewed with some modifications in 1994, which established a special system of deregulation for the automotive industry with the objective of promoting its restructuring and its relative participation in the sector's globalization;
- Redefining the parameters of contractual relations among suppliers;
- Defining new scenarios and entering into agreement with the unions on new rules of the game in labor relations.

The remaining sections of this article discuss the nature and development of these strategies in more detail.

## The Special Characteristics of Labor Relations in the Automobile Industry

The automobile industry's system of labor relations differs significantly, in some respects, from the "paradigm model" that has been prevalent in Argentina since the 1950s. The "paradigm" system was sustained throughout periods of profound political conflict, a succession of military coups, the advent of democracy, and the institutional restructuring of recent years. It is characterized by authorizing collective bargaining rights (the capacity to represent workers legally) to only one union, and by allowing only one agreement to be made regarding salaries and work conditions for each broad area of activity.

With the installation of the first terminal assembly firms in Argentina, however, the automotive industry inaugurated a new model of labor relations. After the arrival of multinational companies in the 1960s, the Fordist system of production was introduced and one "union per company" became the norm in the industry. This modality gave rise to a considerable number of intense worker–employer confrontations in the 1970s. In later years, however, it led to a peculiar system of labor relations that endowed the sector with a marked ability to decentralize negotiations, while allowing its heavily centralized political directorate to avoid having to pay the price for the heterogeneous labor-related situations which that same directorate created and institutionalized in the varying agreements made on a per-company basis. This historical construction, which segmented the union while the "Ford agreement" regarding labor relations was still in effect, is easily incorporated into the new strategies of collective negotiation that automotive companies are at present proposing. In the third part of this article we will elaborate on how the modality of negotiations and labor relations established by SMATA (Sindicato de Mecánicos y Afines del Transporte Automotor, the dominant union in the sector) prepared the way for "articulated" negotiation. Articulated negotiation in this sector aims at guaranteeing employment and stability, establishing prior commitments to collective peace. The parties also sign particular agreements that specify the conditions for the use and recompense of work, as appropriate to the economic and financial situation of each company.

As for flexibility, the sector was one of the first to introduce microelectronics technology and new organizational and management techniques that modified the configuration and the content of work. These structural modifications were not expressed in collective agreements until very recently. Strategies using flexibility in the contracting of the sector's labor have been accompanied by norms of general flexibility imposed in recent years by Argentine legislation. In many cases the union itself, via company agreements, authorizes these forms of transaction.

In the automotive industry, most workers are affiliated with SMATA and the workforce in only one company belongs to the UOM (Unión Obrera Metalúrgica de la República Argentina). The state's continued ambiguity regarding the union options open to workers in the sector has provoked not a few interunion conflicts, most recently in January 1996 following the installation of a new Fiat plant and the signing of a collective work agreement. Fiat proposed the agreement first to the metallurgic union (UOM), and later, when the UOM delayed in accepting the proposed salarial conditions, made the agreement with the mechanics union (SMATA). This is a new way of making agreements, for one is not coming to terms with the representatives of a preexisting work collective but rather with an abstract social representation.

### The Development of the Automobile Industry in Argentina

#### Installation and Consolidation of an Idiosyncratic Industry Model: 1958–74

*The First Phase, 1959–64: Installation of the Industry*

The development of the automobile industry began in the 1950s. In 1951, when the industry was incorporated into the system of industrial protection and promotion in effect at the time (decree 3693/59), there was a high and unsatisfied demand. Moreover, the anticipated rate of Argentina's internal growth indicated a significant potential market. The basic features of the overall industrial picture consisted in (1) acceleration in the process of integrating domestically manufactured parts and inputs into the vehicles produced, and (2) strong tariff protection for the sector. This was equivalent to a typical situation of market reserve (Kosacoff, Todesca, and Vispo 1991).

The automotive industry saw spectacular growth. In 1951 it represented 2.5 percent of the GNP and by 1965 had grown to 10.3 percent. Between 1958 and 1965 its annual growth rate was 24 percent. Its importance led the sector to be dubbed "the engine of the economy's growth." However, the automotive plants in Argentina were far from having the scale and work organization of the plants installed in more developed countries. In manufacturing technology, the local plants were less automated and had a wider production mix. They were forced to recreate, in a local setting, a significant number of technologies relating to products, process, and methods that were not available in the country as they were at the companies' headquarters.

This affected the model of industrial organization from the outset of automotive production and had a negative impact on equipment utilization times and on the turnaround time for capital investments. The result was that the Argentine automotive industry came to operate with a less than optimum technology of production and work organization. Consequently, local engineering efforts were in large part occupied with resolving the technological problems arising both from an inadequate scale of work and from a prototypical industrial organization placed in an industrial setting less mature than that of the developed countries (Katz and Lengyel 1991). Static and dynamic dis-economies of scale and of industrial organization were thereby added, blocking the possibility of emergence from the tight circle of the internal market.[4]

The implantation of terminal assembly companies brought on the development, in this period, of a network of suppliers or subcontractors who manufactured parts for the industry. When the auto parts industry reached full development, accelerated technological efforts were made to create a web of local suppliers that would make it possible to meet the growing legal requirements for the national integration of production. The relationships that the main industries established with subcontractors were completely idiosyncratic when compared with their equivalents in other countries.

As a result of the benefits granted to the industry, twenty-one manufacturing plants were approved in 1960 and began to operate for a market whose size hardly reached 100,000 annual units. Employment in the sector grew from 9,700 people in 1959 to 17,500 in 1960, an increase of almost 100 percent. Of the 21 companies, many eventually left the market in the following years through a long and costly process of buyouts, mergers, bankruptcy, and manufacturing closures, which reaffirms the irrationality both of the original scheme for the organization of production and of the regulatory system that produced it (Katz and Lengyel 1991). Another crucial feature was the complete prohibition of imported vehicles, lasting until 1976, at which time the first relatively massive imports took place.

## Fordism Arrives in Argentina: The Organization of Work and Labor Relations

The model of work organization developed in Argentine industrial workshops over the period 1950–75 could be characterized as *proto-Taylorism*,[5] inasmuch as it did not orient its technical, organizational, and social components toward productivity (understood as technical efficiency proper to a specialization), but rather toward the disciplining and control of the workforce. The arrival of the automotive industry meant the arrival of the Ford model of production, which, though it apparently upheld the fundamental features of Taylorism–Fordism, continued to reinforce the mechanisms of control and discipline of the workforce more than those oriented to the technical improvement of productivity.

The model of work organization—marked more by control and discipline than by productivity—allows us to distinguish the pattern of production management prevailing in Argentina from the one which, based on individual productivity, characterized the Taylorist production of the core countries.

Foreign terminal assembly firms arrived in Argentina country toward the end of the 1950s intent upon establishing themselves and installing a new model of labor relations. Fearful perhaps of the strong—yet conciliatory—trade unionism found throughout the history of labor relations in Argentina, they promoted a union organization that was not centralized or organized by type of work or region, but rather based upon geographically decentralized units organized on a per-company basis. The organization of terminal work processes adopted Fordist forms, which tended to differentiate markedly between the work content of repair shop mechanics and the work done in final assembly operations. To this was added the new type of dynamic generated among the large concentrations of wage earners in the terminal plants. The density of operations and the kind of work done created deep distinctions between terminal workers, repair shop wage earners, employees of sales concessionaries, and those who produced auto bodies. A new model was thereby diffused in Argentine industry—a new model of company and work organization, on the one hand, and of labor relations, on the other. This involved plants housing thousands of workers, Fordist forms of work organization, the timing of production rhythms, etc. The company-based union no longer represented the intercategorical diversity of a sector of workers. These unions no longer specified their interests and claims, and tended to define representation in terms of the salary relation with one or another company organization. The system did little to link workers' interests with their work activities or with the exercise of specific functions and roles. The unions' identity pivoted not on a professional role but on belonging to one or another organizational and productive culture. What took priority was not so much an identity based on "doing" as one based on the differentiation or identification with labor relations within the establishments. In this sense the representation was more social than work-related.

In this type of representation, based on the form taken by labor relations, the central theme is the autonomous perspective the workers were able to achieve, since it was through this perspective that their social identity was redefined.

The model of labor relations that remained in force for years in Argentina was sustained by a collective negotiation system with a "tripartite" nature—made up of state, companies, and unions. Company directors formed employer associations, which took part in collective agreements and in the formation of lobbies. The unions and company associations, whether allied or in conflict, formed pressure groups to assure that the state attended to their sectorial interests. With this model, the salary relation diffused principles of work organization that can be characterized basically as Taylor-Fordist. Profitability depended much more upon the capacity for political articulation as a factor of influence on the overall way the economy was regulated (in the sense of achieving intersectoral income transfers), than upon the configuration adopted by the technical, organizational, and social components of the work organization model. This excessive influence of politics impregnated all the operations of the period's social participants and has continued intermittently to the present day.[6]

The automotive sector, however, deviated from the so-called standard model. The main way was that the companies, due to their size, economic power, and ability to generate direct and indirect employment, had their own space from which to act directly upon the state. In this initial stage they had little need of trade unionism in order to pressure or obtain advantages. At the same time, the multinationals' initiative to form unions by company and not by type of work implied an attempt to change the "idiosyncratic" labor relations system that had been emerging in Argentina, characterized by strong, single, activity-based unions.

*The Second Phase, 1964–75: Consolidation and Breakdown of the Previous Model*

From 1964 to 1975 we observe, simultaneously, a falloff in aggregate investment and an intercompany struggle for market share. Several small companies of national origin had to abandon the market in the 1960s. By the end of the decade only nine manufacturing plants were still in operation—a fact that caused the concentration of capital in the sector to grow significantly. While there were some changes in product and process technologies, these did not modify the idiosyncratic features mentioned above in a way that would allow the local plants to take on the technological and organizational patterns prevailing in more developed countries. On the contrary—according to Katz and Lengyel (1991)—these innovations were incorporated into the existing layouts without producing a significant reorganization of production. The automotive industry continued to exhibit, during these years, low levels of automation, reduced scales of production, a wide diversity of product mixes, long manufacturing times, and an exclusive orientation to satisfy a captive internal demand, given the high level of tariffs.

One significant aspect of the period is that, at the outset of the 1960s, transnational companies continued to stock their warehouses with imported parts, assigning to national companies only that part of the production for which the relevant technology had been sufficiently diffused. The lack of uniform demand produced small markets and profit levels lower than those required by the transnationals. However, the major requirements of national integration demanded by the system placed into effect in 1965 caused an increase in the local purchase of parts and other inherent elements of the automotive industry. Expressed in terms of their production value, they rose from 26.3 percent in 1960 to 35 percent in 1963 and to nearly 50 percent toward the end of the 1960s.

The development of the auto parts sector was accompanied by that of the terminal firms, which overtook the former by internalizing the manufacture of parts in their own establishments (Kantis and Quierolo 1990).

The *coup d'état* of March 1976, and the program to open Argentina to the international economy, as promoted by the military government, left a clear mark in the country's industrial history. A new system lifted the prohibition of importation and fixed tariffs for automobiles at 95 percent and for utility vehicles at 65 percent. These were to remain in effect until 1979, followed by another progressive reduction of 55 percent and 45 percent to be carried out in a decreasing time table until 1982. It simultaneously authorized an increase in the imported content of manufactured vehicles, eliminated restrictions on vertical integration in the "mix" produced, established the regulation of imports by vehicle category rather than by model, reduced import tariffs for parts and subassemblies, opened the possibility of new companies entering the market, and allowed intercompany agreements of compensated marketing. This process—parallel to the restructuring the sector was undergoing internationally—set into motion a profound transformation of the Argentine automotive sector. Its economic concentration increased considerably.[7] Indicative of this process is the fact that the terminal industry's portion of the overall industrial output decreased from 13.3 percent in 1973 to only 8.5 percent in 1984.

This complex situation—involving changes in the sector's regulatory policies, an increase in imported components and units, a system that repressed guild structures—had an immediate counterpart in the area of employment and productivity. There was a spectacular drop in the number of jobs, from 54,556 workers in 1975 (the last year of constitutional government) to 23,620 in the first years of the return to democracy (see Tables 2.1 and 2.2).

Table 2.1

**Production, Employment, and Productivity in the Argentine Automotive Industry, 1959–1975**

| Year | Number of vehicles produced | Employment | Hours per worker | Productivity per worker |
|------|------|------|------|------|
| 1959 | 32.319 | 9.900 | 1.242 | 3.32 |
| 1960 | 88.338 | 17.500 | 1.194 | 4.27 |
| 1961 | 136.188 | 24.400 | 1.270 | 4.39 |
| 1962 | 129.880 | 25.500 | 1.411 | 3.60 |
| 1963 | 104.899 | 28.200 | 1.092 | 3.40 |
| 1964 | 166.483 | 33.493 | 1.262 | 4.97 |
| 1965 | 194.536 | 36.710 | 1.283 | 5.29 |
| 1966 | 179.453 | 39.500 | 1.221 | 4.53 |
| 1967 | 175.318 | 34.528 | 1.241 | 5.01 |
| 1908 | 180.976 | 35.295 | 1.253 | 5.12 |
| 1969 | 218.590 | 40.349 | 1.288 | 5.24 |
| 1970 | 219.599 | 41.561 | 1.315 | 5.28 |
| 1971 | 253.237 | 42.909 | 1.288 | 5.90 |
| 1972 | 268.593 | 46.316 | 1.244 | 5.80 |
| 1973 | 293.742 | 50.626 | 1.265 | 5.80 |
| 1974 | 286.312 | 57.400 | 1.205 | 4.98 |
| 1975 | 240.036 | 54.556 | 1.216 | 3.61 |

*Source*: Asociación de Fábricas de Automotores (ADEFA) (1993).

Productivity saw a significant increase. It rose from 3.61 in 1974 to 7.08 in 1984 (Tables 2.1 and 2.2). Although there was in this period some reorganization of production and a timely incorporation of electronics technology, the increase in productivity was centered in a greater intensity of work and a greater number of hours on the job per worker.

*The Process of Incorporating Technology
and Organizational Innovations*

One of the automotive industry's characteristics on the international level is its marked dynamism in making innovations in products, processes, and materials. In countries like Argentina these innovations take hold with a certain time lag, since the local firms lack research and development sectors. Their incorporation is influenced by the specific conditions of the Argentine market and by a significant process of adaptation, which, according to some research reports, has had a decisive influence on the resulting technological configuration (Katz and Albin 1978). Part of the process of technological change in the terminals requires a substantial adaptive effort on the part of supplier industries. This fact allows us to conceive of the automotive sub-block as an articulated technological unit with

Table 2.2

**Production, Employment, and Productivity in the Argentine Automotive Industry, 1976–1990**

| Year | Number of vehicles produced | Employment | Hours per worker | Days | Productivity per worker |
|------|------|------|------|------|------|
| 1976 | 193.517 | 50.012 | 1.196 | 150 | 3.24 |
| 1977 | 235.356 | 48.765 | 1.326 | 165 | 4.82 |
| 1978 | 179.160 | 38.402 | 1.265 | 158 | 4.66 |
| 1979 | 253.217 | 41.201 | 1.338 | 167 | 6.14 |
| 1980 | 281.793 | 38.851 | 1.426 | 178 | 7.25 |
| 1981 | 172.363 | 28.334 | 1.269 | 158 | 6.08 |
| 1982 | 132.117 | 23.267 | 1.255 | 156 | 5.67 |
| 1983 | 159.876 | 23.449 | 1.361 | 170 | 6.81 |
| 1984 | 167.323 | 23.260 | 1.394 | 174 | 7.08 |
| 1985 | 137.675 | 20.715 | 1.341 | 167 | 6.64 |
| 1986 | 170.490 | 22.129 | 1.455 | 181 | 7.70 |
| 1987 | 193.315 | 21.820 | 1.680 | 210 | 8.85 |
| 1988 | 164.160 | 21.313 | 1.069 | 133 | 7.70 |
| 1989 | 127.863 | 19.281 | 1.241 | 155 | 6.62 |
| 1990 | 99.639 | 17.430 | 1.194 | 149 | 5.71 |

*Source:* Asociación de Fábricas de Automotores (ADEFA) (1993).

strong connections to the transformations occurring in the core countries (Kantis and Quierolo 1990).

In the case of Argentina, the accumulated design lag, when compared to models produced in the developed countries, began to diminish from the time the nation opened to importation in the 1980s. The spread of advances in product technology, together with the reorientation of the final product toward market segments with larger incomes, invigorated the modernizing process.[8]

In the 1980s, the sector initiated a process of partial technological modernization in response to the open-door import policy promoted by the military government. This policy involved a lowering of import duties and resulted in the arrival of foreign models in the market, thereby implanting new parameters in terms of both quality and comfort.

Innovations were introduced in terms of product (creation of new models and modernization of old ones) and in terms of process (modernization and automation of various processes such as painting, plastic component manufacturing, and soldering). Adjustments were made to plant layouts. Given the tendency to reduce components of national origin, equipment was incorporated to control processes and product testing in order to make parts and components homogeneous with those manufactured by the parent companies.

Organizational innovations were implemented slowly and piecemeal in Argentine industry. In the late 1970s and early 1980s, Renault initiated a program of worker participation centered on the presentation of suggestions for the solution of diverse problems. In the years 1980–81, Ford introduced "quality circles,"[9] and Sevel implemented the teamwork concept with the same objective.

Toward the end of this phase and the beginning of the next, we observe a tendency for markets to concentrate in both the automotive and the auto parts sectors, a reorientation of the product, a more efficient organization and use of labor, a presentation of new models and a withdrawal of old ones. For the sector, this was the beginning of a period of industrial restructuring.

To summarize this section, we could affirm—as do Katz and Lengyel (1991, 5)—that "The behavior of the investment on the part of the automotive terminals, from the late 1970s on, exhibits the same spasmodic character as in past decades. This occurred despite the fact that, in the late 1980s, an important qualitative change was made in its orientation, associated with the new strategies of production and internationalization that these firms had been developing since the middle of the previous decade."

### The Second Stage of Development, 1985–90: The Search for Alternatives Motivated by the Shrinking Internal Market

Toward the mid-1980s, investment projects were increasingly oriented toward the control of the automobile parts branches of the sector. This tendency displaced the axis of the sector's activity from the terminal assemblers to the production of auto parts. Investment plans aimed to consolidate a new production pattern which, centered in the manufacture of auto parts, would make it possible to occupy a well-defined space within the schemes of production specialization that were being consolidated on an international level. At this stage in the automotive industry it seemed that companies were going to specialize in parts, whereas the present tendency is to specialize in models. The strategy of specializing in parts was a response to the pronounced retraction of the internal market. For the companies that remained in the country, this alternative offered one of the few possibilities to subsist. These projects, in addition to providing for the terminals' future, were to have an important effect on the increase of exports. In this period, regional specialization and complementary production in tandem with Brazil were just beginning to be consolidated. With the probable exception of Sevel, which concentrated more on its complementarity with the Brazilian market, the specialization policy was to be found in the strategies of the companies' international headquarters.[10]

The terminals' efforts to modernize their technology gained momentum in the mid-1980s, the central feature being an increasing automation of auto body soldering by means of robots and multi-soldering molds. The sector's various companies differed in the degree to which they carried out this automation. Renault took the lead in robotization by making installments in 60 percent of its plants during these years, followed by Sevel with 36 percent and Autolatina with 4 percent. According to Katz and Lengyel's (1991) estimates, the level of automation in the local plants around 1987 was extremely low by international standards. On the average, only 4.3 percent of the stages in the production process were automated in the Argentine automotive industry, compared to 38 percent in Japan, 33 percent in Europe, 31 percent in the United States, and 18 percent in the newly industrialized countries (NICs) of Asia. In terms of robot density, the average figure for Argentine terminals was 0.3 robots per 100 workers, compared to 12/100 in Japan and 4/100 in Europe and the United States.

Part of this technological incorporation was motivated by the creation of new models. From 1980 onward, and in response to the open-door import policy, the industry began a program of partial technological modernization. This resulted in a flow of investments that included layout adjustments, modernization of processes, renewal of machinery and equipment with partial automation (e.g., soldering robots), equipment for process control, and product testing in order to standardize parts and components with those of the parent company, thereby facilitating the incorporation of imported auto parts for the new models. In an international setting of rapid technical change, and given an industrial policy that constrained the options open to automotive companies, the latters' strategy tended to give greater priority to importation than to development and/or technological modernization of local suppliers. Simultaneously, the sector's strategy also tended to increase its stocks provided by plant subsidiaries. This increase in purchases from abroad and from local subsidiaries tended to stimulate an endogenous growth of the productive process within the various plants of one and the same company.

Regarding organizational innovations, all the sector's companies have introduced strategies involving substantial change in management technologies, though they differ in their application times, their depth, and the extent to which they affect company organization and work content. As an indicator of these transformations, we present below the results of a questionnaire answered by the delegates of all Argentine terminals (automotive, trucks, tractors, etc.) in existence in 1991.

Even with the limitations inherent in any poll, the questionnaire's results (CIOSL, ORINT, and FITIM 1990) indicate that these technologies had become widespread around 1991. This was more true of those having to do with quality techniques, quality circles, and so on than with the so-called "hard" technologies (Novick 1991).

In the period under review, then, the new technologies of production and work organization were more widely adopted than those derived from electronics and information technology (see Table 2.3). For example, 91.6 percent of the delegates present stated that they worked with stock reduction programs; 83.3 percent stated that they were involved with total quality programs, and 66.6 percent with quality circles; 58.3 percent of the delegates indicated that their

Table 2.3

## Incorporation of Technological and Organizational Changes in the Argentine Terminal Industry

|  | Yes | No |
|---|---|---|
| **Management Techniques** | | |
| Total quality | 83.3 | 17.7 |
| Quality circles | 66.6 | 33.3 |
| Stock reduction | 91.6 | 08.4 |
| Just In Time system | 58.3 | 41.7 |
| Other management techniques | 33.3 | 66.6 |
| **Incorporated Technologies** | | |
| Electronic mechanisms in machinery used regularly | 83.3 | 17.7 |
| Programmable automation | 50.0 | 50.0 |
| Tool machines with statistical process | 66.6 | 33.3 |
| Manipulators | 25.0 | 75.0 |
| Robots | 25.0 | 75.0 |
| Transfer systems | 16.6 | 83.3 |
| CAD (Computer Assisted Design system) | 13.3 | 66.6 |
| CAM (Computer Assisted Manufacturing system) | 13.3 | 66.6 |
| Other informational technology | 17.7 | 83.3 |

*Note:* The survey was administered to twenty union delegates who work in all of the terminal assembly plants (e.g., automobiles, trucks, tractors, motor assembly).
*Source*: Novick (1991).

companies are implementing forms of the Just in Time (JIT) system; 83.3 percent of those consulted were of the opinion that electronics and information technology is incorporated in the machinery normally used in the plant; 66.6 percent affirmed that their production environment is equipped with machine tools having statistical control, and 50 percent indicated that programmable automation was present in the work environment. Other technologies such as CAD, CAM, manipulating robots and transfer mechanisms are less used in Argentine automotive terminals.

### The Recovery of the Terminal Industry, 1991–95

*Overview: The Special Nature of the Automobile Industry's Regulatory System*

Given the sector's contribution to GNP, its multiple effects on industrial activity, its capacity to generate employment, and its weight in the national economy, the automotive industry is one of the sectors most regulated by the state. Its particular regulatory system is linked to the stabilization of the economy and the opening of markets. In contrast to the regulation of other sectors, liberalization policies have not allowed companies to import automotive goods without restrictions, but allow manufacturing firms themselves to import models from abroad on the basis of progressive annual quotas. These provisions establish a system for liberalizing the market while demanding the modernization of manufacturing plants, in the hopes of avoiding production with outmoded technology. The main elements in the automotive industry's regulatory system are:

- legal authorization to increase by 40 percent the average imported contents per line of cylinder bore;
- an agreement to allow very low tariffs for terminal companies that import vehicles and auto parts, for which the companies must compensate with exports;
- quotas for the import of models not produced locally

The results of this special system for the automotive industry—accompanied by the convertibility plan and the reduction of inflation—can be seen in a spectacular increase in production (based on a market with backed-up demands from the 1980s) and a considerable rise in interindustry commerce, reflected by a drop of approximately 35 percent in automobile prices.[11]

In March of 1991 an agreement was reached between bodies representing the terminal companies (ADEFA), the concessionaries (ACARA), and the sector's unions (SMATA and UOM), producing a number of benefits. On the one hand, the agreement permitted firms to increase the amount of imported content used in vehicles produced, based on a widening of the margins allowed and the possibility of obtaining an additional percentage if the company's import–export performance improved. On the other hand, it established tax breaks to provide an incentive for exports. One of the main objectives of the agreement was to improve the terminal companies' balance of payments.

In the agreement, each party committed itself to the following: (1) the government would reduce the National Highway Fund Tax and the Internal Tax, with the effect of lowering the price for the end consumer by 5.2 percent and 4 percent, respectively; (2) La Asociación de Concesionarios de la República Argentina (Association of Concessionaries of the Republic of Argentina, ACARA) lowered its commission, resulting in a 2 percent drop in the public sales price; (3) the national auto parts suppliers reduced their prices for the January/February period of 1991 by an average of 16 percent, resulting in a 3 percent drop in the public sales price; (4) the sector's unions contributed their share through the salary negotiations being worked out at the time; (5) the terminal assemblers were prohibited from passing on to the consumer's price the increase in dollars for the months of January/February 1991.

Importantly, during this period there would be no layoffs of union personnel in the terminals or concessionaries, except for disciplinary reasons. In addition,

Table 2.4

**Production, Employment, Days Worked, and Productivity in the Argentine Automotive Industry, 1991–1994**

| Year | Production | Employment | Hours per worker | Days | Productivity per worker |
|------|-----------|-----------|------------------|------|------------------------|
| 1991 | 142.380 | 18.317 | 1.485 | 185 | 7.58 |
| 1992 | 259.716 | 22.161 | 1.847 | 230 | 11.81 |
| 1993 | 341.189 | 23.027 | 1.960 | 245 | 14.86 |
| 1994 | 408.777 | 25.734 | 1.870 | n.a. | 15.88 |

*Source*: Asociación de Fábricas de Automotores (ADEFA) (1995).

toward the end of 1993, the government took a number of measures to continue in the direction of deregulation and tax elimination. In this context, the pact known as the Fiscal Agreement was signed between the national and the provincial governments. The latter agreed to reduce taxes on gross income, seals, and so forth, which are applied to all productive activities.[12] In the case of vehicle production, eliminating the gross income tax had the impact of reducing the gross production value by 5.3 percent, if one estimates that the tax was normally imposed at least twice in the production chain. Moreover, the Fiscal Agreement also included reductions on the order of 30 percent in the contributions made by employers to the social security system. This lowered the labor costs of the terminal and auto parts companies from 1994 onward.

*Sectoral Productivity and Competitiveness*

While production between 1990 and 1994 grew by around 310 percent, employment grew by 48 percent in the same period. Productivity saw a spectacular gain: total automobiles produced in relation to workers employed went from 5.71 in 1990 to 15.88 in 1994. The number of hours worked for each automobile produced also confirms this increase in productivity. From 1982 on, the number of hours required per vehicle declined, albeit with fluctuations. While in 1982 the production of a single vehicle took up 221.2 man hours, in 1994 it required 142.6 (see Tables 2.4 and 2.5).

The departure of the multinational companies and the sector's heavy concentration of capital in the 1980s continued into the 1990s. With the production increase, market leadership in automobile manufacturing was concentrated in only three companies (Sevel, Autolatina, and Ciadea, formerly tied to Renault). Autolatina continued to lead the utility segment while Mercedes-Benz led in trucks and omnibuses. Two local companies, El Detalle and Decaroli, participated in the market of chassis production and have seen significant growth since 1981.

Table 2.5

**Evolution of Productivity in the Argentine Terminal Industry**
(hours worked and number of workers per unit)

| Year | Production | Hours Worked (in thousands) | Productivity Index (hours) | Productivity Index (per worker) |
|------|-----------|------------------------------|-----------------------------|----------------------------------|
| 1973 | 293.742 | 64.065 | 218.1 | 5.80 |
| 1975 | 240.036 | 66.374 | 276.5 | 3.61 |
| 1976 | 193.517 | 60.863 | 314.5 | 3.24 |
| 1977 | 235.536 | 64.674 | 274.8 | 4.82 |
| 1978 | 179.160 | 49.609 | 276.8 | 4.66 |
| 1979 | 253.217 | 55.156 | 217.8 | 6.14 |
| 1980 | 271.793 | 55.436 | 196.7 | 7.25 |
| 1981 | 172.363 | 35.975 | 208.7 | 6.08 |
| 1982 | 132.117 | 29.207 | 221.1 | 5.67 |
| 1983 | 159.876 | 32.929 | 205.9 | 6.81 |
| 1984 | 167.323 | 32.934 | 196.8 | 7.08 |
| 1985 | 137.675 | 27.784 | 201.8 | 6.64 |
| 1986 | 170.490 | 32.214 | 188.9 | 7.70 |
| 1987 | 193.315 | 36.661 | 189.6 | 8.85 |
| 1988 | 164.160 | 22.787 | 138.8 | 7.70 |
| 1989 | 127.823 | 23.930 | 187.2 | 6.62 |
| 1990 | 99.639 | 20.812 | 208.9 | 5.71 |
| 1991 | 138.958 | 27.216 | 195.8 | 7.58 |
| 1992 | 262.022 | 40.939 | 156.2 | 11.81 |
| 1993 | 342.344 | 45.155 | 131.9 | 14.86 |
| 1994 | 408.777 | 48.135 | 117.7 | 15.88 |

*Source*: Asociación de Fábricas de Automotores (ADEFA) (1995).

Due to the protective regulation, the increase in internal demand, and the progress made by MERCOSUR, changes in the sector's investment tendencies are emerging with the arrival in the country of new companies and capital. In 1994, after fifteen years, General Motors returned and installed a plant for the manufacture of pick-ups in Córdoba on the grounds of Ciadea (which has a 20 percent share in the new company), and in 1995 laid the groundwork for an automobile plant in the province of Santa Fe. Toyota initiated its project to install a manufacturing plant, also of pick-ups and light commercial vehicles, while Fiat, as recently as January 1996, closed negotiations on a collective labor agreement in order to install in Córdoba a plant that will employ 5,000 workers.[13]

The data on production, productivity, and technological and organizational changes indicate an industry that has undergone a very significant transformation on the level of companies, products, production model (with greater emphasis on subcontracting), organization type, and work content. These technological and organizational changes, however, have not resulted from the installation of a "pure type" of production system. The modernization in question is rather of a "hybrid" and even idiosyncratic nature, considering that it includes diverse technological conditions and even diverse and adaptive forms of work organization, resulting in the coexistence of different models in one and the same plant.

Some authors (e.g., Shaiken 1995), who maintain that the Argentine industry is still not highly competitive when compared to its analogs in Brazil and Mexico, pose the existence of two models. On the one hand, we have the industry that supplies the internal market with automobiles and components, made up of old plants with outdated technology and a still-inefficient production process. On the other, we have the beginnings of a new, though small, industry that exports components to Brazil and the international market. This analysis, resulting from a survey made in 1993, recognizes the new emerging model in recently installed plants such as those of General Motors, Volkswagen, Toyota, and others under construction. This new model implies innovations not only in the techno-organizational area but also in its system of labor relations.

## Changes in Work Organization and
## in Labor Relations in the 1990s

The transformation of work organization processes has deepened in recent years, although such changes have not been institutionalized in the sector's collective agreements. The exception is found in the new work agreements—such as those of General Motors of Argentina and recently Fiat—which are signed before initiating activities and which inaugurate a new model of collective agreements in the country.[14]

It seems strange that, despite the sector's transformation, there are few systematic studies of the terminal industry's work organization models, with the exception of a recent Latin American study (CEPAL 1995) that does not examine the case of Argentina in depth. There are, on the other hand, a profusion of journalistic articles focusing on the innovations in organization and work content resulting from General Motor's "production cells."

Based on a recent study (Bartolomé and Buceta 1995) of the automotive market's four leading terminal companies, we can offer the following synthesis of the industry's present situation:

1. All the companies under study tended to manage their production under a logic that we could generically call "lean production," though in only two cases was there regular use of Just in Time with suppliers for significant portions of the segment of parts, assemblies, and components stocked.
2. Mutually complementary management approaches reinforce quality requirements throughout the supply chain. This obliged the companies to develop functional structures specifically to attend to their relation with suppliers, in

order to develop "Suppliers with Certified Quality" within the sector's patterns of general development.

3. The reduction of stocks—a prime characteristic of lean production—tightens the line and provokes a reevaluation of Internal Logistics. This fact takes on an especially complex significance for companies operating with foreign suppliers. In addition, all the companies have developed Continuous Improvement programs, including the practice of Quality Circles and Suggestions Systems.

4. The corrective maintenance of machines and tools, and the tendency toward multiple uses of tools, has produced an increase in the qualifications of operators, in order for them to take responsibility for the preventive maintenance of the machines. This has led two companies to study the possibility of subcontracting the service, which would then be given by micro-companies independently managed by ex-maintenance workers. In the case of one company, reopening its other plant has meant subcontracting two services: (1) preventive maintenance service—from the outset of activities—contracted to a firm controlled by the corporate group itself; and (2) internal transport. Only one of the companies polled relies on an outside source for information services (internal and satellite networks), thereby making direct connection with its companion company in Brazil for the internal transport of materials and for the consolidation of materials and items (including imported auto parts and those supplied locally); its purpose in this is to supply all its needs, even in sectors as dynamic as the assembly line.

5. Concerning subcontracted activities related to phases of the productive process, one finds that all the companies demand the provision of finished assemblies or sub-assemblies; the activities related to coating, painting, and assembly remained integrated in three of the companies analyzed. Only one plant, recently installed, subcontracts the activities of production and assembly of front and cabin, as well as the painting, which is provided by a local associate.

6. In all cases, the new production logic presupposes a new work organization and changes in layout, though in three of the plants surveyed most of the distribution took place in longitudinal lines. Technological incorporation has been gradual and focused on some segments of the production line (painting and chassis measurement appear to be the most relevant). While most processes are computer controlled, there is no indication of a massive introduction of international cutting-edge technology.

7. All the companies have adopted approaches that—with different names and degrees of implementation—involve a reorganization of jobs in terms of modules or work cells, thereby stimulating widespread intercell rotation and a certain degree of vertical multi-tasking capability (e.g., stock management, preventive maintenance, quality control). In only one case, the cells have autonomy to determine their own objectives (related mainly to matters of

security and quality), for the achievement of which they are paid group productivity prizes. For one of the companies, this reorganization has in turn given rise to "on site" management.

8. At the level of the individual job position, changes in the work process have called for new skills involving practical and socio-relational competence. Demands for greater understanding of the productive and operative process, greater ability to concentrate, ability to work in groups, to listen, to observe processes and persons and communicate orally, added to the requirement for a greater capacity to resolve problems—such demands extend all along the occupational pyramid in order to involve workers more directly in meeting the firms' objectives.

These new job requirements represent, in a sense, deficits for the companies. It should be mentioned, in fairness, that there have evidently been no problems with qualifications related to basic knowledge and specific techniques. This is due to the recruiting strategies used after raising the requirements for formal education; it is also due to internal policies of employee development on the job.

While we have indicated, in general terms, that the industry's work has been simplified, we should also acknowledge that there has been a need to reformulate—and in some cases to create—job positions that are fairly complex and that require the application of specific knowledge and skills. Positions dealing with internal logistics and line balancing (in companies using the JIT and/or the Kan Ban approach), as well as new positions for the coordination of cells or work teams (leader) combine decisively high technical qualifications and a fine-tuned balance of practical and personal skills.

In the area of labor relations one finds significant changes. Even in plants where old agreements are still in effect, the latter are only symbolic where salarial clauses are concerned, and in practice permit greater flexibility in all areas. In fact, some "company agreements" not validated by the Ministry of Labor accept the contracting of temporary personnel. The sales slump of 1995 provoked long suspensions and even layoffs referred to as "voluntary retirement," without any open conflicts.

Another feature of this new stage is the breakdown of the vertical integration model and an increase in subcontracting, or, at least, significant changes in the way it is practiced. All the companies studied leave the manufacture of assemblies or significant sub-assemblies to auto parts companies. In many cases, the auto parts firm itself centralizes and processes the tasks, parts, or assemblies made by other companies that, until recently, used to supply the terminal directly.

On the one hand, this process leads terminals to make greater demands on auto parts companies, while causing supplier plants and subcontractors to change their geographic location. On the other hand, it requires the terminals to undertake complex developments in terms of changes in process.[15] This is particularly important if we bear in mind that most auto parts companies are locally owned and can be characterized as PyME (small businesses).

Finally, the varied composition of the PyME auto parts sector—as regards technological trajectory, market position, production scale, quality, and price—makes it necessary for the companies to have access to information that would allow them to select associates for long-term projects.[16] Several studies of the competitiveness of the sector (e.g., Moori-Koenig and Yoguel 1992) suggest that auto parts firms have little or no knowledge of the terminals' strategies or the dynamics of the market in which they operate, a fact that further limits the terminals' ability to implement their own strategies. Moreover, the Management Chambers have not yet consolidated a role in the transfer of and assistance with information. They are giving preference to traditional means of response (mainly lobbying the state), a set of strategies tied to the internal market model and that are based upon fear of integration with Brazil.

## Trade Unions in the Automobile Industry

### The Development of the Sector's Unionism

In SMATA's fifty years as a mechanics union, one can identify three periods that distinguish its behavior as an intermediary between workers, the state, and employers. The first period begins with the union's inception in 1945 and continues to the mid-1960s. In this period the sector's unionism produced various strategies. In the first years, SMATA developed a policy of gradual growth through the formation of its productive and commercial units, using a conservative strategy that was not ambitious. It conceived of itself as a small union in a sector with scant growth. When the large terminal assembly firms were installed, the sector was transformed in its dynamism and its capacity to induce modernization processes based on the production linkages idiosyncratic to this industry. These new structural characteristics renewed the sector's unionism, which responded by developing two strategies: one that called itself "classist and combative," and the other, which is normally referred to as "corporatist." These approaches were to clash with one another from 1965 to 1975.

The second period, extending from 1965 to 1990, was characterized by the advent, consolidation, exhaustion, and near extinction of an idiosyncratic auto industry model—a model which, in labor relations, worked with the corporatist model of unionism. Other representative forms in the sector's combative unionism were organized as company unions; they were eventually defeated and dissolved, first by legal measures taken by the state,[17] and later through state terrorism.[18] In the automobile sector, then, corporatist unionism consolidated its hegemony. This model of union action developed between 1965 and 1970, entered a phase of sharp internal confrontation with alternate models from 1971 to

1975, and emerged reinforced from this period onward, in spite of the obstacles imposed on unions by military repression.

A third period can be defined from 1991 to the present. Here, corporatist unionism, which today has absolute hegemony in the sector, has delineated a bargaining strategy in which elements of traditional corporatism are combined, in a singular way, with forms of articulated but strongly centralized bargaining. Due to its strategy, it is perhaps one of the unions that has grown the most in this last period—a period that has seen the progressive weakening of unionism and significant changes in the model of labor relations.

### Characteristics of Union Strategies Developed between 1945 and 1965

The first period included the most dynamic phase of the model of import substitution. The vertical union organization, which grouped workers into single unions by area of activity, predominated in the industry and in the private sector. In this framework, the Sindicato de Mecánicos y Afines emerged in June of 1945 as the single union for workers who were repair shop mechanics. Toward 1946 it achieved its position as an independent union—a birth marked by a historical dispute, persisting to our own day, over the best way to group workers belonging to the metal mechanic sector. The state looked at the question of union organization in terms of alternatives: either the power of the metallurgic union would continue to grow, creating its own "automotive" sub-area of organization; or the state could permit the formation of a new automobile union, distinct from metallurgical workers. As it turned out, the mechanics union was granted union status in August of 1946 and was defined as a national, profession-based association of workers, grouping together workers and employees of the nation's automotive industry. It represented, therefore, workers in the automobile manufacturing terminals (automobiles, trucks, etc.), in automobile parts plants, in establishments for the manufacture and marketing of trucks, farm machinery and road equipment, in mechanics repair shops, in automobile dealers, and in auto-related upholstery and electric shops.

In April 1948 the mechanics union adopted its present name (Sindicato de Mecánicos y Afines del Transporte Automotor—SMATA) and in November of the same year signed its first collective work agreement with ACARA (Asociación de Concesionarios de Automóviles de la República Argentina) and the Ministry of Labor. This agreement fixed salaries and work conditions for a number of different occupations: mechanics, lathe operators, repair workers, electricians, ironworkers, welders, metal platists, painters, auto body workers, upholsterers, radiator work, rubber workers, grease work, washers, cleaners, and chauffeurs.[19] At that time the union organized workers in small production units: mechanic shops, concessionaries, and auto parts workers. Toward 1950, the union formulated its internal statutes.

In the 1950s SMATA constituted, grouped, and developed its membership base. Although the union's strategy was to strengthen its numbers, its profile in the context of the worker movement was still less than ambitious. It fought for and gained endorsement from the Ministry of Labor for its inclusion of auto part upholsterers, workers of the Automóvil Club Argentino,[20] and some service station mechanics. Meanwhile it took steps to develop its own social services, made possible through the creation of the "mutual aid society." This process of consolidation and development was interrupted by the military *coup d'état* of 1955. What then remained from the foundation period was the achievement of an independent union status, the first statutes that institutionalized the union, the first collective agreements signed, and the installation of the mutual and the storehouse for members.

The ground had also been prepared for the legal, unionist, and political struggle between the UOM and SMATA for the affiliation of metal mechanics units. The conflict between the two unions for the representation of automotive workers developed over all the periods under review, having its high point in the 1970s when the sector's combative unionism was defeated. Both unions can be considered "strong" because of the size of their membership, their power to mobilize, and the fact that their directors have political weight in the Partido Justicialista, the political party that inherited Peronism. This is why the state ruled, alternatively, in favor of the one or the other. At present, the signing in January 1996 of an agreement between Fiat and SMATA revived a controversy that seemed resolved. At the time of its apparent resolution, the UOM emerged as a general union within the area of metallurgy and auto parts, while SMATA would be a union clearly linked to the terminal automotive industry. But the conflicts over membership persist.

The sector's dynamism in the late 1950s and early 1960s was not reflected in the unions' growth because the new terminals adopted another strategy of union representation for the automobile industry: the company union. Meanwhile, SMATA developed a strategy intended to maintain both the salarial purchasing power and the employment of its members.

Company unionism in Argentina developed a different strategy for representing workers' interests—a strategy that expressed itself in an anti-ownership and anti-bureaucracy stance. It is noteworthy that SMATA at that time did not yet adhere to the corporatist unionism model, as it would in the 1970s and 1980s, with the capacity to deal with the state as an intermediator and pressure group. The expression "anti-bureaucratic struggle" reflects certain politico-ideological convictions as to how to conduct the struggles of workers in relation to management, or how to build the unity of workers in a given occupation.[21] These conceptions do not address the need to build a strong union with an ability to pressure the state to intervene in the sector's regulation or in the determination of its salaries.

At the end of this formative period we find that the three union strategies having the most influence in the union's history were taking defined positions: the conservative-traditional, which originated with the union without taking note of the sector's structural changes in the first half of the 1960s; the corporatist, which began to emerge after 1965; and the combative, which arose, paradoxically, within the company unions.

## Characteristics of Union Strategies Developed during the Second Period, 1966–90

Within SMATA the creation and consolidation of a model of corporatist unionism stretched over a long period extending from 1966 to 1990. In this time frame one can distinguish several sub-periods correlated, on the one hand, to the evolution of the Argentine automotive sector, and on the other, to the possibility of building a strong union able to question hegemonies in the worker movement and in national politics. The novelty of this project was that it was a new union that grew and consolidated itself in the late 1960s when most unions already had long decades of history in the worker movement and in national politics.

In the evolution of the strategies developed within the union there are four sub-periods. The period from 1966 to 1970 can be considered the moment in which a model of corporatist unionism emerged. From 1971 to 1975, there were serious confrontations between the corporatist model of unionism and that of the combative sectors. From 1976 to 1983, within the framework of union repression, there was resistance to the military dictatorship's policy regarding salaries. And finally, between 1984 to 1990, the union began a defensive struggle to protect sources of work, while the industry was in crisis and threatened to shrink to an insignificant size, and while the state abstained increasingly from mediating distributive agreements and sectoral policies. In what follows, we briefly review each of these sub-periods.

By 1966, a new current began to develop within SMATA and became known as the Movimiento de Unidad Automotriz Lista VERDE (Automotive Unity Movement). This movement (MUA) proposed a different role for the union within the labor movement and before the state.[22] It was a moment when an attempt was made to strengthen the union's bargaining capacity based on the corporatist union model typical of the phase of import substitution industrialization. The example they apparently followed, with regard to organization, was that of the Unión Obrera Metalúrgica, which involved centralizing and creating hegemonic power over union management, integrating the members of the terminal assemblers, taking part in the making of sectoral policy, and blocking the affiliation of members toward the metallurgic sector union by preventing— through legal recourses before the Ministry of Labor—the concession of increased membership to the rival union. Toward 1968, then, one finds a new inflection in the concepts orienting the union.

That year, some of SMATA's political leadership took the initiative to give the union a new profile, to transform it into a strong intermediary with the state and with company management in the area of automotive policies. Consequently, SMATA's new orientation lent a new dynamism to its struggle to increase membership and it obtained the affiliation of workers in the terminal assembly firms. This would change SMATA's representation: it went from having no affiliates in the terminal plants to having 40 percent of terminal workers by the mid-1970s. More recently, in 1994, terminal workers represented less than 20 percent of the union's members,[23] although it continued to recruit almost all workers in the industry (the exception being the company Sevel, which remains affiliated to the UOM). However, as the union with the greatest relative growth and most substantial innovations, it strongly influences patterns of collective bargaining in the sector.

This change of strategy in the union's management reveals a new logic of operation both in the sector and at the level of national policy: the union had to assume a different role in relation to company management, the state, and its own members.[24]

Based on this new vision, the mechanics union now conceived of itself as a pressure group capable of determining the sector's public policy and the social organization of its government. It began to enter into a stronger dialogue with the state than with company management. The sector's more specific occupational claims had little relevance. Partly neglecting concrete work conditions and everyday concerns of workers, the union turned its main efforts to the area of employment and the national automotive industry's role within the development model as a guarantee of its future hegemony in the sector.

The essential elements of conflicts within the mechanics union between 1984 and 1990 reflected the development and exhaustion of the corporatist strategy, the last reformulations of militant stances, and the emergence of a new strategy that would consolidate itself from 1991 on.

On the one hand, while the union retreated somewhat from a corporatist strategy, its official leadership maintained a dialogue with the state, questioning its economic and social policies, above all in relation to employment and salaries. On the other hand, the union instigated negotiation in new areas: agreements on company mergers and on union participation in MERCOSUR. In both areas, the state's attitude as an interlocutor became equivocal and the union–company relationship took on a special protagonism. These agreements and new bargaining issues were the practical antecedent for the new model of union action that the union would propose after 1991. Moreover, traditional forms of struggle took place in a sector whose own industrial model had now entered a phase of exhaustion. These *traditional forms of struggle* were in general *defensive,* since employment and work conditions had been adversely affected. Given this combative political line of the union leadership, a militant tendency emerged which, while expressing itself in matters of employment and salaries, also developed other forms of expression and a different way of representing adversaries in collective bargaining. The expression of this tendency tended to compromise the management's control of the plant, as management and the union leadership were represented both as "the opponent" of the rank and file. This combative line was eventually isolated and defeated by the action, sometimes concerted, by union leaders and management.

Furthermore, the nature of the decentralized bargaining taking place at this time, due to the difficulty in linking up production units and small fields of activity, made the practice of even the traditional mode of confrontation appear scattered and uncoordinated.

Faced with the economic decline of the automobile industry, the Plenary of SMATA's Secretaries General for the entire country made a declaration in 1985 announcing its "peaceful and responsible mobilization" in order to promote the financial health of the industry. To achieve this they proposed the creation of policies that would eliminate financial speculation, promote manufacturing activities and internal market growth, and nationalize bank deposits.

Acting on this plan, SMATA's leaders demanded the creation of an Automotive Industry Commission. The Commission was to have company representation through the industry's management chambers—ADEFA (Argentine Association of Automotive Manufacturers), ACARA (Argentine Association of Concessionaries), and FAATRA (for auto parts and components). It was also to have official representatives of the MTSS (Ministry of Labor and Social Security), the Secretary of Commerce and Industry, and SMATA. Its purpose was to study and work out a plan for the reconversion of the auto industry with short-, medium-, and long-term objectives for the sector's production and marketing. The innovative element of this proposal was the introduction of concertation between the state, owners, and workers representatives with regard to sectoral policy. This foreshadowed another agreement, signed in 1991, that was also to be an initiative of the union. Indeed, in this agreement, one finds the foundation for the new role that the union assumed in response to the sector's crisis and its restructuring.

In December of 1987, legislation passed by the National Congress (Law No. 23545, 11 January 1988) restored collective bargaining through commissions having equal numbers of management and worker representatives. This abrogated the existing Law 21307, which had given the executive branch the power to fix salaries for public and private activities. As a result of the new legislation, SMATA denounced all of its previous agreements and called for their renegotiation.[25] The crisis of the automotive industry, the technological and organizational investments being made, and the difficulty workers had in evaluating the latter in terms of emerging strategic changes, made the union feel it would be inopportune to make substantial changes in the agreements since they could not anticipate what problems might result from the transformations under way. In other words, the commissions opened their discussion of the agreements at a time when the union did not want to anticipate the worker's defense strategies; they opted to focus their negotiations more on the recovery of salary levels and the defense of work sources than on the issue of flexibility in the conditions under which the workforce was to be used. The result was that the previous agreement formally remained in effect without regulating the work norms.

The period 1988–90 signaled the end of an automotive production model oriented toward a small, internal, and highly protected market. The local industry had threatened to shrink to a minimal size. In this context, unions were unable to find a favorable "terrain" upon which to negotiate for improvements in workers' conditions. The union thus tended to develop defensive strategies dealing with employment and salary. In these circumstances, the union preferred to explore situations, to experiment, and to improvise "ad hoc" solutions according to the condition of labor relations and the economic and financial situation of the companies.

From 1989 to the first half of 1991, the union's collective bargaining encountered many difficulties. The strategy of the union leadership was to sustain salary negotiations and suspend all bargaining for improvements in working conditions. They concluded that they had already reached the highest level of attainments possible within the traditional production model, and that—in view of the industry's present stagnation and bankruptcy—to discuss the entire claims package would set the union permanently back from the historical advances previously made, in exchange for a paltry gain in salaries. Each salary increase jeopardized a seniority bonus, or vacation pay, or the introduction of multi-tasking for workers. The solution, they imagined, was to suspend institutionalized bargaining for work conditions and to continue to press the issue of salary levels.[26] However, this strategy only managed to delay the legal formulation of the collective contract. The reason was that, in reality, the companies initiated far-reaching transformations in areas in which the old agreements had (and still have) nothing to say, but with which both the workers and the companies' Internal Commissions have been deeply and directly involved. This situation has generated a body of internal agreements taking varied forms, as authorized by the Ministry of Labor and Social Security.

### Characteristics of Union Strategies since 1991

By the 1990s, the automotive sector's unionism began to manifest logic that differed from that of other sectors. The union established itself as a political interlocutor promoting a model that made its influence felt in sectoral agreements on three levels: the nation, MERCOSUR, and in the companies. It had managed to link negotiation by company (decentralized and localized regarding salaries and work conditions) with negotiation by field of occupation (in terms of the sectoral and regional policies of MERCOSUR). The new model proposed by this strategy contemplated acting upon the state as a pressure group, in order to obtain a special regulatory system precisely at a moment when the internationalization of business presented both a threat and a challenge. This regulatory system would produce a gradual liberalization of the sector's economy, would facilitate its restructuring within a time frame, and would avoid a negative impact on employment. Moreover, the union negotiated clauses concerning "social peace,"[27] which took preventive measures against conflictual situations that could arise in the process of industrial restructuring, and established retaining walls against unemployment.

In the midst of the deep crisis that affected this economic sector, SMATA pressed the national government to promote and coordinate a collaborative effort on the part of all the sector's representatives. This gave rise to the Acuerdo para la Reactivación Automotriz (Automotive Reactivation Agreement), signed on 25 March 1991, whose application has produced stabilization, a slight growth in employment, and a significant increase in the sector's production, sales, and productivity.

The setting for the development of this new model of unionism was demarcated by the Acta de Concertación del Régimen para el Sector Automotriz (Concertation Act for the Automotive Sector Regulatory System) signed in April 1990, and by the Acuerdo para la Reactivación y el Crecimiento del Sector Automotriz (Agreement for the Reactivation and Growth of the Automotive Sector) signed in March of 1991. The latter was renewed—after drawn-out negotiations—in August of 1994 for the period 1994–99.

The Agreement committed the signing parties (government and automotive industry sector participants) to make a concerted effort to reduce the dollar price of automobiles by an average of 33 percent in relation to the prices of December 1990.[28] This Agreement gave the union a respite in the area of layoffs and suspensions, but in counterbalance the union was required to renounce open discussion of salaries and what was euphemistically called "social peace."

The recovery in automotive activity produced by the Collaborative Act was not reflected in the union's achievements in the area of claims *(reivindicaciones)*. Negotiations for new work conditions took place at the level of the individual establishment, where care was taken to include the subject in written agreements. Bargaining over salaries was placed "on hold" from the first moment of the Agreement; it was further impeded by the Plan de Convertibilidad (Convertibility Plan, 1 April 1991), which prohibited salary increases from being passed on to prices; and by Decree 1334/91, which authorized only such salary increases as were founded on reasonably estimated (or calculated) productivity levels. When the latter was substituted by Decree 470/93, salary discussions were revived on a decentralized basis; this, it was claimed, was an improvement of sorts for the sector's workers. Importantly, however, decentralized bargaining tended to deepen the heterogeneity of the sector's rewards and payments.[29]

The sector's companies were reluctant to renew the Agreement for the Reactivation and Growth of the Automotive Industry for the period 1994–99. How did the union respond? SMATA resorted to the concept of "sectoral concertation" as a strategic foundation for labor relations, referring to such concertation as "the only way to increase production while respecting the rights of workers."[30]

For their part, the companies pressed for a low-salary agreement. A new five-year Agreement was then reached, called Acuerdo para la Consolidación de la Reconversión, el Empleo, la Productividad y el Crecimiento del Sector Automotriz (Agreement for the Consolidation of Restructuring, Employment, Productivity, and Growth of the Automotive Sector"). The companies' management retracted its demand of denying salary increases, granting a 3 percent increase to become effective in the months of April, May, and June of 1993, a 2 percent increase in October of 1993, and an additional $450 in the second half[31] of February 1994. This salary agreement revived a procedure that had not been used since 1975: the global discussion of salaries with the terminal assembly firms. From 1975 onward, salary negotiation had been carried out by the Consejo Directivo Nacional (National Management Council), the Comisiones Ejecutivas de las Seccionales (Sectional Executive Commissions), and the Miembros de la Comisión Interna de Reclamos (Members of the Internal Claims Commission) in each of the establishments. The union sector pressed vigorously to include globalized salary negotiation[32] within the framework of a production agreement that already discussed, on a global basis, production conditions, activity improvement factors, employment gains, and that singled out only the negotiation of salaries to be particularized by company.

In the agreement's annex the companies and unions committed themselves to the following:

1. Salary increases negotiated by establishment (productive unit) on the basis of goals in productivity, efficiency, and quality.
2. The terms agreed to will be calculated and paid out in regular periods no smaller than a trimester.
3. Company management will offer to co-signing union organizations, when appropriate, the documented information needed to analyze and financially monitor the systems agreed to.
4. The parties to the Agreement will negotiate, in good faith and in a climate of social peace and mutual understanding, the basis and the mechanisms needed for the full operation of this Agreement.
5. Future agreements derived from the present one will remain in effect for a period to be assigned in each case by the parties, in exercise of their collective bargaining autonomy.

In the above Annex one finds the basis for articulated negotiation,[33] where the parties negotiate particular modules per establishment. The articulated negotiation proposed does not leave the parties free to bargain as they see fit, but rather is tied to previous commitments with the "social peace" and guarantees stability so long as the self-disciplined conduct of the parties allows the agreement to remain in force.

Articulated bargaining was more readily accepted by SMATA[34] than by any other, inasmuch as it already formed a part of its historical bargaining practice. The articulated negotiation model chosen by SMATA for the stage beginning in 1990 had two levels. At the macro level, there was a General Agreement for the sector among the principal participants (the state, unions, companies, and sectoral chambers). At the micro level, particular modules were to be negotiated between the union, on the one hand—with the participation of the Claims Commission, the Sectional Executive Commission, the National Management Commission—and the companies, on the other. It is interesting to note that in this type of negotiation, though all levels participated, the roles of the Claims Commission and the Sectional Executive Commission were limited. In other words, SMATA, as an entity on the highest level, did not decentralize negotiations and avoided initiatives which in former periods had produced alternate lines of political and unionist development. It is also noteworthy that SMATA accepted this type of articulated bargaining while establishing a scaffolding to control the negotiations with the objective of limiting the relative autonomy of the different organizational levels involved in negotiations. Curiously, SMATA emphasized that the articulated system of bargaining could imply the breakdown of solidarity for the union's workers, without noticing that what had been changing was only the manner of constructing that solidarity. The Fordist model and, to a degree, the corporatist union model, rested on a mechanical structuring of solidarity. In that model solidarity is produced by the ease with which one worker identifies with another. The new models of union representation call for the construction of a solidarity based on differences. In them it is more problematical to build identification between workers; the kind of participation and communication they require is different from that of the previous model.

The present form of unionism assures employers of the benefits of per-company negotiation—that is, sensitized to the real conditions of profitability and productivity—without the "dangers" of a company unionism that, in Argentina, has had a strongly militant and anti-management tradition. The companies thereby enjoy the benefits of "tailored" negotiations without the risks of governability implied by decentralized bargaining. Under this arrangement, the company's interlocutor is not the Internal Commission, but rather the Secretariat, the Sectional Management Commission, or the National Management Commission. These interlocutors guarantee the company greater ability to distance itself from everyday problems, while proportionally reducing the power and autonomy that a radicalized internal commission could acquire. The union, on the other hand, strengthens its hand in institutionalized bargaining and avoids the growth and articulation of protest policies "from below." For the union, the benefits are the strengthening of its institutional power and the guarantee of employment for the sector. The down side of the system is that the union must accept a clause regarding "social peace" in labor relations and collective bargaining, and it is required to sign agreements on a per-company basis to create temporary employment for defined periods of time.

Therefore, to summarize, in this framework of labor relations, the union gains institutional power, the generation of employment, and a leading role in collective bargaining in exchange for a decentralized and articulated negotiation, social peace, and precarious employment.

*Conflicts in the Sector, 1984–94*

The level of conflict in the automotive sector remained virtually the same in the years 1983 (9 percent), 1990 (10 percent), 1991 (14 percent), and 1994 (10 percent). The percentages are in relation to the average level of conflict for industrial unions as a whole. These are the same years in which SMATA's conflict level also grew in relation to the average level for the nation's industrial unions (see Tables 2.6 and 2.7) Isolation is a prime characteristic in the conflicts undertaken by this union. This invites reflection on the difficulties faced by a union with SMATA's structure in its attempts to forge a solidarity based on occupational similarities among workers. Solidarity is established—if indeed it is—by sub-area (i.e., car dealerships, service stations) and never through inter-establishments. This tends to isolate the demands of the sector's most dynamic workers: those of the terminal plants. Moreover, the union does not handle the solidarity of the workers' interests in such a way as to achieve an organic extension of that solidarity throughout all sub-areas. Thus, conflicts and strike movements tend to be isolated and politically controlled by an organization that centralizes the role of leadership in the National Executive Commission.

It should be noted that SMATA's conflicts, in contrast to other unions, tend to be concentrated in the country's inland, away from the coasts, and especially in the province of Córdoba. This setting diminishes the demonstrative power of its actions, inasmuch as the union's influence on public opinion, and on sectoral public policy or the policies of private industries, is diminished when compared to unions that can mobilize and act directly in the Federal Capital. Indeed, the data in Table 2.6 indicate that 52 percent of the period's conflicts were registered in the province of Córdoba, where union action was concentrated in 1990 and 1991. Of the 10 conflicts recorded in each of those two years, 7 took place in the province of Córdoba in 1990, followed by 9 in 1991.

Conflicts in the automobile industry were concentrated mainly in three years of the period being considered: 1984, 1990, and 1991. The year 1984 was atypical. It was a year of political liberalization, during which workers' pent-up and delayed claims emerged simultaneously. The reasons for the conflicts varied between demands for salary increases, protests for layoffs, delayed payments, work conditions, and issues. In 1990, conflicts centered on demands for salary increases. However, strikes and conflicts in 1991 had various motives, including layoffs, delayed payments, work conditions, and salary increases (Table 2.7).

Table 2.6

**Conflicts in the Argentine Automotive Sector, 1984–1994** (absolute number)

| Zone | 1984 | 1985 | 1986 | 1987 | 1988 | 1989 | 1990 | 1991 | 1992 | 1993 | 1994 | Total (% of 11-year total) |
|---|---|---|---|---|---|---|---|---|---|---|---|---|
| Country | 2 | 2 | | 2 | | | 1 | | 2 | 1 | 2 | 12 (22) |
| C.F.-G.B.A | 7 | 1 | | | | | 2 | | | | | 10 (18) |
| Córdoba | 2 | 1 | | 2 | 2 | 3 | 7 | 9 | 2 | | 1 | 29 (52) |
| Tucumán | | | | | | | | 1 | | | | 1 (2) |
| No information | 2 | | 1 | | | 1 | | | | | | 4 (7) |
| Total (% of 11-year total) | 13 (23) | 4 (7) | 1 (2) | 4 (7) | 2 (4) | 4 (7) | 10 (8) | 10 (18) | 4 (7) | 1 (2) | 3 (5) | 56 (100) |

*Source:* Spangeneberg (1995).

Table 2.7

## Conflicts in the Argentine Automotive Sector, Classified by Motive, 1984–1994

| Motive | 1984 | 1985 | 1986 | 1987 | 1988 | 1989 | 1990 | 1991 | 1992 | 1993 | 1994 | Total (% of 11-year total) |
|---|---|---|---|---|---|---|---|---|---|---|---|---|
| Salary increase | 3 | 2 | | 1 | | 3 | 7 | 2 | 2 | 1 | 1 | 22 (39) |
| Layoffs/suspensions | 1 | 1 | | | 1 | 1 | 1 | 3 | | | 1 | 9 (16) |
| Delayed payment | 3 | | | | | | 1 | 2 | | | | 6 (11) |
| Work conditions | 2 | 1 | | | | | 1 | 2 | 2 | | 1 | 9 (16) |
| Others | 1 | | | 1 | | | | 1 | | | | 3 (5) |
| No information | 3 | | 1 | 2 | 1 | | | | | | | 7 (13) |
| % of 11-year total | 23% | 7% | 2% | 7% | 4% | 7% | 18% | 18% | 7% | 2% | 5% | 56 (100) |

*Source:* Spangeneberg (1995).

Between 1985 and 1989, conflict in the sector decreased dramatically due to the contraction of the automobile industry. The threat of plant closure, combined with suspensions and layoffs, made it difficult to mobilize collective action through the traditional measures of protest and the use of force. The only conflict that stood out, by virtue of its paradigmatic nature, was that of the Ford workers. This conflict was driven by management's policies in two areas: adjustment in response to the sector's recessive cycle, and restructuring in response to the globalization of the international economy. This conflict also brought out the new themes that restructuring imposed on workers in the areas of negotiation and union action: participation, autonomy, self-monitoring, the role of supervision, functional multi-tasking, quality self-control, and the capacity for production management. The Ford conflict also clearly demonstrated the potentialities and limitations for alternatives for workers in a fragmented setting with highly centralized corporate management.

Between 1991 and 1994, although the sector's expansion might have favored the emergence of collective action seeking improvements in living and working conditions, the union's prior commitment to "social peace" clauses tended to dissuade actions that resorted to force. However, it should be noted that in this period, demands relating to labor conditions became more vigorous. The period 1989 to 1991 began with a high level of conflict, which fell to a far lower level between 1991 and 1994. The conflicts registered in 1991 reflected the crisis affecting the sector. The motivation for conflicts that year revolved around layoffs, delayed salary pay, requests for improved labor conditions, and salary increases. The conflicts due to layoffs were concentrated mainly in the terminal assembly firms, since the auto parts workers, owing to their smaller numbers, were less able to take effective action in response to such management measures. Claims related to delayed payments were concentrated in the large plants of Córdoba. In 1992 and 1993, the concessionaire branch of the sector was had some of the highest levels of conflicts regarding salary increases. In May of 1994, SMATA called for a strike and a march before the Ministry of Economy and the House of Government to pressure for the renewal of the Automotive Agreement that had expired in March of 1994.

It is relevant here to highlight the kind of inter- and intra-organizational conflicts that accompanied the process of salary bargaining at the company level. The period's main conflict occurred on 5 and 6 May 1994, when 4,500 workers in Sevel went on a "spontaneous" twenty-hour strike for salary reasons.[35] During the strike the workers at Sevel accused the UOM's directors of conspiring with company management. In the second half of 1994, after a wave of conflicts with the Internal Commission, Sevel signed with the UOM a pre-agreement for salary increases as a means of raising its salaries to a level commensurate with that of other terminal assemblers. This pre-agreement gave rise to a sharp conflict of strategies within UOM, although it allowed it to reposition itself with respect to the Internal Commission of that plant. The UOM, in contrast to SMATA, was willing to negotiate only unified salary increases that applied to the entire metallurgical branch, despite its being aware that the industry's economic situation was deeply differentiated by sub-area of activity and even within a sub-area depending on the size of the establishment. The UOM had maintained this strategy since 1991 in its dealings with the government and sectoral chambers. In 1993 it had accepted—grudgingly—to negotiate salary increase percentages differentiated by sub-area of activity. In 1994 it made the salary pre-agreement with Sevel only. Given this situation, the UOM's executive committee was divided between those who supported salary bargaining on a per-company basis and those who wanted to keep it on a sub-area basis. The central argument was based on the concern that negotiation by company, with its "contagious" logic, would drag in the claims of workers in other companies of the sub-area, thereby jeopardizing their financial situation since their profitability tended to differ from that of the large companies. The tangential problem that the union dealt with was how to avoid the "heterogenization" of the salaries, work conditions, and contract conditions of workers, when the companies they belonged to were differing more and more from one another economically, technologically, and in the manner of conceiving their business. In other words, though the problem may have been expressed only in terms of salaries for the entire workforce, the unaddressed central theme was how to deal with solidarity and justice in a setting that tends to increase differences. The pre-agreement was finally ratified during a heated confrontation between members of the UOM's executive committee and the Internal Commission of the company and union.

The new model of articulated bargaining presented the sector's unionism with new conflicts and problems. The UOM negotiated with Fiat for eight months in 1995 to represent workers in the new plant. The position of the union's executive committee, added to the company's offer to fix entry-level wages below industrywide standards, caused the negotiations to stagnate. Given this impasse, Fiat entered into negotiations with SMATA using the same rough draft of the agreement—with scant modifications—and signed an agreement with that union in the first days of 1996.[36]

## Collective Bargaining

### *Collective Bargaining Agreements in the Automobile Industry*

Historically, bargaining at the company level developed after the terminals began to promote company unions. Union action transformed this initiative into bargaining at the company level. The main objective of the companies was to benefit from noncentralized bargaining—that is, bargaining that was defined by the conditions of each company or establishment. SMATA was virtually the industry's only union without a general agreement for the area of activity. However, from its inception, SMATA signed various nationwide collective agreements with upholstering company associations, automobile concessionaries, automobile parts companies, and auto repair associations (Moreno 1991).

Between 1988 and 1989, thirty-three collective agreements were discussed within SMATA. Agreements on work conditions were to remain in effect for two years, and salary levels for one year, with periodic adjustments for inflation. In most of the agreements, the following benefits were obtained: improved payments for seniority, national holidays, paid leaves of absence, reclassification of workers, and transportation subsidies; also, the union obtained a greater number of union delegates, worker participation in the systems of work methods and work time in terminal plants, the creation of a Medical Board with equal management and worker representation, the establishment of Hygiene and Safety Committees, and so on. In general, the new items in these agreements do not reveal substantial changes in the system of work organization. The demands appeared to stem from a desire to bring up to date the traditional system that negotiations had been locked into for the previous three years. However, there were changes in the terminal plants that were not reflected in these collective agreements.

Bearing in mind the considerable changes that had taken place in the automotive industry—in terms of technological and organizational innovations, product mix, materials utilized, production processes, and the tendency to subcontract—one would expect that, in the new round of automotive sector agreements, transformations would have been introduced in the system of job positions and categories, in the form and content of job training, and in the nature of work flexibility.

However, in the "renewed" agreements—in contrast to new agreements ratified by companies having recently arrived in the country—changes were limited almost exclusively to the following areas:

- productivity clauses (the only legal way to increase salaries since the enactment of the Convertibility Plan);
- a joint commitment to increase quality, decrease costs, and promote exportation
- the need to utilize quality techniques, statistical process controls, and so forth.

The rest of the agreements' contents remained almost identical to their original version, above all in the areas of job classification systems, and in particular references to new methods of work organization that could result in different worker responsibilities. On this point, again, the agreements signed by companies that had recently arrived in the country (the so-called "new agreements") differed greatly from the "renewed agreements."[37]

An analysis of the entire body of the terminal companies' agreements reveals some significant findings. Except for the "new agreements" of General Motors de Argentina and Fiat Argentina, the agreements were in all cases authorized by the Ministry of Work and, in effect, extended the collective agreements signed in 1975 without modifications.

In each of these agreements, the following were indicators of a tendency toward change: (a) the system of categories agreed upon; (b) negotiation concerning new production systems; (c) negotiation concerning productivity; (d) clauses regarding the "social peace."

*The System of Occupational Categories*

The system of 8 to 10 occupational categories originally agreed upon in 1975 remained in force in most of the agreements—that is, prior to the introduction of new technologies based on electronics and the transformation of work organization. With the gap widening between job activities and their traditional definitions, the strategy of formally preserving the old agreement's structure (with regard to occupational categories and the definition of job positions) obliged the internal claims commissions to make a steadily growing number of requests to the union for studies on work and task assignments. Moreover, the system of categories for automotive mechanics and metallurgical workers remained the same as in agreements of the 1970s.

This probably explains why the union did not want to negotiate the entire body of clauses in the agreements, for it was convinced it could not renew most of the provisions of the "Fordist agreement" and, at the same time, would have to openly accept "work flexibility" in the plants themselves. However, in the "new agreements," the classification system corresponded to the new models of production. The 8 to 10 categories of the previous model, then, were reduced to four: (1) entry-level employee with multiple skills; (2) experienced employee with multiple skills; (3) specialized technician with multiple skills; (4) senior specialized technician with multiple skills.

The mention of work activities that imply self-discipline and self-monitoring began to appear in agreements as practices required of workers. The agreements also specified the body of knowledge that applicants would be required to have in order to occupy positions at each level in the classification. In the previous wage scale system used for metal mechanics, the criteria for promotion were fixed by "knowledge" and "know-how" acquired through experience in resolving problems associated with the position or occupation, measured by accumulated seniority in the company and, in some cases, by the management's internal forms of evaluation with union approval. In this second model, a higher educational level is required for acceptance, and a certain level of preparation is stipulated for promotion, along with "the unanimous approval of the companions in the work group." This point is central because it denotes, on one hand, the need to internalize social and productive control within the workforce without externalizing it in the figure of a supervisor. It also denotes, on the other hand, this production model's need to achieve greater horizontal and vertical cooperation, coordination, and communication among workers. This characteristic is intimately tied to the company's objectives in the areas of quality and productivity, inasmuch as it is one of the principal means by which such objectives are achieved.

*The Emergence of "New Production Systems" in the Agreements*

Globalization of the economy and the increase in competition undoubtedly presented companies with new challenges. Their strategy in response was to involve union organizations and workers in the pursuit of an overriding objective: to make the company more competitive. Union organizations participated in these agreements with the objective of sustaining, and hopefully increasing, employment levels. In these agreements there were clauses that began to institutionalize a requirement for the worker to be able and willing to complete multiple tasks— roles that were in most cases insufficiently described.

In most agreements ratified between 1990 and 1994 there were references to new production systems—above all to the strategy of "quality" implemented by the companies, and to the "shared responsibility" being assumed in that area. Apart from what has been stated above regarding union strategies of this period, there were few references in the agreements to work organization methods. These were made explicit only in the sector's "new" agreements, which stated that "work in the plant will be organized and based on multifunctional teams and/or work cells, each one with clearly defined attributes and purposes, the guidelines for which are found in the standardized work and the technological, organizational and administrative systems of continuous improvement."

*Bargaining and Productivity Clauses*

An analysis of the automotive sector's agreements, both the "old" and the "new," gives interesting indications of the factors that the parties considered to be key in the area of productivity. The "renewed" agreements conserved the traditional Fordist logic, both in the identification of sources and in the methodology for calculating their estimation and distribution. Most of these agreements, then, identified sources and proposed incentives that produce greater work intensity and traditional calculations of estimated parameters and the distribution of results (that is, they related physical production to the number of workers or hours worked).

The agreements recently signed and tied to the new system, however, showed greater variety in the nature and type of factors considered to be sources of productivity, and in the methodologies used to estimate the sources and to calculate their distribution. All of them tended to include the subject of quality as a source of productivity. Defects or loss of product quality (e.g., defects index, client satisfaction index, loss of parts, index of quality objectives achievement) were regarded as a factor in the loss of productivity. Moreover, we begin to find a significant presence of calculation methods that segmented the workforce in terms of both responsibility for productivity and the benefits of its distribution. Obviously, this non-Fordist manner of calculating and of explicitly assigning responsibilities constituted a "hard" factor in the social construction of productivity as an object and a concept. The workforce, then, was differentiated into individuals, production cells or section cells, plant, and establishment; and corresponding to this differentiation, agreement on the distribution of benefits.

The "old," the "renewed," and the "new" agreements gave evidence of two ways of conceiving and implementing productivity. The old agreements were still anchored in a Fordist kind of reasoning, which conceives of work as the sum of simple tasks (even though work processes and organization in the plants concerned were undergoing great changes). In the new agreements, the worker was required to be willing to realize complex tasks that integrated a wider range of operating phases and varied job roles.

Another change in the way of conceiving and increasing productivity involved the workforce's homogeneity and heterogeneity. The previous system tended toward a greater homogeneity and, in any case, installed intersectoral heterogeneity. Today, the heterogeneity is intrasectoral and intracompany in terms of efficiency parameters and rewards for attained objectives (see Tables 2.8a and 2.8b).

*"Social Peace" as an Objective of the Agreements*

One of the most important indicators of change in the sector was the presence of clauses referring to "the social peace" in all the agreements studied. To illustrate, we have provided examples of the social peace clauses from a number of different contracts:

- Agreement A: "Both parties declare their firm intention to avoid any kind of conflict."
- Agreement B: "The parties agree on the need to work together to promote an atmosphere of understanding, mutual respect, excellence, and harmony in relations."
- Agreement C: "The parties concur in the need to carry out their activities within a framework of harmony in labor relations, avoiding tensions and conflicts that would inevitably affect the objectives mentioned . . . , for which reason they commit themselves during the entire period this agreement is in force to preserve a framework of full social peace."
- Agreement D: "This common effort, which is expected to lead to rising

65

Table 2.8a

**Methods for Evaluating Productivity and Worker Rewards in the Terminal Industry**

**Part A: "Renewed" Agreements**

| Company | Way of Calculating Productivity | Reward or Compensation for Productivity |
|---|---|---|
| Ciadea (ex-Renault) | Real Hours paid by Company/ Standard Hours of Production (') | Up to 8% accumulated over 3 yrs. upon reaching 100% of the improvement standard |
| Sevel (Fiat & Peugeot) | Standard Hours/ Total Hours Paid (MOD + MOI) | Annually, 10% of increase in Productivity + 3% Salary Increase |
| Autolatina (Ford & Vokswagen, prior to the dissolution) | Participation in company profits (") | 10% paid quarterly |
| Mercedes-Benz (Trucks) | Efficiency Index<br>Quality Index<br>Index of Indirect Workers' Variability | Up to 4 — 5%<br>From 5 to 6 — 10%<br>From 7 to 8 — 12%<br>From 9 to 10 — 14%<br>From 11 to 12 — 16%<br>From 13 to 14 — 18% |

* The standard hours measured in the formula are those corresponding to the production obtained and approved at+ the discretion of the marketing director for its sale.
** The second part of this agreement was supposed to be signed in June of 1994 to set the system in motion, but was never signed.

Table 2.8b

## Methods for Evaluating Productivity and Worker Rewards in the Terminal Industry

### Part B: "New" Agreements

| Company | Manner of Calculating Productivity | Reward or Compensation for Productivity |
|---|---|---|
| General Motors de Argentina | I. Productivity index<br>total N of vehicles produced/<br>total N employees in Agreement | Rewards increasing from 1994 to 1998<br>Beginning multi-task employee (10–35%) |
| | II. Index of Defects in Vehicles Produced<br>III. Achievement of Sales Objectives for locally produced vehicles<br>IV. Customer Satisfaction Index (on basis of polls) | Complete multi-task employee (25–60%)<br>Specialized multi-task technician (15–55%)<br>Complete specialized multi-task technician (25–60%) |
| | Reward for competitiveness (evaluation using indicators of the industrial management type).<br>UTE (monthly calculation) | Rewards for 1997–98 period: |
| Fiat Argentina | • Worker efficiency (hours produced)<br>• Worker productivity (hrs. produced over hrs. present)<br>• Unit (quarterly)<br>• Quality (codified losses)<br>• Absenteeism<br>• Loss of parts paid for (cost of parts destroyed at level of UTE and establishment)<br>• Quality of service | • 15% anticipated increase<br>• 11% of total salary |

Toyota Argentina

Formula for achievement of productivity and quality objectives:

$$PL = \frac{(NVF)}{NTC \times (NDW + HW)} - \frac{(NVF - NVR)}{NVF}$$

References:
PL:  Production Level
VF:  Vehicles Finished
WA:  Workers under Agreement
DW:  Days Worked (expressed in hours)
HW:  Hours Worked
VR:  Vehicles Repaired

15% of the basic remuneration of each worker

Chrysler Argentina

Index of Productivity
(by cell and in general)

$$UP = \frac{PP}{MH} \times QO$$

the Units Produced (UP) without defect equals Productivity Program (PP) divided by the number of Man-Hours (MH) directly worked, multiplied by the Quality Objectives index (QO)

Progressive:

1996–97: Only per cell (up to 10%)
1997–98: Per cell (10%) per plant (10%)
1998–99: Same as previous year
1999–2000: Per cell (up to 12.5%); per plant (up to 12.5%)

The remuneration level is in all cases far below the salary earned by sectoral workers in the oldest companies.

levels of quality, competitiveness and productivity, objectively evaluated, will be carried forward in regular meetings. . . . Opinions will be expressed in an atmosphere of mutual respect, sincerity and understanding, promoting thereby the social peace, and avoiding any kind of confrontation."

- Agreement E: "The parties agree on the mutual objective of maintaining harmonious and orderly relations in order to preserve the social peace and avoid the occurrence of acts that might lead to conflictive situations."

While these clauses may not eliminate conflicts in themselves, they signaled a union strategy of "cooperation" and a preoccupation with the elimination of the use of force. These clauses were also linked to a highly "rule-based" behavior on the part of Argentine unionism. The breaking of an agreement was reported to the corresponding authority, and there was constant bargaining prior to the possible declaration of open conflict. In the new production models, the emblematic figure *par excellence* is the peer-judge. The peers, constituted as internal clients, act in a double capacity as judges and participants, both in the techno-productive capacities involved and in the attitudes shown toward the work at hand. Every worker, then, is required to become involved, bringing into play his or her ability to establish communicative relations that can be systematically incorporated into horizontal and vertical forms of production coordination. The social peace is the foundation of a production system that attempts to function with low stocks and with methodologies of continuous improvement or increasing quality. The social peace represents the control of conflict and the possibility of making a system governable, though that system was designed to be tense.

### The "New" Collective Agreements

The return of General Motors to Argentina after seventeen years meant something more than the return of capital that had been withdrawn. The agreement signed by the union at the national level, by the regional Córdoba union where the new plant was installed (within the Santa Isabel Plant of Ciadea—formerly Renault), and by the new company constitutes a new model of collective agreement. The GM collective agreement is novel not only in relation to the sector's "renewed" agreements (which remained unmodified in most of their clauses since 1975), but even in relation to the "new" agreements signed in recent years.

A multitude of newspaper articles, the Ministry of Labor, and even the nation's president in his speeches, have exaggeratedly proclaimed this agreement to be a paradigm for a new kind of labor relations. The agreement is built around techno-productive flexibility. It includes flexible work schedules regulated on an annual basis. It centers the work process in an organization based on production cells, and gives the company a strongly horizontal structure.

An analysis of General Motors' "new agreement" reveals some interesting features:

1. There are only four categories of workers (compared to ten in the other companies).[38]
2. It establishes an annual work cycle (equivalent to 252 eight-hour days), rather than a daily or a weekly one. The system for *licencias* (leaves, absences) and even authorizations for extraordinary *licencias* must be coordinated by members of the "work team."
3. The agreement regulates work organization through the creation of "multifunctional teams and/or work cells," each one with "clearly defined attributes and purposes, the guidelines for which are found in the standardized work and the technological, organizational and administrative systems of continuous improvement."
4. Internal mobility, the company's "internal market," is regulated in such a way that a job is offered to an outside candidate only if none of the existing employees is qualified. In all worker categories, promotions must be unanimously approved by the cell companions concerned.
5. Objectives and productivity achievement parameters are specific to each cell and have specific quarterly goals in terms of: indices of accidents and observance of safety rules; general indices of absenteeism; indices of order, cleanliness, and organization at the worksite; the application of several systems—Just in Time, visual controls, standardized work, and continuous improvement; reduction of costs, time periods, and losses; indices of quality, of attention to internal clients, and others particular to each cell.
6. In terms of labor relations, the union is explicitly recognized as an interlocutor. At the same time, a mixed follow-up commission is created, composed of two company representatives and two representatives of SMATA. It is interesting to point out some of the functions of this commission: to promote joint effort; to evaluate the results of programs in the areas of productivity, quality, efficiency, effectiveness, and training; to generate respect, solidarity, cooperation, and mutual progress; to support the introduction of innovative methods oriented to attain the joint objectives of the company and its employees; to analyze customer service.
7. The company explicitly commits itself to maintain programs of professional training and cultural development. The agreement lists course subjects and the number of hours to be received by each worker. (There is a total of 95,000 hours, of which 30,000 are given to what is called "the process of education for quality.")
8. The company commits itself to guarantee the "stability" of its workers' jobs; even if there is a fall in demand, it agrees to assign workers, if necessary, to other tasks.

**Conclusion**

This chapter has offered an analysis of the ways in which new models of organization, production, and labor relations were formulated and contextualized in transnational automobile firms throughout the industry's development in various stages.

The first phase, 1959–75, corresponded to the implantation of "Fordism" in Argentina. An automobile "package" was imported, indicating the prototypes of the autos to be produced, the organization of the production system, and the institutional forms that labor relations had to adopt within those plants. The companies promoted the installation of a "company" unionism, which, given the nature of the Argentine labor relations that preceded this institutional form, was transformed into a "union per company."[39] The organizational form of the "union per company" allowed the national leadership of the mechanics union to carry out negotiations in a decentralized manner while maintaining an iron grip on the political management of the sector's membership, even when radicalized internal commissions emerged in some companies.

Labor relations were not the only component to undergo redefinition when this "package" was transferred to a country in which import substitution was the prevailing model of development. Its socio-technical components were also subjected to demands very different from those of its original context in the United States and Western Europe. On the one hand, high import duties protected internal investments from production conditions abroad, thereby eliminating part of the sector's intercapitalist competition. On the other hand, a relatively small but avid internal consumer market did not manage to provide enough business for the number of direct investors that competed for that market. This small, avid internal market did make it possible, however, to offer relatively few models that were cheap to produce at relatively high prices, which made any form of production organization profitable. That is why, in this first phase of development, there were no special restrictions in terms of economy of scale; neither were there cost overruns due to an excessive vertical integration, nor due to low standards of work productivity or to other production factors. The import substitution model of development, and the need to favor and finance the sectors that lent a dynamic impulse to the industrial economy as a whole, acted as elements that defined sectoral strategies on a macroeconomic scale, above and beyond the capital–labor contradictions inherent in the need for productivity, discipline, and control of the workforce. All these elements combined in such a way that the predominantly Fordist manner of organizing work did not become the axis of capital–labor conflicts or of the period's labor relations. On the contrary, the period's points of contention—both in the most corporatist and the most combative forms of automotive unionism—had to do with these strategic macroeconomic negotiations. In general, the conflicts of this period took place in the general framework of a boom in massive claims, and concentrated around intersectoral rivalry[40] for income distribution.

Precisely because of the dynamics of the import substitution model's components, as described above, the automotive production system based mainly on Fordist socio-technical principles did not resort to any of its typical measures to increase efficiency and to raise productivity in the sector. The low productivity levels of the 1960s (4.27 autos per worker per year), 1970s (5.28 autos per worker per year), and the 1980s (7.25 autos per worker per year) were addressed with specific policies only in the mid-1980s, thereby attaining in 1994 an annual level of 15.88 autos per worker.

During the automotive industry's second phase of development, 1976–90, the globalization of the international economy and the formation of regional markets by the period's end—in this case, MERCOSUR—began to place increasing pressure on the strategic decisions taken by firms in the sector. Here again, internal capital-labor relations had little bearing on the sector's restructuring; such relations were instead subordinated to the strategic positions that the parent companies were taking, and to the business opportunities being proposed to the latter by the local subsidiaries. This was a period marked by a lack of definition—or rather by provisional and contradictory definitions. At this time, a strategy emerged that would be consolidated in the 1990s: the automotive companies established in the country began to transform their technology and work processes, taking little account of local markets in the areas of work, consumption, and products. New work and production methods were defined around various strategies (i.e., specialization of local companies in the production of components, parts, or sub-assemblies; development of new models intended for market sectors with greater purchasing power; development of models intended for export or regional exchange; development of utility lines). All this development broke up the vertical integration model and prepared the way for a production model calling for a linkage between local, regional, and international suppliers. This linkage had to be especially well calibrated in terms of technical requirements and programming. As a result, the profitability and viability of production began to depend both on its capacity for logistical organization and on the companies' internal capital–labor relations. And it was in this sense that labor relations became particularly important for the sector.

This redefinition of the companies' production strategies required new forms of institutional coordination between the state, automotive sector companies, and unions. The sector's companies based in Argentina needed state policies to bring about a regulated opening to foreign trade in order to finance restructuring. For this reason, their reconversion had less to do with conditions of the labor market and internal consumption than with the possibility of efficiently integrating the latter into regional strategies required by globalization. The new constraints with regard to productivity and profitability were not related to a new capital–labor relation that emerged within the pale of social relations in Argentina; they were, rather, related to the increasingly globalized regional markets.

In this context it is particularly interesting to analyze the contribution that labor relations made to the formulation of this model. During the phase when Fordism was establishing itself in Argentina, the "per company" union gave the sector's labor relations system a special ability to decentralize its collective bargaining, while allowing the union's national executive committee to avoid the costs of heterogeneity that "per company" unions created in the sector's labor market. This modality in labor relations facilitated the establishment, in the last decade, of articulated collective bargaining, anticipating one of the strategies that apparently will be adopted by the CGT (Confederación General de Trabajo— General Confederation of Labor) according to its latest public statements.[41]

These changes have affected labor relations in numerous ways and at different institutional levels. At the macro-institutional level, the companies and unions have pursued a corporatist strategy to bargain with the state in order to obtain a graduated deregulation of the sector, the objective being to generate sufficient profits to bring about the sector's modernization so that it can be competitive on a regional level. The union played a central role in supporting and promoting the process that led to the signing of these agreements. To bring about the agreement, the union contributed by ceasing to pressure management for the recovery of salaries eroded by the cost of living; by accepting "social peace" clauses according to which it would avoid and control any form of conflict within the plants; and by accepting—explicitly or tacitly—various kinds of flexibility in the contracting and use of the workforce. In exchange, the company management sector accepted clauses that required a certain stability in the sector's employment level.

At the level of the production unit, labor relations helped to legitimize and socially construct new forms of flexibility in production, giving rise in turn to new ways of obtaining productivity increases and new standards of quality. In order for the sector to be technically and economically compatible with international standards, its reconversion required the introduction of electronics technology and the adoption of new models of organizational techniques grounded in qualifications and work intensity. These modifications were accompanied by new ways of contracting and using work time, with the intention of adjusting the flow of production to the greater uncertainty that weighs on present-day product markets and consumption markets.

Labor relations at the company level helped to legitimize and to bring about a consensus regarding new sources of productivity, by instituting and laying down provisions for forms of work performed in cells and by teams. The regulation of such units applied not only to the socio-technical interchange among their members, but also to the ways in which their members are involved in quality management, continuous improvement, and work time management.

## Notes

1. ADEFA (1993; 1995). The data refer to aggregate vehicle production for categories A (automobiles and utility vehicles) and B (heavy transport and passenger vehicles).

2. By comparison, in 1994, Ford and Volkswagen had used overtime as a means to increase the productive capacity of some of their subsectors. This recourse increased the

length of the workday to twelve hours and included Saturdays as workdays. In 1995, they were obliged to balance the smaller plants, resulting in a 20 percent drop in their production and a reduction in the use of overtime.

3. Agreement of the automotive sector signed in 1991, renewed in 1994, and in effect until 1999.

4. To illustrate with quantitative data: A local company employed 3,500 workers to manufacture 12,000 vehicles per year, which indicates an average annual productivity level of around three vehicles per worker. Meanwhile, international standards during this period were five times greater than the performance levels achieved locally.

5. We call this period "proto-Taylorism" to distinguish it from the models of Scientific Work Organization used by the core countries. In the latter, the division of labor, the worker's loss of autonomy, work content, and work conditions are centrally conceived in order to diminish down time and increase productivity and profitability.

6. As we shall see, "articulated bargaining" refers to agreements that have a "general module" on minimum work conditions and salaries, and "particular modules" regarding work conditions and salaries with benefits superior to those established in the general module and applicable only to those companies that are expressly included in the agreement.

7. As indicated earlier, the automotive industry attempted to establish twenty-one companies in the 1950s, of which only nine remained in the late 1960s: Chrysler, Fiat, Peugeot, General Motors, Citroen, Renault, Ford, Volkswagen, and Di Tella (a company of national origin licensed by the English company Morris). In this period we have the following: Volkswagen acquired Chrysler; Safrar (ex-Peugeot) left Argentina and merged with Fiat Concord, which sold parts of its equity in 1979. This gave rise to the birth of Sevel Argentina (a national economic group that achieved a 25 percent share of the automotive market, maintaining the brands and licenses of multinational companies). General Motors closed and left the country in 1978. Finally, Citroen Argentina closed in 1979. Years later, a medium-sized company with national capital attempted, unsuccessfully, to re-establish Citroen's popular model.

8. Considered as a whole, the technical coefficients corresponding to "radios and TV," "communications devices," "air conditioners," "watches," "measuring instruments," and "other electrical devices" rose by 4 percentage points in relation to total items consumed, going from 1 percent of the total product purchase in 1973 to 5 percent in 1984 (Kantis and Quierolo, 1990).

9. Due to the significant conflict in the Ford plant in 1985, attributed by many to the results of Ford's implementation of quality circles, companies that later adopted this work technique (and not only within the automotive sector) gave it a different name: work groups, corrective action groups, etc.

10. The gear box manufacturer supplying Autolatina made a heavy investment to radically modernize its plant in order to cover the demands not only of the regional market, but also of its parent company's headquarters.

11. However, the price was still 20 percent higher than that of the Brazilian market.

12. This pact and the consequent elimination of taxes was tied to provincial policies and agreements with the national government. This was advantageous for the automotive industry because Córdoba and Buenos Aires—two of the provinces in which the terminal industry is established—were among the provinces signing the pact.

13. The process of change in the sector is not finished. Fiat announced its decision to separate from the Sevel group (Fiat–Peugeot) and establish itself autonomously. At the same time, Autolatina (Ford–Volkswagen) has announced its dissolution and its decision to go back to constituting two separate companies.

14. See section on Collective Agreements in this chapter.

15. The data on subcontracting is taken from a study realized by Bartolomé and Buceta (1995).

16. In the case of an assembly company, logistics-related activities become especially important. The requirements of JIT and the complexity of production made it necessary to create the Department of Logistics and Internal Materials Management, which handles production programming. A company was contracted to act as consolidator. Its function is to supervise the general stocking of materials, both imported and locally supplied, coordinating the shipping in order to then gather and place the materials in the plant's warehouse. Following Kan Ban requirements, it divides them up, assembling the parts kits, and making the Kan Ban boxes to be delivered in line. All these tasks are carried out by the "Consolidator's" personnel, who must stay in constant touch with line requirements, replacing boxes by direct observation of what is needed or receiving orders through an electronics network connected to the office of Internal Logistics and Line Balancing.

The synchronization in the operations of the Consolidator and Internal Logistics presupposes a constant flow of information coming from the work cells—information that must foresee problems and possible complications in terms of the time and quality of the importation of materials (delays in Customs processing and shipping and handling conditions). Moreover, it must also anticipate eventual problems related to external activities (back cabin assembly and painting). Logistics activities take on a dimension that goes beyond traditional warehousing; they now have a decisive impact on the global goals of production programming.

17. The reference here is to the military government's decree to dissolve the automotive sector's company unions in 1972, and the state's immediate placement of the workers of these two companies into the UOM and SMATA unions. In 1974, during the period of constitutional government, the "combative" leadership of SMATA's Córdoba delegation was suspended and expelled from the union by SMATA's National Directory, with powers granted by an assembly of delegates from the entire country.

18. The members of these combative leadership groups were pursued, imprisoned, and "disappeared" by the military dictatorship of 1976 and 1983. Among them was one of the leaders of this movement, Renee Salamanca.

19. See, in particular, subsection on the mechanics union in Jauregui (1984).

20. A large service company for auto travelers, Club Argentino has developed along the country's main routes and gas stations, offering varied automobile services, including a network of emergency road services.

21. The following emerged in the context of company unions: SITRAC (Sindicato de Trabajadores de Fiat-Concord), and SITRAM (Sindicato de Trabajadores de Materfer), both of Córdoba; and SITRAP (Sindicato de Trabajadores de Perkins), and SITRAFIC (Sindicato de Trabajadores de Fiat Caseros), which aligned themselves with currents that were combative and anti-bureaucratic.

22. In an interview, José Rodríguez, present leader and a follower of the movement's founder, H. Kloosterman, stated: "The neglect in our organization between 1955 and 1968 made our union lose strength. In 1968 that changed. It was this period when the union was really re-made and went from 18,000 to 14,000 members." See Jauregui (1984, 17).

23. This was due to the pronounced drop in employment experienced by the sector.

24. In particular, for the leadership that extended its hegemony at the national level (MUA—Movimiento Nacional de Unidad Automotriz), the union would create: (1) "A role involving the defense and tutelage of workers' interests and rights on a professional plane"—a role played through collective bargaining, collective work agreements, claims directed to judicial and administrative organizations and to company management, and, as a last resort, by means of direct action; (2) an "educational and promotional role," intended to improve the workers' technical and professional capacity; and (3) a "political

role" in the sense of participating in the process of government at the national level.

25. Records show that SMATA processed the renewal of 44 collective agreements, of which 36 were with individual companies and 8 were with chambers or for the occupation as a whole. Of these 36, the new ones numbered 13. This indicates a tendency within the union to determine degrees of decentralization in bargaining. One should note the difficulty this union faces in preparing representatives for the discussion of agreements when the bargaining is carried out on a company level.

26. SMATA's record for 1990–91, page 9, states: "If we include the entire Collective Work Agreement in the discussions today, we will probably have to give up, in exchange for an increase in salaries, the gains we achieved through many years of effort."

27. This subject will be taken up at a later point in this chapter.

28. The main points of this agreement were developed earlier.

29. As a result of Decree 470/93, productivity was no longer to be the sole and exclusive criterion used when negotiating salary increases. Other factors were also to be admitted—such as an increase of investments, professional improvement, the incorporation of technology that tends to increase the overall efficiency of the production system. Moreover, the agreement provides for the possibility of "articulating" the bargaining— that is, the agreements would have a "general module" on minimum work conditions and salaries, and "particular modules" regarding work conditions and salaries having benefits superior to those established in the general module and applicable only to those companies that are expressly included in the agreement.

30. See the magazine *Avance,* No. 9, August 1994, a publication of SMATA.

31. The relation of the peso to the U.S. dollar at this time was 1:1.

32. From SMATA's records, 1992–93, p. 7.

33. See the section on the negotiation of collective agreements in this chapter.

34. The records of SMATA, 1992–93, state on page 8: "This new modality of articulated negotiation, while it may be objectionable in its tendency to undermine the principle of solidarity, does not have a fundamental effect on our Organization, considering the various conventional kinds of negotiation that SMATA historically has maintained (by activity, national or zonal, by company or groups of companies in a certain area of activity)."

35. As a consequence of these measures, 17 workers were discharged by the company with the accusation of being "instigators of the use of force." The workers were held by police, denied communication, then discharged by the company without further consideration.

36. Information from the UOM, *Diario Clarín,* 22 January 1996.

37. According to the union, in spite of the fact that the old categories are partly or completely outmoded, the union prefers the tactic of not introducing modifications in the agreements, but rather maintaining the stipulations regarding the old, outmoded categories as a "written norm."

38. See analysis of occupational categories in the agreements.

39. This is a fundamentally important difference for a proper understanding of the automotive union's strategies. Both the American and the Japanese models of the company union use a labor relations system that is applied exclusively within the plant or productive organization. Argentine "per company" unionism uses a labor relations system that, while negotiating within the company, refers the negotiation primarily to the general union for that particular occupation. The company's union, then, depends on the nationwide occupational union to ratify the internal agreements or to place them within the national framework of action for the occupation. This way, the agreements made with a particular company of the sector, in Argentina, must be ratified and signed by the leadership or the regional or national directory of the union. The power of each company's internal commission, then, is limited to a function known as "claims commission."

40. This intersectoral competition took place between exporting agricultural sectors and industrial sectors who were oriented toward production for the internal market and were therefore interested in raising the purchasing power of some population segments.

41. In negotiations conducted by the Confederación General de Trabajo (CGT—General Confederation of Labor) in March of 1997 regarding the modifications that the CGT would accept in the collective bargaining system, this entity stated to the media that it would promote the signing of a framework agreement for each occupational activity, and would accept the negotiation of agreements by company, with the exclusive participation of the union pertaining to the occupation involved.

Glauco Arbix and Iram Jácome Rodrigues

3 | # The Transformation of Industrial Relations in the Brazilian Automotive Industry

## Introduction

One of the main questions posed by economic restructuring for unions is the trend toward a reduction in employment. In Brazil, this trend has taken place alongside a significant increase in productivity over the course of the past few years. Overall, Brazilian industry employed 6.12 million workers in 1987, falling to 4.81 million in 1993. More than 1.3 million jobs in industry were lost in only seven years, representing a 21.2 percent labor reduction in that sector. In addition, Brazil's GNP for industrial production fell around 5.5 percent during the same period (Coutinho and Ferraz 1994, 33).

In the automotive sector, there has also been a gradual decrease in the number of workers employed since the eighties: in 1980 there were 133,700, while in 1985 this number fell to 122,200; in 1987 employment in the sector reached 113,500, but by the beginning of 1992 the figure had fallen to 109,300 (Sindicato dos Metalúrgicos 1992). This systematic reduction in the number of jobs has become one of the fundamental characteristics of the process of economic restructuring under way in Brazil. As such, it represents a permanent challenge for union efforts.

Translated by Elizabeth McQuerry. Some sections in this chapter are reprinted with permission from *Los efectos laborales de la reestructuración productiva,* ed. Héctor Lucena (Venezuela: Universidad de Carabobo and Asociación de Relaciones de Trabajo, 1996).

At the same time, industrial modernization during the 1990s has opened up many new possibilities for unions, which, in an effort to avoid a potential source of conflict among themselves, did not seek a unified agenda during the eighties. Initial discussions on the flexibilization of production have pointed toward the "multi-skilled worker" as a new profile for the work force. This profile includes an "enrichment of the tasks on the factory floor," greater worker "participation" in defining productive processes, broadening of "team activities," and "intensification of the work pace," among other characteristics. This dynamic has been especially intense since Brazilian economic opening began in 1990. Productivity increases and improvements in efficiency and product quality are the immediate goals.

Exposed to international competition, the Brazilian automotive industry—which had relied on a closed market, state benefits, and subsidies since its founding in the 1950s—is being driven to modernize at a faster pace; deverticalize old structures; rationalize organizational structures; implement tercerization; modernize installations, processes, design, product mix, and range of vehicles; as well as avail itself to the apparatus of global sourcing. In other words, all the rationalization methods inspired by the Japanese and widely used today by American and European businesses: just-in-time, kanban, kaizen, CCQ, CEP, and others. In the majority of cases, unfettering these processes inside firms has produced a fundamental change in labor relations.

In the midst of these sweeping changes, an unprecedented event in the country's history occurred at the end of 1991 when workers, organized through the Sindicato dos Metalúrgicos (Metalworkers Union), organized a tripartite body (composed of the state, and representatives of capital and labor) that was able to define industrial policy directions, bringing about the recuperation of the Brazilian automotive industry. This body was called the Sectoral Chamber; in a virtuous cycle from its birth in 1991 through 1994, it defined relations between the state and society in Brazil. These interactions were a rare demonstration of economic and political efficiency.

In the search for alternative policies to intervene in the industrial restructuring process and the fight against unemployment, the Sectoral Chamber expressed an important point of articulation in the strategy of workers linked to the CUT (Central Única dos Trabalhadores—Unified Workers' Central).[1] This chapter attempts to discuss these new policies that have come to light as a result of the maturing of the ABC region's union movement.[2] These policies are also salient in current discussions on reforming labor relations in Brazil.

### New Styles of Union Action

The rapid transformations occurring in the international automobile industry and intensification of world competitiveness standards are producing an extreme diversification of markets and of the productive system itself. These developments are being propelled by unforeseen economic and technological changes. Although an industrial transformation has been under way in most of the industrialized world since the 1970s, restructuring only began to take place in Brazil in a generalized and more intense manner in the current decade. The opening of Brazil's economy took a decisive turn at the beginning of 1990 and since then has not stopped provoking shock waves in both production and in the union environment, the consequences of which are still far from clear.

This text explores the changes occurring in the automotive industry in the ABC region of São Paulo, with a special focus on the new agreements being elaborated in the nineties. In particular, this research focuses on the four large automotive assembly plants responsible for almost one-third of the metallurgical work force in the region: Ford, Mercedes-Benz, Scania, and Volkswagen. Our purpose is to respond to the following questions: (1) When and why did this process begin? (2) How has it developed? (3) To what extent can this union strategy be effective in the fight against unemployment? (4) What do the agreements and negotiations represent for reforming labor relations in Brazil?

Above all, it is important to point out that changes in relations between capital and labor are occurring in the midst of a rapidly transforming global economic environment. Over the last twenty years the automobile complex has been one of the key sectors in industrial reordering, propelling technological and organizational innovations that are subsequently disseminated to most all other productive sectors in goods and services.

In the current transition period, the main tendencies (positive and negative) of the movement that Pérez labeled a veritable "storm of creative destruction" (Pérez 1989) are asserting themselves in crude fashion. In the world of production, profound disequilibriums are being systematically introduced, fragmenting workers and their activities, increasing exclusion and unemployment, reaching into the safety net of solidarity that has sustained union activity for more than one hundred years. This is the root of the burning impasse for the union movement around the world today.

Today's conjuncture of labor relations in Brazil was constructed, above all, during a period of conflict that has transversed the nineties, and in which diverse forms of struggle by workers stand out. Among other factors, these struggles affirm labor's identity before owners and the state. Since its first appearance in 1978, this movement, known as "new unionism," has questioned union structure, defended open negotiation between capital and labor on the one hand and, on the other hand, has demanded and sought the development of a grassroots organization that would strengthen unions from the plant level up.

It was this new unionism that emerged in the ABC region of São Paulo alongside the 1978 strikes. The Sindicato de Metalúrgicos de São Bernardo do Campo (São Bernardo do Campo Metalworkers Union, now the Sindicato dos Metalúrgicos do ABC, or Union of ABC Metal Workers) was, at that moment, the main example of this new union standard and the automotive companies were the privileged space for the development of this practice. For the most part, workers in the automotive industry continue to be organized through unions linked to the CUT in the ABC region near São Paulo, where the country's main automotive assembly plants are concentrated.

There is, however, a fundamental difference between the labor activity at the end of the 1970s and the 1980s and that taking place in the nineties. Today we are witnessing an important change in union posture and in the attitude of entrepreneurial circles about issues of industrial conflict.

In a country like Brazil, with its huge inequalities in income distribution, the salary question has occupied and will continue to occupy a prominent place on labor's agenda. Nevertheless, efforts to fight unemployment have been increasing in importance since the beginning of industrial reconversion in the middle of the 1980s, even becoming the main issue in the nineties. Indeed, the struggle to maintain employment levels has become a key question for the union movement. From this point of view, the restructuring under way in the ABC region (especially in the automobile assembly plants we investigated) begins to take shape as a strategy of resistance to unemployment—albeit on the sectoral level and with a strongly defensive character. This strategy can be observed in the broadening of issues under negotiation and, moreover, in the signing of recent agreements on flexibilization of the work day.

**Employment and Productivity Trends in the Sector**

The Brazilian automotive sector has a strong impact on industrial employment in the country. It is estimated that for every job in the Brazilian automotive industry, 29 jobs are created in the larger productive complex linked to the sector. The industry association ANFAVEA calculates that for a total of 120,635 workers employed in 1993 in sectors linked to the production of autos (106,738) and agricultural machines (13,897), 5.2 million jobs were created (ANFAVEA 1994). According to ANFAVEA, presupposing an average number of 3.0 dependents per worker, almost 16 million people would be directly or indirectly sustained by the activities generated by the automotive sectors. Clearly these figures are not precise, but they do give us an idea of the importance that the automotive industry has in the Brazilian economy.

Table 3.1 demonstrates the total number of workers in the automotive assembly plants in the ABC region from March 1987 to July 1995, and the number of union workers in the ABC area. There is a flagrant discrepancy between the gradual reduction of jobs and the increase in productivity and successive record production levels in the automotive industry.

The data in Table 3.2 indicate that automobile production took off. At the same time, the automotive sector made marked improvements in sales and productivity, surpassing the stagnation that characterized most of the 1980s (Table 3.3).

Table 3.1

**Employment Trends in the Brazilian Automotive Industry**

| Year | 1987 | 1988 | 1989 | 1990 | 1991 | 1992 | 1993 | 1994 | 1995 |
|---|---|---|---|---|---|---|---|---|---|
| Automotive Assembly Plant Workers in the ABC Region (average per thousand) | | | | | | | | | |
| | 59.6 | 55.3 | 55.2 | 58.0 | 53.9 | 52.0 | 49.5 | 48.7 | 47.9 |
| Total Unionized Metallurgical Workers in the ABC Region (thousands) | | | | | | | | | |
| | 196 | 194 | 196 | 189 | 162 | 149 | 145 | 143 | 146 |
| Average Work Force Reduction in the Automotive Assembly Plants in the ABC Region (1987 = 100) | | | | | | | | | |
| | 100 | 92.8 | 92.7 | 97.4 | 90.4 | 87.2 | 83.1 | 81.7 | 80.5 |

*Source:* DIEESE, unpublished data.

Table 3.2

**Goals and Actual Production of Automobiles** (thousands)

| Year | Goal | Result |
|---|---|---|
| 1990 | — | 914 |
| 1991 | — | 960 |
| 1992* | — | 1,073 |
| 1993* | 1,200 | 1,391 |
| 1994 | 1,350 | 1,581 |
| 1995 | 1,500 | 1,635 |
| 2000 | 2,000 | — |

*Years sectoral agreements were in effect.
*Source*: ANFAVEA.

It is important to point out that the decrease in the number of workers in the segment directly linked to the automotive sector is occurring at a different rate and at a slower pace than in the rest of Brazilian industry. One of the most important factors, if not the most important, can be found in the institutional changes that took place in this period. Above all else, these changes were the product of an adverse situation for the automotive sector.

**Workers Confront Change**

Interviews with members of internal commissions[3] in the automotive assembly plants provide valuable information for understanding the process behind the changes faced by workers. First, the broadening of the boundaries of democracy in society demonstrated the limits of the strategy of rejection and confrontation that had defined the eighties. Unions began to perceive that in order to be better

Table 3.3

**Top Six Production Years in the Sector's History** (thousands of units)

| Year | Result |
|------|--------|
| 1992 | 1,073 |
| 1979 | 1,128 |
| 1980 | 1,165 |
| 1993 | 1,391 |
| 1994 | 1,581 |
| 1995 | 1,635 |

*Source:* ANFAVEA.

citizens themselves they needed to articulate alternatives and not simply negate proposed directions. According to one member,

> I think that everything started to change when *the model began to weaken,* this was the *anti-model,* the model of radicalization, because in that period the owners did not have the slightest intention of sitting down and having a conversation with the union movement. So now it's okay for everyone to negotiate, I think this started happening in 1988 with CUT's Congress. This Congress showed the need for the union movement to not only speak out against issues but to *elaborate alternatives* for issues that we were against, and this approach was hammered out here in the Mercedes-Benz plant and in other companies. . . . We are going to resist but we are also going to put forth alternatives (emphasis added).[4]

In the same interview, the internal commission member observed that the majority of agreements that are being signed today, like the agreement on work teams, for example, took more than two years of negotiations to be implemented by Mercedes-Benz. In his own words:

> Officially we signed the agreement in January/February of 1995, but the work teams are being established in a very suspended form because they touch upon so many things there inside [the plant] that are not pressing, thus I think that *this is a point that I have to think of as positive,* the company takes firm but slow steps . . . and so does the union, because for them it is also new, a novelty, [and] it is taking tentative steps. . . . Thus, for us, change began around 1988, I don't know the exact moment but it began to build and take shape, materializing through the activities of the sectoral chambers, through a proposal for an industrial policy for the automotive sector. . . . (emphasis added)[5]

The following interview with a São Bernardo union leader points out the change from a confrontational unionism, which practiced the discourse of *"no,"* toward a union action based upon proposals. At the same time, negotiation was elevated to a privileged position in the environment of change under way inside companies. Moreover, the interview shows that the agreements by the automotive sectoral chamber represent an advance in relations between capital and labor. Referring specifically to the profit-sharing agreement, this representative of workers at Mercedes-Benz observed:

> It was not the agreement in itself that changed anything between workers and the company. This relationship had been changing over the last several years. [U]ntil 1978 the metal workers movement was dormant. In 1978, Lula appeared and the movement was reborn, and the company was already preparing itself in that period for a new reality, for a more active, more actuated union movement. One company director was in Germany for a year preparing strategy, getting to know the company's reality there, getting to know the reality of social relations and capital/labor relations in Germany as a component of preparing for a new labor reality unfolding here in Brazil and, mainly, here in this region. Thus, workers learned that revindication was not only a question of salary but was also related to the nature of the employment crisis. It was this way until, say, 1990, despite having had a minor intensity conflict at the end of the eighties.[6]

This deposition placed discussion of productive restructuring, a critical theme in this new standard of firm/union interaction, at the foundation of attitude changes and of the guidelines for negotiation.

Mercedes-Benz was the last automotive assembly plant[7] in the ABC region to recognize the internal commissions. Conflicts over the effects and impact of economic restructuring profoundly redefined the relationship between the company and its workers. In the end, the internal commission was only recognized after innumerable manifestations and strikes. Tense throughout the eighties, this new relationship established fairly strict guidelines for discussion. Basically, these included issues such as: (i) discipline; (ii) absences; (iii) salaries; (iv) promotions; and (v) dismissals.

Changes in the organization of work and production accomplished during this period were rarely discussed because the interest shown was small, on the part of both the unions and the company. On the other hand, the agenda in the 1990s was significantly broadened to include: (i) salaries; (ii) worker mobility; (iii) work conditions; (iv) deverticalization; (v) tercerization; (vi) cellular manufacturing; (vii) work teams; (viii) kaizen; (ix) profit sharing; and, most importantly, (x) flexibilization of the work day.

As a result of these negotiations, the following agreements were signed after 1992: Logistics (December 1993); Deverticalization/Tercerization (April 1994); Cellular Manufacturing (July 1994); Kaizen (February 1995); Work Teams (March 1995); Profit Sharing (July 1995); and Flexibilization of the Work Day (December 1995).

If there was progress in the negotiations, there was not a cessation of conflict. In fact, the conflict began to assume a different character as a result of the behavioral changes on the part of both the company and the workers. Tensions continued, largely due to the adoption of "Japanese" techniques, which, when enacted in the Brazilian environment, placed hundreds of workers at the firm's mercy by reducing the number of available jobs. These tensions can be seen in the heavy-handed action by firm leadership in September 1995 in dismissing more than 1,200 metalworkers, virtually denying the existence of negotiations and interactions with the internal commission and the union. Abrupt and painful actions like that by Mercedes-Benz only reaffirm the need for a broader institutional framework than the industrial unit (i.e., factory) for balancing products and by-products of the industrial reconversion under way in Brazil. For better or for worse, governmental orientations weigh heavily in this discussion as they unfortunately become rules through the "let it bleed" policy, which leaves the initiative and responsibility for defining the direction of industrial restructuring in the hands of the firms.

It is always useful to remember that the agreements at Mercedes-Benz opened new roads for the union movement in 1995. The agreement on Work Teams, signed by the firm and representatives of workers on 17 March 1995, affirms that "the parties view Work Teams as the realization of a complex of activities by a semi-autonomous groups of workers subordinate to a master technician, they seek to carry out a certain part of firm production and/or services, are allied in the obtainment of significant productivity gains, product quality, and quality of life in the work place." It is important to remember that the implementation of Work Teams will be carried out in strictly defined areas and "will be initiated by pilot projects," and that "each group will have previously defined the team of personnel, work conditions and the set of responsibilities, adding direct and indirect responsibilities, and will determine the beginning and ending boundaries for its activities."

Work Teams are a way of organizing work within firms that aims toward

> the holistic realization of a determined set of responsibilities and, as a result, aims to overcome the fragmentation of work by progressively broadening the possibilities for decision making by participants, and seeks to improve the professional qualification of workers through: (i) group autonomy of methods of carrying out work, internal distribution of activities and allocation of existing productive resources geared toward improvements foreseen in the first clause, and without harming the productive flow of previously established, or post hoc groups or sectors; (ii) slow growth of new activities by means of adequate prior training and respect for the abilities and potential for growth among the professionals who comprise the work team; and (iii) institutionalization of a spokesperson as a technical representative of the work team and interlocutor with other groups and higher up superiors. (Agreement on Work Teams, 17 March 1995)

On the point of work qualifications, the agreement foresees that "workers involved in the implementation of the pilot project will be trained for Work Teams through classroom instruction, as well as practical training in work areas." Regarding continual improvements, the "work team can make suggestions for improving products, work methods and organization in its respective area. The leadership will bring these suggestions to the relevant internal bodies." In this sense, "groups will have autonomy to adopt certain suggestions germane to work methods, since this does not require additional resources nor does it decrease indicators of group performance" (Agreement on Work Teams, 17 March 1995).

This agreement became a guide for other internal commissions in that it put forth business's need to increase the work pace and create semi-autonomous work teams while, at the same time, giving workers sufficient decision-making power in questions related to internal firm activities such as "suggestions for improving product, work methods and the organization of respective work areas." On the other hand, this form of work organization opens possibilities for workers to exercise more creativity in the production realm, and slowly, at least in theory, it begins to change the entire organizational framework of work processes based on the notion of Taylorism.

The same can be said of the agreement on Cellular Manufacturing, which introduced new concepts for the organization of work in firms. Cellular Manufacturing is the idea that "the machines and equipment will remain duly grouped according to an arrangement and lay-out sequence compatible with the productive process, in agreement with the category of auto parts being produced."

The negotiations that have been going on between Mercedes-Benz and its workers—which are more or less reproduced in the discussions under way in the other automotive assembly plants—generally represent demands by the process of economic globalization to effect product improvements and reduce costs so that firms can increase competitiveness in domestic and international markets. At the same time, these negotiations speak to a new unionism in the ABC region supported by an extensive organization inside companies.

In this sense, internal commissions, in particular those established in the automotive assembly plants, have been very active in significantly broadening their attributes and responsibilities, reaching the point of functioning like a real company union. Although the official position of the ABC metalworkers union, CUT, and the internal commission members is against the creation of company unions, it is impossible to deny that this reality practically exists. Internal commissions in the automotive assembly plants have meeting rooms and communication equipment, their members are released from work to conduct activities relevant to political and salary issues, and their members are elected by all workers in the plant—not only by unionized workers. It is evident that in all the automotive assembly plants researched, the internal commission is the "number one" representative of the workers, because it is the commission that negotiates the individual benefits, all matter of internal problems, and internal frictions with the firm, affecting the daily lives of thousands of laborers.

This reality can be seen in an interview with a distinguished member of the internal commission:

> [W]e are not a union, but we are happy with what we have. In the union we have an overarching political identity. But if, by chance, another leadership comes to power, and we become the opposition, we will operate as if the internal commission were a different union. (Interview with T. Secoli, 8 March 1995)

Thus, it is from these examples and the interactions among the firm, union, and internal commission that new compromises are emerging in the general framework of industrial restructuring. This is equally true for Mercedes-Benz as for other automotive assembly plants in the ABC region. Above all, it is important to note that internal commission representatives from Mercedes-Benz have a reflective vision of this process. In general, they consider it important to participate in these recent discussions and sign agreements on the most discussed issues. In large part, they see this process as a unique way to minimize the losses that they believe industrial restructuring has brought about. Put another way, a negotiated reorganization of production is better than restructuring carried out in the absence of a union, internal commissions, and workers. For the commissions, negotiations open up a way to help ensure that the effects of the changes that everyone knows are inevitable do not become even more negative for workers.

Asked about the significance of these changes, a member of the internal commission responded:

> Our evaluation is that these changes will come, without or without our agreement. Thus, the internal commission at Mercedes-Benz is involved and negotiates not because of its own will but due to the lack of an alternative. If we organized work according to our own ideas, it would be totally different from what is being implemented today. Thus, based on what we have seen in other parts of the world where these changes have occurred, we know that where change was carried out without union involvement, it was very bad for workers. Our hope for interacting with these changes is to try to soften up the bad that they bring and not have any big expectation that now we're going to control the factory, that the worker is autonomous, or that he is in charge of everything. Our vision, our objective, was to minimize the negative impacts on employment, mainly to not lose jobs, to not allow professional disqualification, increased work pace, etc. Changes in the organization of work do not always enable workers.[8]

This presents a central question: What will be the least painful scenario for workers? To negotiate, or to reject changes? Facing this dilemma, union leaders in the ABC region opted to participate in discussions and negotiations about changes in the organization of production and work in the automobile industry, foreseeing the possibility of intervening, even if only minimally, in this dynamic. Nevertheless, this same deposition recognizes that these changes

> undeniably bring some new opportunities. The way work was organized before was that the worker goes into a firm, drills something and stays there doing the same thing for eighteen years; this type of model is also not good for workers. The way work was laid out prior to productive restructuring did not interest us. It is necessary to be honest to recognize this but, at the same time, we don't have great illusions about these innovations. . . .[9]

Another respondent, also a representative of the internal commission, observed:

> We were very concerned about multi-skilling and labor flexibility. This is a very concerning situation in the day-to-day implementation of work teams because we are worried about competition among workers. I am very worried about what will happen when the worker feels that he has autonomy, that he has decision-making power in his work area. Lots of competition is going to be taking place among workers themselves.[10]

An attitude of caution regarding the changes being implemented can be gathered from the interviews. Workers feel that firms want to change only according to their own interests, interests that are not identical to those of labor. At the same time, workers realize that the organization of work is cruel and that it should be changed, but they do not know exactly how to proceed. This is the basis of the contradictory perception of many commission members. For years they thought of production and work as issues for the plant. They did not want, nor were they invited, to give their opinions. Today they try to negotiate, albeit from a defensive position. However, their confidence and preparation is damaged every time that an agreement is not abided by.

Nevertheless, it is through this more generalized contact that the importance of new rules of negotiation between the union, internal commissions, and automotive assembly plants emerges. The ratified agreements represent the possibility of a new social contract, broadening both the scope and openness of negotiations between owners and employees in important sectors of the Brazilian economy.

## The Firm as the Nerve Center of Change

The transformations taking place in the automotive assembly plants in the ABC region are directly inspired by methods and processes successfully used by Japanese corporations in the war against American and European dominance in the world automobile industry. Although the restructuring currently under way may not have the same form and character of that taking place in the most advanced economic centers, it must be recognized that the changes are intensifying the pace and volume of investments. The outline of the new industrial environment can be seen in the number of new automotive assembly plants[11] that have announced investment plans in Brazil and the Southern Cone. In addition, planned improvements to preexisting assembly plants such as the new Volkswagen plants under construction in Resende and São Carlos, expansion of the Scania and Ford plants, and modernization of the Mercedes-Benz plant are indicators of this trend.

This new landscape, in which new production concepts are being tested, is already fostering a significant differentiation in the work force as well as subsequent diversification of interests and demands among workers themselves. Under these circumstances, the "flexibilization" desired by firms is not guided by the type of labor relations grounded in broad-based unionism. In the global economy as well as in Brazil, firms are endeavoring to reorganize production and proceed as if they were the center of organizational and technological innovations. By the same token, they view work force "flexibilization" as a competitive advantage.

A goal of flexibilization is the effort to weaken the state's power to influence organizational structures. As a corollary, flexibilization seeks to displace the *center of gravity* of industrial relations from the *macro,* societal level to the *micro,* plant level. The weakening and deliberate retraction of governmental action, leaving firms free to act as they wish, is best understood through this change in society's power center. Clearly, this position is not inevitable. In reality, it is a political choice that at base is a solid alliance between the government and the class of "modernizing" entrepreneurs. In Brazil, this alliance has endured because it balances the absence and existence of society's mechanisms of protection. This is what propels the tropical version of intensive globalization. The literature on industrial restructuring is full of critiques, yet so poor in linking vital problems with growing unemployment, exclusion, and the marked deterioration of the basic quality of life.

For workers and their unions, the image of a deregulated world only serves to augment uncertainty, brutally increasing the difficulties of carrying out an effective labor relations reform. Precisely because of this situation, fear of the future should stimulate democratic action in the search for new institutional interaction between workers and firms, not deter it.

## Deregulation Propels Conflict

The CUT, through its particular brand of unionism, in 1992 and 1993 began to sketch out industrial policies of national importance via the Sectoral Chamber. The automotive chamber began to take on the contours of a neo-corporatist arrangement in which social concertation was relatively successful (Arbix 1995).

The positive results for the automotive industry (i.e., the sector's evident recuperation), for the government (i.e., increased tax collection and affirmation of its ability to articulate policy), and for workers (i.e., salary increases and the cessation of dismissals) all began to make possible the development of a comprehensive strategy for the union movement.

Social concertation took hold in the automotive chamber due to: (i) highly politicized negotiations, not only in terms of the government's and business's participation, but more fundamentally because their decisions were based on *mutual legitimation,* which strengthened all three parties in the arrangement; and, (ii) negotiations involving *political trading* that lowered the conflict level throughout industry, and affected labor relations and changed relationships inside the larger factories. The activities and decisions by the Sectoral Chamber balanced old problems in a new way. The chamber's experience showed that the functioning of a system of tripartite concessions, whose economic and political efficacy allowed the lasting creation of an agreement and decreased uncertainty for all actors along with a positive economic impact, was possible.

Generally speaking, the Sectoral Chambers also opened new roads for democratic reform in the antiquated system of labor relations by showing that sectoral negotiation can be achieved. This accomplishment invited workers and business owners to change their shop floor interaction and paved the way for the possibility of defining differentiated strategies in both firms and unions. As a rule, the chambers did not break down in the usual dialogue of the deaf. This experience, however, was interrupted.

Changes in the political sphere, mainly those in the last part of the government of President Itamar Franco (1992–1994), when Fernando Henrique Cardoso was appointed to head the Ministry of Finance, set in motion a reaction against this trend. In the beginning, latent conflicts over strategy came to light slowly. With the presidential victory by Cardoso, by then the ex-Minister of Fazenda, all the fluid and the most democratic interactions between the state and society began to dry up. The union movement was a favorite target for the growing anti-negotiation mind set that began to shape what could be called a strategic rejection of concertation. This scenario would be inconceivable in any Social Democratic program but was developed at full steam by the Brazilian government.

Like all the other chambers, the positive attributes of the automotive chamber were gradually exhausted. Tripartite interaction was delegitimated by state action, which rescued bipartite relations in clandestine negotiations between entrepreneurial sectors and the state. Even though it has not been presented as a concerted program, some of the government's recent actions and positions allow us to analyze a "rough draft" of the Cardoso government's official labor relations policy. This includes: (i) rejection of an industrial relations policy based on compromise; (ii) erection of restrictive legal barriers to union actions, especially concerning the right to strike; (iii) affirmation of the firm, especially large firms, as the most appropriate arena for discussion of labor relations—away from the union and away from the sectoral, categorical, state, or national level; (iv) change or flexibilization of labor legislation to permit rearrangement inside firms of the work day, work duties, holidays, productivity, tercerization, and collective contracts; and, (v) reduced state protection of unions.

If these ideas were mechanically transformed into government projects, several factors would impede their establishment. First, the forces against changing the current union structure are significant and have a spillover effect beyond the union sphere. Second, the fate of Força Sindical (Union Power), one of the main sources of government support among unions, is practically sealed by the current union structure. Third, even among supporters of the CUT, whose official position is the transformation of the heavy-handed corporatist model, there is strong resistance. (Indeed, this can be seen in research carried out by the union itself— e.g., DESEP-CUT 1994). Fourth, business generally maintains a friendly relationship with the established system of categorical labor representation,[12] largely due to its enduring stability. A fifth reason is that the Brazilian National Congress is very sensitive to the maintenance of this stability. If we add up these "natural" obstacles to governmental action in search of the judicious reduction of union power, we will have all the ingredients for an explosive recipe. The conclusion to be drawn from this situation is that reforms of this type could only be carried out in an environment of heightened conflict.

**Pragmatic Construction of New Labor Relations**

Except in certain sectors and localized niches, the automobile industry in Brazil continues to be organized along Fordist lines. Like the classic example of countries where mass production was the dominant mode, metalworkers in Brazil were concentrated in huge plants and thus became the dynamic element in unionism, frequently assuming national leadership regarding salary and political questions. The new realities shaped by worker actions in the 1980s and 1990s, the hybrid union structure (Martíns Rodrigues 1991) created by the 1988 Constitution, and domestic political changes constantly demonstrate the inadequacies of current labor legislation and labor relations.

The state still continues to be a central factor in protecting unions, maintaining the system of categorical labor representation, and in sustaining a normative and mediator role for Justiça do Trabalho (Labor Court). This form of labor representation allows unions to benefit from the state, as well as for businessmen to cultivate their own clientele. Ironically, open negotiation is made more difficult by Justiça do Trabalho, an obsolete institution surviving only as a bureaucratic-political instrument that often incites conflict, as was the case in the national strike by petroleum workers in 1995.

In the face of the flagrant rigidity of labor relations, businessmen have repeatedly pointed to "flexibilization" as the grand alternative for modernizing Brazil's productive infrastructure. While it allows for union freedom outside the factory gate, business's brand of flexibilization generally does not include the right to organize at the work site. Metalworkers in the ABC region have shown that they understand "flexibilization" in a different way. Until the beginning of the 1990s, the ability to have a practical influence on the course of industrial restructuring almost exclusively depended on decisions by firms. The ABC union has been patiently trying to change the style of its actions, carving out new environments inside large factories in the area. As a leader of metalworkers commented about the gradual broadening of power by internal commissions: "It is no longer possible to suffice with the premise of Lula: 'The union should be at the plant doors,' but in order to survive today it [also] has to exist inside every plant." The new mentality being developed promotes advances in the union environment and was the aim of a recent resolution in the CUT's Third National Congress of Metalworkers: According to a metalworkers leader in the ABC region commenting on the gradual broadening of power by internal commissions,

> In order to confront productive restructuring, CUT must dispute the content of the ideas of "quality" and "productivity" with firms that attempt to impose them on workers. According to the resolution on this point at the union's third national congress, the purpose of improving product quality is the betterment of living and work conditions of those that work directly in production.[13]

Through this debate, the CUT Metalworkers Congress again generalized for the entire country an experience that had originated in the ABC region. This experience suggested negotiation, both inside and outside plants, as the best way to respond to each of the technological and organizational innovations that are being planned by firms. The tragedy is that this path risks losing its way. While there is still time to correct its course, the unions may be unable to adapt.

Through this dynamic that has spread from plants and from discussions hammered out inside unions, we can point out that: (i) direct participation by worker representatives in the elaboration and alteration of productive processes and the organization of work continue to become more important; (ii) this trend is developing quickly inside union movements linked to the CUT, reaffirming the policy lines that the CUT leadership has been carrying out since the beginning of the 1990s; and, (iii) these negotiations and outcomes are not mechanical visions that attempt to force agreement between measures to flexibilize production and the automatic establishment of a specific set of labor relations.

These elements, although limited to the ABC region and taken from the experience of one of the most organized professional groups in the country, urgently point toward the negotiated construction of new labor relations and industrial policies. In this sense, agreements to flexibilize the work day signed at the end of 1995 in the big automotive assembly plants in São Bernardo qualitatively surpass previous agreements and are the most important compromise signed over the last few years.

In the ABC region, the November 1995 salary campaign was initially marked by intransigence and a lack of confidence. The breakdown of dialogue at the Mercedes-Benz plant in September, when the firm dismissed workers in large numbers[14] and in a unilateral fashion, weighed heavily on the workers. Ford was the first automotive assembly plant to accept flexibilization of the work schedule, establishing a 42-hour workweek, and, starting in January 1996, establishing a band of flexibilization, the limits of which were between 38 and 44 hours. This means that the work schedule may vary according to demand but workers should collect for 42 hours of work. At Volkswagen, flexibilization of the work schedule resulted in a variation of 36 to 44 hours. Finally, in February Scania began to reduce the work schedule to 40 hours per week with flexibilization between 32 and 44 hours and with job security through June 30, 1996.

The flexibilization at the end of the year was based on the April 1995 agreement signed by the ABC union with all the automotive assembly plants in the area. This agreement sought to guarantee a progressive reduction of the work schedule without a salary reduction, and foresaw a 43-hour workweek in January 1996 and a 42-hour workweek in October of the same year. The negotiations went much farther than had been anticipated. The significance of the schedule reduction can be seen in the cessation, although provisionary, of dismissals while more than a thousand jobs were preserved, in addition to bringing about a real 10 percent increase in the average hourly wage.[15]

### Final Considerations

What are the possibilities for effective democratic reform in capital–labor relations in a changing world? This question does not have a single response. However, based on the experience of automotive firms in the ABC region, we can say that the strategy of "cooperative conflict" (Rodrigues 1993) is capable of charting new paths. On the one hand, firms need to improve the quality of their products, lower costs, and become more competitive. On the other hand, the union and the internal commissions want to preserve jobs, create new employment, and improve quality of life for those they represent.

The practical activity of negotiation is not a one-way street. Nevertheless, resistance among the two parties directly involved has not been an impediment to concertation. This was evident in our research on the automotive assembly plants in the ABC region. Negotiations in the automotive sector provide many lessons for the entire union movement and for entrepreneurial circles. It is possible to say that these agreements and negotiations, which are also beginning to take place in other firms, can be seen as the beginning of a true transformation of labor relations in Brazil. Transformation can only be effective, however, if the framework of the existing but outmoded corporatist legislation is dismantled.

There are, however, significant obstacles to overcome. The first of these obstacles is the rapid pace at which these changes are being implemented. Pressured by national and international competition, firms may try to solve their problems in the quickest way possible by increasing tercerization and dismissals or by carrying out some sort of organizational arrangement. Trampling negotiations may precipitate unnecessary job loss and increased unemployment. This is the permanent tension that is part of the daily life of workers in the ABC region. The second obstacle pertains to the precariousness of strategic planning. There are hundreds of examples of firms that "downsize" and, after a short period of time, are driven to gear back up to their former capacity. Opportunistic dismissals hasten the loss of confidence. Third, productive restructuring negotiated in the four automotive assembly plants studied here can help firms and unions to find a point of equilibrium, a fundamental element for the future of labor relations in Brazil.

The difficulty in finding this equilibrium point is that the regulatory functions of the state would have to be reconquered. But the direction being put forward by the government points toward the strategic rejection of concertation and imposition of the state's plenipotentiary reason in defining future paths for the country, leaving other alternatives aside. Put another way, the distance between the government and a social democrat profile is enormous.

## Notes

1. Founded in 1983, CUT is by far the largest of the existing union structures in Brazil. Its main leaders maintain strong ties with the Partido dos Trabalhadores (Workers' Party), or the PT. The current president is Vicente Paulo da Silva, leader of the metallurgical workers in the ABC region.

2. The ABC region refers to the industrialized cities of Santo André, São Bernardo do Campo, and São Caetano do Sul located in the periphery around São Paulo. Diadema is often added to this list of cities with strong union activity.

3. In Brazil, unions cannot organize or exist within a factory. However, "internal commissions" (or *comissões da fábrica* in Portuguese) have sprung up inside factories, often after periods of intense or protracted conflict, as a kind of worker representation committee. Internal commissions are independent from unions and represent all workers in a plant—not just the unionized ones. Although technically not a factory union, internal commissions discuss work conditions, wages, security, and related questions with management but they cannot legally negotiate or sign agreements on behalf of workers.

4. Interview with Tarcísio Secoli, director of the Sindicato dos Metalúrgicos do ABC (8 March 1995).

5. Ibid.

6. Interview with Pedro Marconi Filho, assistant director of Personnel and Social Services for Mercedes-Benz in Brazil (26 July 1995).

7. This process began in 1984 and the first commission elected by Mercedes-Benz workers took office the following year.

8. Interview with Sérgio Nobre of the internal commission at Mercedes-Benz (8 March 1995).

9. Ibid.

10. Interview with Itamar Santana of the Mercedes-Benz internal commission (8 March 1995).

11. Manufacturers that have announced plans for production in Brazil are the French producer Renault; Korean automakers Kia, Asia, and Hyundai; and Japanese producers Toyota, Mitsubishi, and Honda.

12. The current system of union representation in Brazil is based on corporatist notions of organizing society. As such, labor representation is categorical in that only one union can legally speak for workers who perform similar types of labor (e.g., metalworkers, plumbers, electrical workers) within a defined geographical area. In Brazil, this is referred to as *unicidade sindical*.

13. Third National Congress of CUT Metalworkers (Águas de Lindóia, August 1995).

14. The result of these dismissals was a general strike lasting eight days. The strike ended only when 140 workers had been rehired and changes in the compensation proposal had been made.

15. Estimates from the Sindicato dos Metalúrgicos and the Interunion Department of Statistics and Socio-economic Studies subsection.

Mauricio Cárdenas P.

4 | # Restructuring in the Colombian Auto Industry: A Case Study of Conflict at Renault

## Introduction

Throughout the decade of the 1980s, important changes occurred in the Colombian automotive sector. The economic recession that began in 1983 resulted in a steep decline in auto sales, and initiated a new phase of restructuring in the industry. Following the severe contraction in the domestic market and the failure of the Andean Pact members to deepen import substitution (Jenkins 1987, 229–37), transnational producers moved quickly to reduce employment, and to seek various concessions from union leaders. Toward the end of the decade, automobile firms had also initiated campaigns to redefine industrial relations on the shopfloor, embracing many of the concepts associated with flexible production.

The restructuring policies introduced in the 1980s and early 1990s often provoked serious labor disputes, particularly at Renault, one of the major transnational firms operating in Colombia. Indeed, after many years of conflict between the union and management, by 1993 Renault was forced to take extraordinary measures to weaken union resistance to its restructuring plans. Why did managers adopt this strategy? What future—if any—do unions have at Renault and other firms producing automobiles in Colombia? How will workers be affected by liberalization and other changes being introduced in the sector?

Some sections in this chapter are reprinted with permission from *Los efectos laborales de la reestructuración productiva,* ed. Héctor Lucena (Venezuela: Universidad de Carabobo and Asociación de Relaciones de Trabajo, 1996).

This chapter examines the evolution of labor–management relations at Renault-Colombia. The analysis begins with a focus on the development of labor militancy at Renault during the 1970s. After this, we will examine changes in the company's human resources policy, including its agenda to eliminate the union. We will also examine the various strategies that Renault's union adopted in response to those programs. To anticipate, a central conclusion of this study is that economic liberalization and regional integration policies have forced the company to reconsider its human resource and industrial relations systems. Unfortunately for Renault's union, the competitive pressures generated by liberalization have entailed its demise as well.

## The Formation of Unions at Renault: Trends during the 1970s

Renault's first union in Colombia was founded in 1970, shortly after the expansion of the company's operations in the country. The original union was established with the support of the UTC's (Union of Colombian Workers) national organization of metallurgical workers. Soon afterward, Renault promoted a competing company-level union that lacked ties with any sectoral labor organization. Under Colombian labor law, the company-sponsored union was permitted to take the lead in collective bargaining with management, displacing the competing organization with ties to the UTC. As a result, in April 1971 the company-level union, with the support of CTC (Confederation of Colombian Workers), started negotiations that led to the adoption of the first collective bargaining agreement for Renault's plant in Envigado. However, shortly afterward, local union leaders in Envigado clashed with advisers from the CTC, charging the leadership of the confederation of being complicit with the government, business leaders, and owners. In the aftermath of this conflict, the union was expelled from the CTC and became independent (Sáenz 1986, 59–60).

In 1973, the union organized in Envigado initiated a campaign to unionize workers at Renault's plants in Bogotá and Duitama, cities that are geographically distant from one another. The workforce in Bogotá was not organized. However, workers in Duitama had already signed a contract with a different union in 1971, and had close ties to the UTC's national organization of metallurgical workers, the competing union in Envigado. As a result, the 1973 deliberations around the workers' demands for the signing of a new contract in Duitama were rather tense. In moves that paralleled those taking place on the national arena, rivalries and mutual recriminations characterized the relations between the competing labor sectors in Duitama. At that point, the Envigado delegates were compelled to leave the negotiations and it would take another year before a group of workers in Duitama was able to establish a competing, and more radical, organization—in a way that was similar to the outcome in Envigado. The spark for such actions was a dispute over workloads (Sáenz 1986, 61–64).

Indeed, in October 1974, the Duitama plant workers initiated a wildcat strike, protesting what they claimed was a deliberately unbalanced workload between shifts. Because of the divisions among the workforce, no coordinated response occurred when management fired those involved in the stoppage. However, the opportunity was seized by those pressuring for links with the Envigado union to establish a local branch, as had already occurred in Bogotá. When the Duitama contract was up for renewal in 1975, the local branch of the company-level union had the most membership (as verified by the Ministry of Labor), leaving the UTC-linked organization with no legal right to lead the bargaining process. At that point, nonetheless, the company refused to engage in negotiations with the radical union independent of the UTC; in response, the workers struck once more. The work stoppage was declared illegal by the Ministry of Labor, the company received authorization to fire anybody involved in the strike, the plant was occupied by military personnel, and negotiations for a new contract were postponed for six months because of the loss of legal recognition *(personería jurídica)* by the company-level union's local branch.

Despite the signing of a minority agreement with the company by the UTC-linked workers' organization in Duitama (to which only 76 workers belonged, out of the 473 Duitama plant workers in May 1975), leaders from both rival organizations participated in a new strike in September 1975. This time, the company fired close to 200 union leaders and members from both organizations, losing any clout it may have had over the remaining union members, unifying its labor interlocutors in the process. The Duitama contract would only be signed in 1976, after the company-level union was again granted legal recognition (Sáenz 1986, 64–8).

Collective bargaining took place simultaneously in the Envigado and Duitama plants and at Renault's Bogotá national headquarters for the first time in 1977. No major incidents occurred during the negotiations because workers had adopted a unified position in collective bargaining. At this point, Colombia's autoworker unions (the other ones being those at the Chrysler and Fiat plants, later acquired by General Motors and Mazda, respectively) were ranked among the strongest in the country. This was reflected in higher-than-average wages, co-management aspirations of the union members, and coordination of union activities (including common legal assistance).[1]

As a result of the 1977 bargaining process, and under the leadership of the independent company-level union, a national executive board was created to coordinate activities at the three regional branches in Envigado, Duitama, and Bogotá. Nevertheless, the October 1978 meeting at which the delegates were supposed to elect the board members was broken up by a military operation, forcing its postponement and relocation. Several of the delegates were interrogated and their homes were raided on grounds that they were linked to "subversive activities." Just two months earlier a National Security Statute had been issued by the new presidential administration, permitting such actions (Sáenz 1986, 69–70).

Table 4.1

**Number of Workers at Renault's Plants and Offices**

| Year | Duitama | Bogotá | Envigado | Total |
|------|---------|--------|----------|-------|
| 1970 | 23  | 129 | 281   | 433   |
| 1971 | 26  | 186 | 422   | 634   |
| 1972 | 46  | 266 | 484   | 796   |
| 1973 | 206 | 403 | 786   | 1,395 |
| 1974 | 640 | 481 | 899   | 2,020 |
| 1975 | 607 | 544 | 824   | 1,975 |
| 1976 | 710 | 469 | 862   | 2,041 |
| 1977 | 771 | 463 | 953   | 2,187 |
| 1978 | 781 | 477 | 1,035 | 2,293 |
| 1979 | 835 | 478 | 1,269 | 2,582 |
| 1980 | 874 | 467 | 1,307 | 2,648 |
| 1981 | 667 | 567 | 1,298 | 2,532 |
| 1982 | 620 | 389 | 1,120 | 2,129 |
| 1983 | 620 | 389 | 1,120 | 2,129 |
| 1984 | 458 | 361 | 987   | 1,806 |
| 1985 | 453 | 355 | 951   | 1,759 |

*Source:* Renault's union archives.

In May 1979, as the national executive board of the company-level union submitted demands to initiate a new round of bargaining, the Ministry of Labor granted negotiation status to the Envigado branch of UTC's metallurgical workers' union. Thus, despite the protests of the company-level union, parallel negotiations took place once again. A year later, leaders of the independent company union reformed their statutory chart so that the national executive board would be based in Medellín and a new Envigado branch created. However, the Ministry of Labor did not give its approval to these statutory changes and eleven leaders lost their immunity, being immediately fired by the company. These events were followed by further labor unrest and lawsuits against the company, but the fired leaders were not rehired (Sáenz 1986, 70–71).

## Industrial Conflict and the Emergence of the Debt Crisis: 1981–88

### *Overview: Toward Militancy and Labor–Management Conflict*

The rapid growth of the domestic demand for automobiles in the late 1970s and the lack of significant competition entailed an increase in employment at Renault. Between 1975 and 1977 the number of workers at Renault increased from around 600 to close to 1,200 (see Table 4.1). By 1980 this figure climbed to 2,000 and a year later to 2,300. It would fluctuate around this level throughout the rest of the decade, although with a changing composition. For instance, at its peak, the Duitama engine manufacturing plant had close to 800 workers; by the end of the 1980s it had reduced to almost half that number, whereas the company's payroll as a whole went back to 2,000.[2]

In preparation for the 1981 bargaining process, the company-level union decided to move its headquarters to Bogotá. This time the Ministry of Labor gave its approval to the required reforms and the company unsuccessfully appealed the Ministry's decision. Negotiations started in May and almost three months later were broken, leading the company-level union to declare its first legal strike ever. The stoppage lasted 25 days and only ended when management agreed to keep in the contract strict job security clauses defended by the union (Sáenz 1986, 72–73).

It is not surprising that the union staged its first legal strike in 1981. Management had refused to accept the union's requests to have a say in personnel decisions. The five-year administration of the company by a French expatriate (who had placed it at a dominant market position) had ended sourly the year before. The managing director had clashed with powerful political appointees close to the government and had left a weakened management hierarchy. Strengthened by the workers' unity that had been cemented during the labor conflicts of the previous two years, the union took advantage of the situation and adopted an aggressive posture toward the new top manager, another French expatriate. At that point, Renault's union had close relationships with some of the most militant and powerful unions in the country, including the oil workers union, the union representing workers in the largest textile company, and the most dynamic steel manufacturer's union.[3]

The 1981 strike represented a turning point at Renault's labor relations. The launching of a new car model was sabotaged by workers and Renault had difficulty maintaining market share as a consequence. Claiming a market crisis due to the economic recession, Renault decided to request authorization from the Ministry of Labor to lay off more than 300 workers in 1982. When the Ministry did not grant the authorization—an apparent union victory that reinforced the job security clauses kept in the 1981 contract—the company managed to negotiate individual terminations with a total of 342 workers (132 of them from the Duitama plant). This contributed to further labor discontent, especially among the more senior workers targeted by the personnel reduction policies.

Changes in working conditions and the national political economy only seemed to complicate relations between the union and management. Shortly before Renault's union's 1981 strike, the daily production quota had gone up from 80 cars to 134. The introduction of new models had resulted in a 15 percent reduction in the number of man-hours needed in the assembly line to maintain a similar level of production. Import liberalization policies had created a more competitive market, with Renault losing share. The union had radicalized because of the risk of layoffs, a restrictive personnel policy (which included the introduction of armed guards inside the plant), a politically repressive external environment (which entailed the occasional imprisonment of Renault's union leaders), and the increasing influence of extreme left movements on the workers. The presence of retired military in the personnel department had also impeded the introduction of more professional approaches to the conduct of industrial relations. Indeed, the company would have to go through another strike before recognizing the need to create a so-called human development area, which was established in 1982. From then on, but especially after the Japanese became partners of the company in 1990, there was a continuous concern to improve the leadership skills of those in supervisory positions.

In spite of attempts to create labor peace, a new strike took place in 1983. One of the reasons was that after the completion of all legal stages of the bargaining process, Renault had failed to accede to the union's demand that the 1982 layoffs be reversed. (A few years later, Renault would have to compensate laid off workers because their dismissal had not received the Ministry of Labor's approval but had been "negotiated" individually; those affected would successfully dispute the company's decision in court.) (Sáenz 1986).[4] This time, the work stoppage lasted only a few days but reflected the new mood. From then on, *the implicit agenda of the industrial relations managers would be the elimination of the union.* The union's explicit agenda would be to avoid layoffs and protect favorable contract clauses that had been negotiated during the boom years of the 1970s.

The company's anti-union philosophy was spearheaded by the Human Resources Office. After the 1983 strike the firm's financial manager was appointed as the new human resources manager. He himself had come previously from a position in the industrial development government agency (Renault's partner) and hired external consultants in order to redefine the company's labor policies and prevent further conflicts. The consultants reviewed the performance of plant supervisors and recommended their being replaced. This decision received strong disapproval from the union, and rather than contributing to an improvement in labor relations, caused them to deteriorate further. As a matter of fact, according to a former industrial relations manager at Renault, what was driving the conflicts of the early 1980s was the lack of adequate personnel recruiting and selection procedures during the dynamic late 1970s. In her view, the company's reliance on retired military officers to control and discipline workers had also contributed to an adversarial climate and to the supervisors' disaffection with the company policies.[5]

### The Impact of the Debt Crisis

To be sure, the emergence of the debt crisis only heightened tensions in the firm. The economic recession of the first half of the 1980s reduced the size of the domestic market for automobiles. Production dropped from 42,727 vehicles assembled in 1980, to only 28,149 in 1983, with a recovery in 1984, when 45,147

Table 4.2

**Domestic Car Sales, 1985–1990** (number of vehicles)

|  | 1985 | 1986 | 1987 | 1988 | 1989 | 1990 |
|---|---|---|---|---|---|---|
| Renault | 16,826 | 17,501 | 15,101 | 15,693 | 12,320 | 8,673 |
| General Motors | 8,330 | 15,580 | 20,783 | 26,005 | 22,362 | 21,040 |
| Mazda | 13,437 | 10,338 | 16,004 | 18,000 | 18,360 | 18,980 |
| Total | 38,593 | 43,419 | 51,888 | 59,698 | 53,042 | 48,693 |

*Source:* Colombian Industry and Commerce Superintendence.

Table 4.3

**Net Profits from Domestic Car Sales, 1985–1990** (Colombian millions $)

|  | 1985 | 1986 | 1987 | 1988 | 1989 | 1990 |
|---|---|---|---|---|---|---|
| Renault | 377 | 1,343 | 498 | (700) | (3,137) | (6,557) |
| General Motors | (5,963) | (3,493) | 2,847 | 8,455 | 6,403 | 8,402 |
| Mazda | (1,771) | (7,154) | 710 | 3,700 | 2,120 | 7,294 |

*Source:* Colombian Industry and Commerce Superintendence.
*Note:* Figures in parentheses are estimates.

vehicles were produced. In Renault's case, after reaching an annual peak production of approximately 19,000 cars at the end of the 1970s, the figure was reduced to 15,000 at the beginning of the 1980s, and to only 9,000 by the mid-1980s. As a result of these changes in the domestic market—and in addition to the layoffs that had contributed to the 1983 strike—Renault decided to downsize, relocate personnel, and even to temporarily suspend production. Workers from Duitama were pressured to either resign or move to Envigado (more than 700 km away); and on February 1, 1984, more than 250 workers were placed on a paid leave of absence for several months (Sáenz 1986, 41).

The company announced publicly that the suspension of work in most sections of the Duitama plant was the result of a strike carried out at its main subsidiary, an autoparts supplier located in Itaguí, a Medellín suburb. However, by July 1984, 93 workers of those on paid leave had been fired and 11 had been relocated to the Envigado plant. At that point, an additional 50 workers were offered the possibility of relocation; those who did not accept the offer were compelled to resign. To make sure they would not refuse, the company offered them a 30 percent increase in the severance payment that according to the contract should be paid by the company in such cases, a similar offer to those made in some of the previous layoffs (Sáenz 1986, 50–56).[6]

From a commercial standpoint, Renault was in a shambles too. The rapid growth of a traditional competitor, General Motors, and the successful entrance of Mazda to the Colombian market with locally assembled cars, had reduced the French company's market share to its lowest level since Renault's establishment in the country (see Tables 4.2 and 4.3).[7] According to managers who left the company at the onset of the new administration, deficient decision making affected every aspect of the business, not just in Colombia but also in other Latin American countries where Renault facilities were located as well. It is no wonder that workers in the Colombian plants feared the new administration's policies.[8]

### Things Fall Apart: 1987–88

In June 1987 a new strike was ratified amid the breakdown of collective bargaining between the union and management. According to union sources, it was the first time in Colombian history that a dispute over occupational health and safety had led to strike action. During the strike, Renault's union received solidarity assistance from Kapitol's and General Motors's unions in the sector, as well as from the CUT (Sole Workers' Confederation) and the French CGT (General Confederation of Workers).

One of the union leaders has claimed that after the 1987 strike the company developed a strategy to prevent workers from being in close proximity to the union leaders, with the aim of forcing workers to search for solutions to problems directly with management. Indeed, after the strike ended, the company decided to change the lunch schedule in the Envigado assembly plant. The union resisted the change and claimed that it should have been previously approved by the Ministry of Labor's regional office. According to the union leaders, this was a way for management to set obstacles to the lunchtime union talk with the workers. After the union managed to delay production once in early September 1987, Renault deducted the lost time from workers' paychecks and threatened to report the incident to the Ministry of Labor so that legal action could be taken. The union responded by requesting that any schedule changes be discussed with union representatives and by threatening to retaliate with more production delays if paycheck deductions occurred.

At a meeting of the labor–management committee in November 1987, the union complained that the lack of sufficient personnel at the plant was endangering the fulfillment of quality goals set by the company itself in order to regain market share after the strike. During the months following the strike, the company had tried to increase production to make up for that lost during the work stoppage; accordingly, the company had offered monetary incentives to the groups that surpassed the program production goals. The union, in turn, had publicly recommended the workers not to surpass the goals to avoid allegations by management that there was surplus personnel in the plant.

Relations between the union and management quickly deteriorated again toward the end of 1987. After seven workers were dismissed by the company in December 1987, union leaders took over the Renault president's office to protest the decision. According to management representatives, the dismissals were not part of a layoff plan but a way to sanction absentee workers. According to the union leaders, those losing their jobs were being persecuted for their militancy.

The basis of the conflict was the company's dissatisfaction with productivity levels and the union's concern with job security. According to a union source, management wanted to increase production, reduce permanent personnel, and use more temporary workers. In particular, after workers of one section had been able to produce their daily quota in a little over half of the shift's duration, the union expressed concern for the risk this represented for job security in the immediate future. The union also complained that the company's assertion that certain positions in the plant were not production-related had entailed additional hiring of temporary employees. Finally, the union denounced publicly the existence of death threats against its top leaders. In the midst of this situation, nevertheless, the ritual end-of-the year management–labor meeting was held to discuss production plans and manpower requirements.

At that point, the union anticipated that management wanted to increase the daily production goal to a level comparable to that of the two competitor firms in the country. All along, particularly after the 1987 strike, the union leaders had tried to persuade the workers not to work overtime or accept incentives to raise production levels given their fear that the company would have additional justifications to reduce personnel. However, judging from the editorial comments in the union's newsletters, most workers were not paying attention to the union leaders' calls for resistance.

By March 1988, after one union member was dismissed and others were considered for sanctions because of resisting workload increases, a group of nineteen Renault workers engaged in a hunger strike. The timing of this action, which had minor effects on the continuity of production, coincided with a national protest organized by the UTC against human rights violations. According to union leaders, the hunger strike was also a way to continue protesting the company's recent violation of a contract clause that prevented it from hiring temporaries. Because the strikers set up a tent at the plant's entrance and their supporters damaged the company cars parked there, the police intervened. However, such intervention further radicalized the union, whose leaders submitted a complaint to the attorney's general office alleging that the human rights of its striking members had been violated by the police. They had already made public their request to the rest of the workers not to cooperate with the company by refusing to accept extra time assignments and by practicing work stoppages once the daily production quota of 84 automobiles was completed. Given the ineffectiveness of the police intervention to end the hunger strike, by the fifth day Renault representatives accepted the mediation of the Ministry of Labor to negotiate with the union about the magnitude of the sanctions that had caused the strike. Two days later the company representatives agreed to pay for all medical expenses incurred by the strikers and scheduled a meeting with the labor leaders to discuss the conditions under which the workers would support an increase in production.

Despite frequent negotiations between representatives from the union and management, workers staged two wildcat strikes at the end of March 1988. In a letter to the Ministry of Labor requesting its intervention so that legal action could be taken against the labor leaders, Renault's industrial relations director argued that "these are not the only two occasions in which our workers have suspended their activities." In fact, since the previous year, the union leaders had protested the company's unilateral decisions to relocate and dismiss personnel and had pressed management to keep all positions filled. The union leaders had also argued that management should discuss all manpower decisions related to expansion and diversification projects with them. Because of the company's resistance to accepting the union terms, several demonstrations and wildcat strikes had taken place between late 1987 (after the thirty-five-day legal strike) and early 1988 (when the hunger strike took place).

In June 1988 Renault's union newsletter *El Automotor* denounced the assassination of a union leader in early May, suggesting that he had received death threats; it also claimed that other union leaders have received similar threats with a warning that "the company is going to be cleaned up." As a result of the assassination, an eight-day strike took place. The September 1988 edition of *El Automotor* also denounced the fact that management was continuously resorting to layoffs, forced negotiation of early retirement, and sending workers on vacation before their scheduled vacation. Renault, in turn, complained to the Ministry of Labor about the circulation of threatening fliers that invited violent acts against the managers in charge of personnel decisions. In order to prevent labor unrest from affecting production activities, military units occupied the Duitama engine manufacturing plant for three days, coinciding with the national strike led by the CUT.

Despite these problems, by November 1988 the company had managed to raise the daily production quota from 84 to over 100 vehicles. In the Duitama engine manufacturing plant, a reorganization of certain product lines *(bielas)* had multiplied labor productivity significantly. However, the risk of a shutdown at the Duitama plant would be kept alive, particularly after the company failed to penetrate export markets. Indeed, throughout most of that year the company would license (i.e., lay off temporarily) entire work groups from Duitama on grounds that there were not enough production activities to keep them occupied.

These trends not only provoked calls for more strikes, but also led to isolated incidents of "everyday resistance," which included the intentional damage of cars coming off the assembly line. Indeed, two weeks after the union had submitted the biannual list of petitions to renew the collective contract, in June 1989 the executive vice president of Renault sent a letter to the attorney general requesting that he take action with respect to a series of violent events involving Renault's personnel. The vice president denounced an armed attack against one of the plant workers, followed a few days later by another armed attack against a French technician visiting the Envigado plant. The vice president also pointed to the appearance of posters with threatening remarks toward Renault's industrial relations manager on grounds of "his violations of the collective contract and his role in laying workers off." In addition, he referred to the damages caused by unknown assailants to 17 cars coming out of the assembly line. Finally, the vice president claimed that these incidents were an attempt to affect negatively "the existing good labor management relations in the company."

**Restructuring and the Introduction of Hybrid Models of Flexible Production: 1988–94**

*Implementing TQM*

As one step in securing labor peace, Renault officially started a total quality management (TQM) process in 1988 with the support of a local consulting firm, a Crosby licensee itself. The first training seminars took place in the Duitama engine manufacturing plant in Boyaca Province. Shortly thereafter, the consultants conducted seminars at the Envigado assembly plant in Antioquia Province. By November 1988, Renault's top managers in Colombia had established a TQM committee and officially proclaimed TQM as the company's new management philosophy. Throughout 1989, several TQM coordinators and close to a thousand workers were trained in principles and tools already put into practice at Renault's French headquarters and its other subsidiaries (*NotiSofsa* 1989, 2–4).[9]

Along with the review of technical and production standards, Renault launched a program to obtain workers' suggestions, with the aim of improving quality, industrial safety, productivity, flexibility, cost management, and efficiency levels. Individual and collective economic incentives were created to stimulate the successful implementation of workers' suggestions (*NotiSofsa* 1989, 3–6). In February 1989, Renault purchased the company's stock owned by the Colombian government's industrial development agency for 52 million dollars, becoming the sole owner of the Colombian operation. To offset the accumulated losses and to guarantee that the company would be competitive and profitable again, the French top manager announced at the end of the year a plan to reduce fixed costs and personnel. According to him, Renault had just negotiated the early retirement of more than 20 executives and was considering a similar approach with blue-collar workers, especially at the Duitama engine plant where only 300 workers were required out of the current 450. At the company as a whole there were still 1,200 blue-collar workers (*La República* 25 November 1989, 2A; Ramírez 1994).

These announcements came at a time when Renault had its worst year ever in

Colombia: record financial losses and continued decline of market share. Whereas the three domestic car manufacturers experienced a combined 10.8 percent reduction in sales during 1989, Renault's decline was over 21 percent (from 15,693 vehicles sold in 1988 to only 12,300 in 1989). The peso's devaluation was a significant contributing factor, since the cost of assembly parts imported from France increased 35.6 percent in just one year as a result of the changes in exchange rates (*La República* 31 March 1990, 1A–2A).

### *Becoming Partners with Toyota: Introducing Reforms in the Labor Process*

In order to revitalize the company, the French headquarters office invested in new equipment (fixed assets increased more than 50 percent in 1989 and total new investments reached US $40 million) and negotiated with Toyota Motor Corporation the sale of 25 percent of the stock (around 15 million dollars), which was concluded in May 1990.

Toyota's participation in the Colombian automaker brought about a significant reorganization of the labor process. The previous system gave one supervisor responsibility for up to 70 workers in a production area; this system was replaced with smaller work groups led by a skilled worker. The union's role in dispute resolution was also diminished. Under the old arrangements, a union steward would represent a concerned worker, and there was approximately one steward for every five workers; after the reforms, the average worker was expected to talk about problems with his group leader. According to Renault's union, Toyota had conditioned its acquisition of the 25 percent of the company's stock upon raising workers' productivity by laying off 30 percent of the workforce. In that direction, in early 1990 the company laid off temporarily groups of workers deemed redundant.

As a part of the Japanese management philosophy implemented in 1991, the company also appointed qualified workers as "monitors" of their groups in order to improve supervision, and to provide "fill-in" workers for absentees. The union complained that this was done without any consultation of union officials. By early 1992, Renault was talking about the establishment of a more humane organization in which supervisors would take care of the personal problems of their workers, not just the technical ones.

By the end of 1992, the company attributed the gains in productivity and quality during the year to the successful implementation of the Kaizen system. One example was the improvement of the acceptance rate from 18 percent to 40 percent of finished cars. In other words, final quality inspection determined now that only 60 percent of assembled cars, rather than 82 percent, had to be adjusted before leaving the plant for distribution. In the company's journal, workers were recognized for their contributions to improvements like this and for their willingness and ability to perform multiple tasks and suggest changes that enhance quality or reduce costs. The journal also highlighted the opportunities given to the workers' families to visit the plant, and included a children's section in its contents.

## The Merger with Sintrauto and Conflicts in 1991–92

What was the union doing during this period? Along with the CUT, the CGT, and other workers' organizations in the sector, Renault's union sponsored in September 1990 a public forum about the future of the automobile industry under the *apertura* (liberalization). Government and company representatives were invited to the debates, as well as autoworkers' union delegates from Brazil, Chile, and France. However, Renault's management representatives did not participate in the forum. At the end Renault's union announced publicly its merger into Sintrauto, an industrywide union (although still restricted to a few autoparts companies led by Kapitol). The merger would be formalized in March 1991.

In 1991, just before the beginning of the next round of collective bargaining, a Chilean expatriate was appointed Renault's general manager in Colombia. He had participated in the restructuring of Renault's subsidiaries in Spain, Chile, and Venezuela. He had also been a student leader and a dean at a Chilean university, so he was familiar with the ideological and political views of the left. Accordingly, his priority was to lead a process of organizational change in Colombia geared to regaining the workers' commitment with company goals and leave the politicized union leadership without followers. His "baptism by fire" was the 1991 bargaining process, which was settled in Caracas (coinciding with the peace negotiations between the Colombian government and the guerrilla movement, one of whose groups controlled Renault's top union leadership) only after a two-month strike had taken place.[10]

The 1991 bargaining process was the first time that top management made it explicit to union negotiators and workers that without dramatic changes in work rules, the company might not survive. In particular, management pointed to several key obstacles, including rules that limited their prerogative to hire temporary employees, rigid job descriptions and disciplinary procedures, the lack of correspondence between wage and productivity levels, and redundant personnel.[11]

When the contract was finally signed in December 1991, management and the union had reached an agreement whereby temporary workers might be hired in case production needed to be increased beyond the previously programmed level, though in a proportion not exceeding 15 percent of all permanent workers. According to the new contract, the union would have the privilege of getting information from management about production and sales plans before their implementation; workers, in turn, could nominate candidates for the temporary positions, making the company give priority to the workers' relatives in the corresponding selection processes. With respect to the possibility of relocating workers due to the adoption of new technologies, the elimination of operations, or changes in production levels, the new contract contemplated retraining options and gave decision-making autonomy to management.[12]

### Growth, Restructuring, and the Politics of Union Elimination: 1992–95

*Reorganizing the Company*

While Renault was successful in securing major changes in the collective bargaining agreement, it was still forced to adopt additional restructuring plans as a result of continuing market share losses and the ensuing financial trouble. Some changes were driven by liberalization in the market. For example, the sale of its local company gave management greater flexibility in adjusting to the anticipated flooding of the domestic market by imported automobiles due to the drastic tariff reductions initiated in 1990 and the economic integration with Venezuela agreed to in 1991. Indeed, tariffs were reduced in only one year from 300 percent to 75 percent, except for Venezuela, a country with which a zero-tariff agreement started to operate in September 1991. Because of the uncertainty this generated among consumers, the sale of both locally produced and imported cars fell for a few months, and it was not until the end of the first quarter of 1992 that the market reacted favorably to both imported and domestic cars.

What steps did management take? To begin with, most of the administrative offices located in Bogotá were relocated to Medellín in order to reduce general costs and allow closer contact with the assembly plant. This also contributed to the establishment of a "Just in Time" (JIT) production system, implemented with the advice of Toyota engineers. During that year the first locally manufactured Toyotas were sold in the market.

A plan was also implemented to integrate the production of Renault and Toyota lines, increase productivity, and establish work groups that were more knowledgeable of the whole process and could make more autonomous decisions. One of the changes included relocating to the Envigado assembly plant an entire section from the Duitama engine manufacturing plan.

The 1992 restructuring plan also brought about a fresh round of layoffs. At the beginning of 1992, the Envigado final assembly plant had an annual production capacity of 38,000 automobiles. At that point, Renault had plans to reduce the payroll from 1,400 workers to around 700. Before this point, the hourly labor force had already been reduced from over 2,000 by divesting from the Duitama engine manufacturing plant (in 1990) and by absorbing the Itaguí body assembly plant (in 1989). In turn, the new owners of the Duitama plant (Colombian investors) would lay off 140 workers between 1991 and 1993 by resorting to individual negotiations (Ramírez 1994, 19).

The company did make modest efforts to compensate workers who were adversely affected by restructuring. Renault and SENA (the National Technical

Apprenticeship Service) signed an agreement in 1992 whereby the company agreed to invest 25 million pesos during a six-month period to provide retraining for dismissed workers and those who had accepted early retirement. The expectation was that the new skills and the advice given by SENA would allow workers to establish small businesses. The program had originated after the 1991 workers' strike, when the company requested authorization from the Ministry of Labor to lay off 414 workers. When this information was made public in early 1992, the union alleged that the company had not discussed it with the union leadership. Despite the fact that the Ministry restricted the authorization to only 169 workers, a union official claimed that as of mid-1992 an additional 245 workers had been "voluntarily" retired after the automaker offered them individual indemnifications. As far as those covered by the Ministry's authorization, the company also offered them retraining at SENA, and in some cases promised workers who established small business that they might be eligible to provide supplies to the automaker.

By the end of 1992, over 100 of those laid off accepted the company's offer of a discount-priced vehicle as part of the severance payments owed them. There were also pledges to support the relocation of displaced workers through the establishment of a "socio-labor adjustment committee." However, since the union filed a lawsuit against the company's request, no committee was created. In the end, when the Ministry made a partial approval of the request, the company funded SENA's retraining activities for unemployed workers.[13]

### Eliminating the Union

As might be expected, the restructuring plan introduced during this period generated severe tensions between labor and management. When it was time to begin contract talks in September 1993, union leaders were prepared to adopt militant tactics to pressure management to avoid making concessions and to maintain current benefits, continuing the posture adopted in previous talks. However, Renault took the offensive and sought to eliminate the union altogether. Union leaders miscalculated management's intentions, as an alternative compensation pact was ready to be signed by nonunion members and those workers who decided to leave the union at the last minute. Suddenly, the union was representing less than a third of the company's workers, the minimum level required to begin a legal strike. How did this come to pass?

Between June and November 1993, management hinted strongly that those workers who left the union would receive higher wage and benefit increases than unionized workers, and this—according to company sources—caused membership to drop steadily from 66 percent of the workforce in the middle of the year to only 6.5 percent toward the end of the year (Ramírez 1994, 39).

Despite the fact that the union was no longer able to act formally as a collective bargaining agent, it did hold meetings that hindered work activities; in

Table 4.4

**Domestic Car Sales, 1994–1995** (number of vehicles)

|                | 1994    | 1995    |
|----------------|---------|---------|
| Renault        | 18,615  | 21,469  |
| General Motors | 40,552  | 41,660  |
| Mazda          | 28,924  | 24,227  |
| Imports        | 55,334  | 44,269  |
| Total          | 143,425 | 131,625 |

*Source:* General Motors.

response to that, management sued the union's leaders (*El Tiempo* 13 November 1993, 3B). In November 1993, 687 workers, out of Renault's 828, made public a letter sent to management in which they rejected the union's call for a strike. According to management sources, at this point only 54 workers remained as union members, making it illegal for them to initiate a strike.

**Conclusion**

Several broad conclusions emerge from the preceding analysis. First, throughout Renault's history, management decisions were informed initially by the quasi-monopolistic dominance of the company in the Colombian market, and subsequently by the financial crisis derived from the loss of that dominance. The emergence of economic liberalization and regional integration forced the company to reconsider its human resource policies, and ultimately contributed to the end of labor conflict in the firm.

Second, while liberalization reduced Renault's market share (see Table 4.4), the company survived the process. The tariff reductions and the economic integration process with Venezuela shored up the company's position in Colombia. New models were imported from France and Venezuela, which helped the Colombian subsidiary meet the competition in market segments where its locally produced vehicles were at a disadvantage. Simultaneously, the most traditional model, which had been under production for twenty-one years, was discontinued.[14]

By June 1993, the market for automobiles, both imported and domestic, had been transformed due to tariff and sales tax reductions. As a matter of fact, despite the enormous growth of the imports' market share (from 13 percent a year earlier to close to 42 percent in June 1993), production and sales of domestic cars had virtually doubled. Sales of domestic cars increased from approximately 22,000 vehicles in the first semester of 1992, to 42,000 in the first semester of 1993. Renault's growth was proportionately higher: including

Toyota vehicles, sales grew from 3,733 units to 8,933 (*El Espectador* 4 July 1993, 12A). The company has continued to recover some of its market share, becoming in early 1996 the second largest automaker in Colombia (the first in the ranking is General Motors and the third is Mazda).

Finally, in the aftermath of the elimination of the union, labor relations at Renault have become more peaceful—at least on the surface. Proactive human resource management policies have been adapted from other successful non-union environments, and the violent and conflictual history of the 1970s and 1980s has been left behind. Still, a central question that remains is whether it was necessary to undertake such drastic measures (e.g., the elimination of the union) to facilitate change in the company?

## Notes

1. Interview with Clara Inés Medina, former Industrial Relations Manager at Renault, Bogotá, May 1993.

2. Ibid.

3. Ibid.

4. Ibid.

5. Interview with Teresa de Cortés, former Industrial Relations Manager at Renault, May 1993.

6. It is also interesting to note here that after five years as general manager, the French managing director who had been witness to two labor strikes was replaced by another Frenchman in 1986. At that point, labor relations had turned so sour that one of the key roles of the human resource management personnel at the Envigado plant was to make sure that workers did not sabotage the assembly line. The appointment of a computer engineer as the new head of the area did little to improve the labor climate.

7. Renault's share in the domestic car market had grown from 11 percent in 1970 to 55 percent in 1974, reaching its peak in 1979 with 75 percent. Ever since that time, the greater dynamism of its competitors (General Motors, Toyota) resulted in a declining market share for Renault, although the company did enjoy a slight recovery in the mid-1990s. Indeed, whereas Renault's share of the market dropped from 42 percent in 1985 to only 17 percent in 1990, it bounced back to 24 percent in 1995.

8. Interview with Medina, March 1993.

9. As we shall see, Renault also seized the opportunity to acquire full equity in the 2,033-employee company in 1989. Without the influence of the Colombian government agency (which had served as Renault's partner during the preceding twenty years), it was easier to revamp the company's managerial style. Indeed, one of the official TQM principles stated that "those who do not show commitment to the new policies are not true company members."

10. Interview with Juan Cunill, General Manager at Renault's Colombian subsidiary, Medellín, May 1993. In addition, it is should be noted here that for the third time in Renault's history, the bargaining process concluded with a (legal) strike in 1991. This was the longest one too: 89 days, compared with only 35 days in 1987 and 25 in 1981; for the first time in history management took the initiative in the bargaining process by "denouncing" the contract, demanding changes in a number of work rules. Indeed, in an internal document, Renault's management had argued that "with personnel reductions and reforms of the collective contract alone we will not solve all of our problems . . . we are

searching to reframe some procedures that are hindering the efficient functioning of the company . . . the main clauses we need to reform include those concerning disciplinary actions, absenteeism, hiring of temporary workers, and coverage of health benefits."

11. Interview by Camilo Escobar and Carlos Londono, Business School students at Los Andes University, with Julio Saavedra, former Administrative Vice President at Renault, Bogotá, May 1995.

12. See SOFASA, "Actas extra-convencionales, Convención Colectiva 1991–1993," Bogotá, 1991.

13. Later that year, in November 1992, a guerrilla attack against the industrial relations manager of the Envigado assembly plant forced his retirement from the company (some of the previous industrial relations managers had been retired military officers, who practiced *allanamientos,* creating a militarized atmosphere within the plant when there was labor unrest).

14. Interviews by Diana Marcela Díaz and Ana María Páez, Business School students at Los Andes University, with Augusto Trujillo and Germán León, managers in the sales and marketing departments at Renault, Bogotá, March 1992.

John T. Morris

# 5 | Economic Integration and the Transformation of Labor Relations in the Mexican Automotive Industry

## Introduction

The automobile industry has led Mexico's transformation from a highly protected economy based on import substitution to a moderately successful export-led economy. However, in spite of the dramatic changes in this sector and its growing importance to the overall health of the Mexican economy, the automotive industry illustrates the considerable limits to converting Mexico into an export base for advanced industrial products. While the industry has been transformed from a backwater of U.S. transnational operations to an integral part of a revived North American car complex, it has yet to expand beyond the confines of the northern half of the Western hemisphere, and certainly falls far short of broader globalization. Clearly, this is the result of the continuing geographical segmentation of the global car market, or what one study labels "glocalization," as opposed to globalization (Ruigkrok et al. 1991). This process reveals some of the fundamental weaknesses of relying on automobile production to lead the transition to a liberalized (re)industrializing economy.

The relative success of Mexico's automobile industry compared to other Latin American countries is partly the result of the relatively early initiatives taken to

Some sections in this chapter are reprinted with permission from *Los efectos laborales de la reestructuración productiva,* ed. Héctor Lucena (Venezuela: Universidad de Carabobo and Asociación de Relaciones de Trabajo, 1996).

restructure the industry. While Argentina was still struggling with a bureaucratic-authoritarian regime that tended to favor financial operations and to punish industrialists (Maxfield 1989), and Brazil was coping with the massive political mobilization of auto and steel workers in its highly concentrated auto complex in the so-called ABC region of Greater São Paulo (Humphrey 1982), automobile transnationals in Mexico were already seeking new production sites that provided easier access to the large United States market, as well as the benefits of greenfield sites (e.g., low wages, new contracts). Clearly, Mexico's unique proximity to the United States made it a perfect industrial platform for the world automotive industry because of increasing costs of development and the Japanese competitive challenge.

The automobile industry in Mexico has passed through several clearly identifiable stages in the course of its development. Originally, this development resulted from rather limited goals in terms of production and productivity, technology and skill, and social and political organization. However, by the late 1970s the automobile companies, owned partially or totally by foreign multinationals, appeared tentatively to be initiating a program of reorganization that anticipated many of the changes that would soon impact the political economy of the entire nation. By the late 1970s the automobile industry began expanding beyond the old industrial heartland of central Mexico, particularly toward northern locales, in the pursuit of export markets. While this expansion and geographical diversification antedated the recession unleashed by the debt crisis beginning in 1982, many of the subsequent developments in the automobile industry were shaped by this crisis. Nevertheless, expansion and transformation of the automobile industry had begun by the time the administration of outgoing President José López Portillo notified lenders in the summer of 1982 that Mexico would not be able to meet its obligations.

Since 1982 the automobile industry has passed through two phases: massive contraction followed by massive expansion and diversification. This contraction and expansion since 1982 should not obscure the longer-term structural changes that had begun well before 1982. Consequently, although it has suffered significantly from the contraction and virtual disappearance of the domestic market resulting from the economic crisis triggered by the currency crisis that has engulfed Mexico beginning in December 1994, the industry's exports have risen dramatically.[1] Indeed, the integration of the Mexican auto industry with the U.S. market, a result of almost two decades of restructuring, has been crucial to the survival of the industry during 1995 and to the preservation of jobs. Still, the recent crisis demonstrates the continuing importance of the domestic market in Mexico for the viability of the auto sector.

In spite of the relative success of the Mexican auto industry, especially amid the current economic turmoil, the transformations that underlie this success have impacted significantly the wages and working conditions of the work force. Whether, on balance, these changes have been positive or negative is difficult to specify, but in general, real wages have suffered steep declines throughout the 1980s and into the 1990s. Only after 1991 did real wages begin to grow again. Also, the introduction of more competitive production processes based on flexibilization of the work force and work organization has brought only mixed results. On the one hand, there seems to be an increase in occupational safety and health, and greater training and education for workers. On the other hand, it has been suggested that newer flexibilized collective labor contracts have reduced or eliminated some of the traditional "Fordist" protections enjoyed by workers previously. Also, the restructuring, relocation, and expansion of the Mexican automobile industry has been based on the reinforcement of worker representational structures that have restricted rank-and-file control of their unions. Most notable in this regard is the dominance of the "official" labor confederation in the organization of all of the major plants in the auto sector. The increase in official union organization, combined with the increase in the number of "white" unions (company-controlled unions) and the prevention of union representation in the maquiladora industry, has represented a significant cost to the rank and file.

## State Regulation and the Mexican Automotive Industry: From *Desarrollo Estabilizador* to NAFTA

Public policy relating to the automobile industry in Mexico has experienced a dramatic shift in orientation since the government first took deliberate steps to promote and shape it in the early 1960s. In that period, the PRI government was seeking to deepen its import-substituting model of industrialization by rationalizing the industry according to the needs of a relatively small domestic market. This was important to maintaining the economic model because at the time automotive imports represented a high percentage of the total value of imports—11 percent (Bennett and Sharpe 1985, 2). By the late 1970s, however, it was clear that ISI was exhausted and that the weight of the country's burgeoning debt would require expanded industrial exports or at least, in the case of the automobile manufacturers, no net outflow of foreign exchange.

### *The Automobile Manufacturing Decree, 1962: Deepening Import-Substitution Industrialization and the Automobile Industry*

A 1962 decree, known commonly as the Decree of National Integration marked the first major attempt by the government to structure the industry according to national priorities, leading to the first major transformation of the automobile industry in Mexico. Even though it attempted to make the industry cohere better with the requirements and limitations of the national economy, the consequent increase in domestic manufacture of both finished vehicles and parts unintentionally laid the foundation for the subsequent internationalization of the automobile sector.

Until the late 1950s, when Adolfo López Mateos assumed the presidency, the Mexican auto industry was primarily composed of assemblers of so-called "complete knockdown kits," but the need to stabilize Mexico's postwar pattern of economic growth and deepen import substitution led to an attempt to limit the number of manufacturers and models, and to promote national companies both in vehicle assembly and parts manufacture. Bennett and Sharpe's fascinating account of the bargaining and strategies employed by automobile multinationals, their home governments in the United States, Germany, and Japan, and the Mexican government shows that the original initiative was not entirely successful because of significant concessions granted by the government. For instance, the government allowed Nissan to file its application to be one of the limited number of producers two years after the deadline (Bennett and Sharpe 1979). Still, although the 1962 decree did not ultimately limit the number of firms that would be allowed to produce, the requirement of government approval had the effect of restricting the number of producers (ten of the eighteen applicants were approved), and it did ensure the presence of national firms (five of the original ten were 100 percent nationally owned).

Other important provisions of the 1962 decree included the prohibition of imports of finished vehicles, the establishment of production quotas for assemblers, and price controls on domestic vehicle sales. Perhaps the most significant element of the 1962 decree was the requirement that vehicles incorporate at least 60 percent locally manufactured content. Furthermore, the terminal firms were limited to the machining of motors and the final assembly of vehicles. These firms were required to incorporate specific parts manufactured by domestic suppliers (created with the help of the multinationals) into finished vehicles. These included engines, transmissions, shock absorbers, radiators, batteries, rear axles, and drive shafts.

The industry experienced significant growth over the next decade, with approximately $500 million dollars in foreign direct investment. Sales more than tripled from 65,000 units to 236,000, while employment grew almost fourfold from 8,000 to 30,000. Additionally, sales of nationally produced parts increased from $17 to $320 million (Mortimore 1995, 59).

### The Decree for the Development of the Automotive Industry, 1972

The decree of 24 October 1972 was an attempt to resolve several problems confronting the industry, especially its balance-of-payments deficit, but also a growing conflict between the terminal industry, dominated by the multinationals, and the predominantly national auto parts industry. First, it formalized the *acuerdo* of 1969 that linked increases in each assembler's production quota (share of domestic market) to its export performance. Second, it raised import "offset" levels, requiring assemblers to export vehicles with increased levels of domestically manufactured content, measured as a percentage of the value of imported content. For 1973 this "offset" level was 30 percent, and rose to 60 percent in 1976. Third, vehicles were required to contain parts manufactured by Mexican suppliers equal to the value of imports. These second two requirements (import offsets and domestic parts content) made it more difficult to raise levels of exports because of higher costs for domestically sourced parts. Conversely, exports without domestic content would not necessarily improve the sectoral balance of payments. Additionally, the 1972 decree established incentives for domestic sales, and continued attempts to rationalize the industry to better fit the domestic market by limiting the number of makes and models in the compact sector to three and four, respectively.

The automotive industry continued to expand over the period from 1972 to 1977 with sales reaching almost 300,000 units and employment reaching 40,800, while exports of auto parts surged to US $118 million. The industry had expanded at more than twice the rate of the whole manufacturing sector since the early 1960s, increasing production between 1970 and 1975 by almost 87 percent, and representing 7 percent of the value of manufacturing by 1977. Still, the industry was unable to resolve its balance-of-payments problems in spite of improved export performances. The assemblers were unable to meet their export requirements for 1974–75, leading to a severe balance-of-payments crisis in 1976.

### The Decree for the Promotion of the Automotive Industry, 1977

In response to the balance-of-payments crisis, the government issued a new decree in 1977, which marked the beginning of the reorientation of public policy away from import substitution and the Mexicanization of the auto parts industry. Still, as with the 1972 decree, this measure included contradictory elements in the form of both incentives and restrictions on the assemblers.

Although this decree still maintained, and even enhanced, the role of the state in industrial promotion, it marked the beginning of a dramatic change in policy that would ultimately lead to a significantly reduced role for public policy. It imposed an "annual foreign exchange budget," requiring a sophisticated accounting system that included imported content in purchases from domestic suppliers and royalty payments to external sources on the part of assemblers. Assemblers were required to produce balanced foreign exchange budgets by 1981, and to increase their proportion of Mexican auto parts equal to 50 percent of the value of exports. Additionally, the 1972 decree created a new Intersecretariat Commission to oversee the industry.

Still, other provisions more clearly denoted the change in policy emphasis and the reduced role of the state. These included the elimination of price controls and a new system of calculating domestic content based on the cost of new parts instead of direct production costs. Most notable was the loosening of the limits on the number of lines and models, a central feature of the 1962 decree. The industry responded by expanding the number of makes from 15 to 19, and models from 36 to 47 (Mortimore 1995).

Although this proliferation of makes and models created significant ineffi-ciencies, with export performance stagnating at the $400 million dollar level, the 1977–82 period came to be viewed as the "golden era" for domestic market sales, most likely a result of the dramatic expansion of domestic demand result-ing from the petroleum boom that spanned the same period. Production during this period reached 585,000 units, and employment more than doubled from 40,800 to 94,300. The combination of contraction and streamlining of the indus-try in the 1982–88 period caused many workers and commentators to regard the 1977–82 period as the benchmark for prosperity in the industry.

Most notable in this period was the dramatic expansion of engine production capacity, most of which was dedicated for export to the United States. This solved two problems for the domestic producers and for the developing North American auto complex: it helped U.S. multinationals meet the foreign exchange budget requirements in Mexico, while helping them to respond to the growing Japanese challenge of low-cost automobiles in the "home" market in the United States.

## The Program for the Rationalization of the Automotive Industry, 1983

The economic crisis that began in 1982 produced two sets of responses by the government: one short-term, the other medium-term. The short-term plan, the Program for the Defense of Productive Plant and Employment, 1983–84, focused on alleviating the gravest problems of underutilization of installed capacity, debt, and lack of liquidity on the part of producers. It also sought to stimulate exports. The medium-term plan, the National Program for Industrial and Foreign Trade Promotion (PRONAFICE) was intended to link policies of immediate economic reordering and medium-term structural change, in order to promote a more open and internationally competitive pattern of industrialization that would generate self-sustaining growth (CEPAL 1992).

The Program for the Rationalization of the Automotive Industry was an-nounced on 15 September 1983, and incorporated into PRONAFICE. The auto-motive decree was the first significant attempt by the government to support the vehicle assemblers in integrating Mexican operations into the rapidly changing international productive system (Mortimore 1995, 61). Vehicle assemblers were permitted to introduce new model lines for export, with 20 percent of production eligible for sale in the domestic market, provided that the new lines became completely self-sufficient in foreign exchange by 1987 and maintained at least 30 percent local content according to the cost of parts. Local content requirements for existing models were raised from 50 percent in 1984–85 to 60 percent beginning in 1987, but these requirements could be reduced for particular existing models that improved their export performance. The provisions for new models combined with the new flexibility in domestic content for existing models provided significant incentives for manufacturers to increase exports. According to Mortimore, the increased flexibility of regulations recognized for the first time the importance of corporate strategies. Furthermore, the decree established the Consultative Committee for the Automotive Sector, which allowed assemblers to participate in decision-making processes related to the industry.

Other provisions required that 25 percent of passenger vehicles be "austere," cheaper models with no optional equipment; prohibited V-8 engines for domestic consumption; and limited the importation of luxury equipment. Undoubtedly, these were intended to combat inflation and domestic consumption. As a package, the 1983 decree contained both incentives and restrictions that produced both positive and largely anticipated results, as well as some negative ones.

The decree coincided with dramatic growth of installed capacity in the industry, especially in northern areas. In reality, much of the planning and construction of the new plants was already under way before the announcement of the decree (see Table 5.1). Still, the decree reinforced the unfolding two-tiered system consisting of the old industrial heartland in and around Mexico City, and a new, modern sector in the north, particularly in border states. The first tier produced largely outdated models for the national market, while the second tier was oriented toward external markets. It should be emphasized that the industry (and the economy in general) was shaping policy in 1983, rather than policy directing the industry. The construction of many of the new northern plants had already been completed or was well under way by September 1983. The momentum of structural changes in the industry worldwide (particularly the Japanese threat) combined with the financial crisis beginning in the summer of 1982 prompted the new administration of Miguel de la Madrid to abandon more decisively the import substitution orientation of previous industrial policy. After 1982 it became clear that ISI could no longer be stabilized or deepened, as was hoped during the period of *desarrollo estabilizador* beginning with presidency of Adolfo López Mateos (1958–64). However, the search for lower costs and expanded, more integrated markets had already begun by the late 1970s as automotive developmental costs increased dramatically under the weight of stricter design regulations for safety and environmental protection.

Although some would emphasize the limits resulting from the contradictions in the 1983 decree that promoted the development of a two-tiered system (e.g., Mortimore 1995), it should be noted that there might be compelling reasons for both the government and the multinationals to maintain this system, at least in the medium term. For the government, it was important to protect the thousands of relatively high-paying manufacturing jobs in central Mexico by ensuring the maintenance of the market for the car models produced there. Indeed, the gov-

Table 5.1

**Principal Plants of the Automobile Industry in Mexico, by Location, Year of Inauguration, Products, Number of Workers, and Union Affiliation**

| Firm | Location (State) | Year | Products | Number of Workers | Union Affiliation |
|------|------------------|------|----------|-------------------|-------------------|
| Chrysler | Federal District | 1938 | Pickups | n.a. | CTM |
| Chrysler | State of Mexico | 1964 | Cars | n.a. | CTM |
| Chrysler | Coahuila | 1981 | Engines, trucks | 1,200 | CTM |
| Ford | State of Mexico | 1970s | Cars | 4,200 | CTM |
| Ford | Chihuahua | 1983 | Engines | 811 | CTM |
| Ford/ Mazda | Sonora | 1986 | Cars | 2,100 | CTM |
| GM | Federal District | 1935 | Pickups | 2,100 | CROC |
| GM | State of Mexico | 1965 | Engines | 2,787 | CTM |
| GM | Coahuila | 1981 | Engines | 5,525 | CTM |
| GM | Coahuila | 1981 | Cars | n.a. | CTM |
| GM | Guanajuato | 1992 | Pickups | n.a. | CTM |
| Nissan | Morelos | 1966 | Cars | 3,100 | Independent |
| Nissan | State of Mexico | 1978 | Engines | 857 | CTM |
| Nissan | Aguascalientes | 1984 | Engines | 3,000 | CTM |
| Mercedes- Benz | State of Mexico | 1990 | Cars, buses, trucks | n.a. | CTM |
| Renault | Durango | 1984 | Engines | 460 | CTM |
| Volkswagen | Puebla | 1966 | Cars, engines | 10,100 | FESEBES |

*Sources:* Herrera Lima and Cruz Guzmán Sánchez (1994); Moreno Brid (1992); Roxborough (1984); Collective Contract, General Motors–Silao, Guanjuato (1992–1994).
*Note:* CTM = Confederation of Mexican Workers.
CROC = Revolutionary Confederation of Mexican Workers and Peasants.
FESEBES = Federation of Goods and Services Unions.

ernment launched two general plans in 1983 and 1984 for responding to the economic crisis: the Plan Nacional de Desarrollo (1983–88), and the Programa Nacional de Fomento Industrial y Comercio Exterior (1984–88). Both were designed explicitly to protect existing jobs against the ravages of economic contraction, while exploring new ways to renew growth (i.e., by promoting exports). For the producers, in the midst of the national economic crisis during which the national market contracted markedly, it might have made sense to continue to offer models for which production machinery and equipment had already been completely amortized.

Importantly, the automobile sector still relies heavily on the domestic market. As a result of the peso crisis that began in December 1994, the domestic sales of automobiles in Mexico have fallen by 70 percent, prompting desperate attempts to minimize the impact. In addition to extending the interest-free grace period for payment of new vehicles by dealers, Ford de México has reduced the sticker price of new models by about 20 percent in dollar terms by excluding expensive options such as compact disk players, sunroofs, and leather seats. As a result, the company has gained market share, while suffering only a 50 percent loss in overall sales (*Business Week* 1997).

## The Decree for the Promotion and the Modernization of the Automobile and Autotransport Industries, 1989

Announced less than a year after Carlos Salinas de Gortari assumed the presidency, the 1989 automotive decree represented the most decisive break with import-substituting industrialization, implementing a gradual but definite liberalization of automotive production both in terms of export requirements and domestic parts content requirements. The most dramatic innovation of the new decree was allowing the importation of completed vehicles, but under certain restrictions. Assemblers with positive trade balances (including up to 30 percent of foreign direct investment) initially could import finished vehicles equal to 15 percent of domestic sales. However, for every dollar in the value of imported new cars, the assemblers were required to export $2.50 for 1991, $2.00 for 1992–93, and $1.75 for 1994. The increased ability to market individual vehicles on both sides of the United States-Mexico border allowed assemblers to integrate their North American operations by consolidating the Mexican operations into their corporate strategies.

Beyond allowing the importation of vehicles, the 1989 decree specified three additional important changes. First, the decree lowered the domestic content requirements to 36 percent for national models, while export models continued with the 30 percent minimum local content. Second, the list of obligatory domestically produced parts was eliminated, freeing assemblers to select their own domestic or foreign suppliers. Third, the limits on makes and models were eliminated.

Through this decree the *técnicos,* who were ascendant in the government, explicitly recognized that the structure of production costs worldwide and the growing internationalization of the automobile industry made dramatic deregulation the best approach for improving Mexico's balance of payments. As in 1983, the government seemed to be responding to the dynamics of the industry, while attempting to mitigate some of the negative effects of liberalization.

The question of the degree to which the government was shaping the industry or vice versa is important. Mortimore (1995), quoting Scheinman (1993), suggests that the new administration of Carlos Salinas had forced the automobile producers ("some of the world's most powerful multinational corporations") to serve the needs of the Mexican economy. This may be true, but it did not contradict the basic logic of the evolving industry. If the industry is spending more money on research and development, and needs to spread those costs over bigger volumes of the same designs, the only way the needs of the Mexican economy could be served is to respect these trends. It has been the central argument here that by the late 1970s it had become clear that important changes were under way in the international organization of the industry. So, by the time of the 1983 decree the industry had become so dynamized that it would have been difficult to resist the changes (Jenkins 1987). Of course, other factors shaped decisions to alter industrial policy related to the auto industry, including the inauguration of a new president, and the incentives and constraints of economic crisis. Still, the direction and momentum of the emerging North American automobile complex restricted the range of policy choice on the part of Mexican administrations.

The implications are significant. If government policy *reacted* to dynamics in the industry rather than *shaped* those dynamics, could such apparently momentous policy initiatives such as the adoption of the North American Free Trade Agreement (NAFTA, or Tratado de Libre Comercio, TLC) affect significantly the development of the industry? Indeed, it would be a mistake to think that the automobile transnationals themselves were not important authors of the sections of NAFTA that affected them. What were the main features of the emerging industry? The industry had been rapidly acquiring the features of "glocalization," a general term used to denote the regional, subregional, and even local character of industrial organization in the contemporary period. For the Mexican automotive industry, specific features include integration into a regional, not a global, system of production and distribution. Additionally, domestic social and political institutions, like the official union structure, have become adapted to the changing demands of the industry, not displaced by them.

### North American Free Trade Agreement (NAFTA), 1994

Although the NAFTA officially represents a further reduction in the regulatory role of the Mexican state in the economy overall, its liberalizing effects on the automotive industry were minimal because the consolidation of the North American auto complex had largely been achieved. Rather than reducing regulatory restrictions, NAFTA might be better understood as increasing regulation in order to limit competition. In fact, for the well-articulated regional auto complex, NAFTA reflects more the discriminatory and protectionist tendencies of trade blocs than an attempt to completely internationalize the industry.[2] As stated above, the contours of this auto complex were already quite well defined before negotiations for the trade agreement even began in the early 1990s.

The agreement specifies that over the first fifteen years, imports of completed vehicles to Mexico will be restricted to the companies already operating there. The large presence of the U.S.-based Big Three (General Motors, Ford, and Chrysler) has served to consolidate the regional complex. Of course, Volkswagen and Nissan will enjoy similar advantages in the regional market. Also, the agreement requires regional content of up to 62.5 percent, again providing a significant advantage to the U.S.-based companies (Mortimore 1995, 63).

It is important not to interpret the 1989 decree and NAFTA as ceding control over the development of the industry to the rhythms of the automotive sector and the strategies of the multinational corporations. Mortimore (1995, 63–64) argues that NAFTA, taken together with the 1989 decree, suggests that:

> [T]rade flows now result more from considerations of corporate strategies than the demands of national policy. In other words, corporate strategies of the auto TNCs (transnational corporations) operating in Mexico have become the central elements defining the nature of the industry, [and] national automotive industrial policy has become more of a contextual factor.

Mortimore implicitly suggests that prior to 1989 public policy was formed relatively independently of the dynamics of the industry and of corporate strategy. However, there is significant evidence that policy had begun to more fully respond to the needs of the industry as early as 1977. So the decree of 1989 and NAFTA should be more appropriately regarded as a continuation of at least fifteen years of regulatory policy that has steadily reduced policy restrictions on an industry that has steadily increased its dynamism.

In summary, although executive decrees and trade agreements have been important to the consolidation of the North American automotive complex, they have typically followed changes that already had been in motion. This is especially true since the late 1970s. Theoretically and empirically this is important, because it suggests that the renewed dynamism of the automotive industry cannot be easily controlled or redirected as production and distribution systems are restructured in the contemporary period. Mexico's particular experience suggests that it plays a special role in the global, or at least regional, restructuring of the industry, a role that is unlikely to be played by any other country in the region, despite domestic politics or policies.

## The Mexican Automotive Industry in Global Perspective

Mexican production of automobiles has grown considerably since the 1970s, increasing at a rate significantly above the annual average of less than 2 percent for the industry worldwide. Perhaps more importantly, the Mexican industry has become much more efficient while achieving international standards of quality.[3] Furthermore, Mexico's exports have increased significantly, especially since the mid-1980s. The success and importance of the sector, however, should not obscure serious limitations of automotive industry growth in Mexico. Most concerning of these limitations are the industry's continuing balance-of-trade problems, the lack of domestic sourcing for capital goods, and the restricted range of Mexico's foreign trade in automobiles. Ironically, these problems are the results of the same forces responsible for the very success of the industry in

Mexico. Although much attention is paid to government policies such as NAFTA, these policies did not completely or unilaterally shape the industry. Nor did they lead the industry. It is more likely that policy *followed* the powerful forces (increased global competition, more stringent emissions control requirements, and the development of more rapid transportation and communications) that had been acting on the industry since at least the mid-1970s. This is an important point, because it suggests that while public policy can certainly have a negative impact on the industry, its overall effect in shaping and promoting the sector are limited. Currently, the automobile industry is consolidating a North American regional automotive complex that relegates Mexico to a limited role in the global industry.

This section reviews changes in worldwide production, both overall growth and changes for individual countries. It then reviews Mexico's performance, including unit production of automobiles, the value of production, the distribution of motor vehicle growth according to product type, the value of exports and imports by product type, and the countries of destination and origin of those automotive products.

### The Global Automotive Industry since 1980

Tables 5.2a and b summarize worldwide motor vehicle production since 1981, with production data for thirteen countries in Europe, Asia, and North and South America. Except for two significant declines resulting from global economic recessions in 1981–82 and again in 1990–92, worldwide production of automobiles has risen steadily from about 38 to over 49 million units. Although this represents an increase of more than 26 percent over the period, the average annual increase has been less than two percent. This might be an underestimation of the actual growth in the industry, because the global economic recession of the early 1990s, which affected the United States first and had a much deeper impact on Europe and Japan after 1992, was followed in 1994 and 1995 with renewed strong growth in autos globally. Still, even if worldwide production reached 50 million units in the past two years, it would not raise worldwide motor vehicle growth since 1980 over 2.0 percent annually.[4] This stagnation of motor vehicle production is even stronger in the production of passenger vehicles (see Table 5.3).

Most notable in the fourteen-year period surveyed is the stagnation of production in the core countries of the industry, and the diffusion of production to areas in the immediate periphery (the "near abroad") of the traditional centers. Both Japanese and U.S. motor vehicle production maintained a level of about 12.5 million units and 11 million units, respectively. Japanese production peaked at 13.49 million units as recently as 1990, but declined steadily through 1993, and likely continued at lower levels through 1995 because of economic recession and the transfer of production overseas, particularly to the North American continent.

Table 5.2a

**Volume of Global Motor Vehicle Production, by Country, 1980–1986**
(thousands of units)

|  | 1980 | 1981 | 1982 | 1983 | 1984 | 1985 | 1986 |
|---|---|---|---|---|---|---|---|
| **Total** | **38,514** | **37,230** | **36,113** | **39,755** | **42,058** | **44,811** | **45,297** |
| Japan | 11,043 | 11,180 | 10,732 | 11,112 | 11,465 | 12,271 | 12,260 |
| United States | 8,010 | 7,943 | 6,986 | 9,225 | 10,925 | 11,653 | 11,335 |
| Germany | 3,879 | 3,897 | 4,063 | 4,154 | 4,045 | 4,446 | 4,597 |
| France | 3,378 | 3,019 | 3,149 | 3,336 | 3,062 | 3,016 | 3,195 |
| Spain | 1,182 | 987 | 1,070 | 1,289 | 1,309 | 1,418 | 1,533 |
| Canada | 1,324 | 1,289 | 1,276 | 1,525 | 1,829 | 1,933 | 1,854 |
| South Korea | 123 | 134 | 163 | 221 | 205 | 378 | 602 |
| Italy | 1,612 | 1,434 | 1,453 | 1,575 | 1,601 | 1,573 | 1,832 |
| United Kingdom | 1,313 | 1,184 | 1,156 | 1,289 | 1,134 | 1,314 | 1,248 |
| Russian Federation | 2,199 | 2,198 | 2,173 | 2,178 | 2,206 | 2,232 | 2,226 |
| Brazil | 1,165 | 781 | 850 | 896 | 865 | 987 | 1,056 |
| Mexico | 490 | 597 | 473 | 285 | 358 | 459 | 341 |
| Argentina | 282 | 172 | 132 | 160 | 167 | 138 | 170 |

*Sources:* American Automobile Manufacturers Association, *World Motor Vehicle Data*, 1994 and 1996 editions.

U.S. production peaked at 11.65 million units in 1985. It declined steadily to as low as 8.81 million units in 1991, but recovered to almost 11 million units in 1993. It likely rose to well over 11 million units in 1994, a boom year for auto sales in the United States.

The European countries experienced a similar but slightly different pattern. While some countries, such as Sweden, stagnated, many of the bigger producing countries expanded, although at moderate rates. Germany (the Federal Republic of Germany) realized steady growth from 3.88 million in 1980 to 5.19 million in 1992, the year before the dramatic contraction of the European automobile market that lasted through 1994. This represented a 34 percent increase over the fourteen-year period, or an average of 2.61 percent annually (not compounded). Motor vehicle production in France grew much less dramatically and less evenly than in Germany, reaching peak production in 1989, but at a level notably higher than that achieved in the early 1980s. Italy also reached peak production in 1989, achieving a growth rate higher than in Germany until 1989–90, but was extremely negatively affected by the European recession of the 1990s. By 1993 Italian production was far lower than in the early 1980s. In the United Kingdom, after flat production levels between 1.2 and 1.3 million units for most of the first half of the 1980s, production rose to a higher plateau of about 1.55 million.

The explanation for the slow and uneven growth in auto production in the

Table 5.2b

**Volume of Global Motor Vehicle Production, by Country, 1987–1994**
(thousands of units)

|                    | 1987   | 1988   | 1989   | 1990   | 1991   | 1992   | 1993   | 1994   |
|--------------------|--------|--------|--------|--------|--------|--------|--------|--------|
| **Total**          | **45,903** | **48,210** | **49,101** | **48,554** | **46,928** | **48,088** | **46,785** | **49,440** |
| Japan              | 12,249 | 12,700 | 13,026 | 13,487 | 13,245 | 12,499 | 11,228 | 10,554 |
| United States      | 10,925 | 11,214 | 10,874 | 9,783  | 8,811  | 9,729  | 10,898 | 12,263 |
| Germany            | 4,634  | 4,625  | 4,852  | 4,977  | 5,034  | 5,194  | 4,032  | 4,356  |
| France             | 3,493  | 3,698  | 3,920  | 3,769  | 3,611  | 3,768  | 3,156  | 3,558  |
| Spain              | 1,704  | 1,866  | 2,046  | 2,053  | 2,082  | 2,123  | 1,768  | 2,142  |
| Canada             | 1,635  | 1,949  | 2,002  | 1,921  | 1,888  | 1,961  | 2,247  | 2,322  |
| South Korea        | 980    | 1,084  | 1,129  | 1,322  | 1,498  | 1,730  | 2,050  | 2,312  |
| Italy              | 1,913  | 2,111  | 2,221  | 2,121  | 1,878  | 1,686  | 1,277  | 1,534  |
| United Kingdom     | 1,389  | 1,544  | 1,626  | 1,566  | 1,454  | 1,540  | 1,569  | 1,695  |
| Russian Federation | 2,202  | 2,147  | 2,061  | 2,117  | 2,052  | 1,950  | 1,619  | 1,114  |
| Brazil             | 920    | 1,069  | 1,013  | 914    | 960    | 1,074  | 1,391  | 1,581  |
| Mexico             | 395    | 513    | 641    | 821    | 989    | 1,083  | 1,081  | 1,122  |
| Argentina          | 193    | 164    | 128    | 100    | 139    | 262    | 342    | 409    |

*Sources:* American Automobile Manufacturers Association, *World Motor Vehicle Data*, 1994 and 1996 editions.

core producing countries over the past decade can be found in the increase in production in adjacent, less developed countries. This diffusion of production should not be understood as necessarily part of the "globalization" of production. Clearly, the major markets (e.g., North America, Europe, and the Far East) have expanded geographically both in terms of production and distribution. However, the most visible pattern is the consolidation of regional markets, not the complete globalization of production. This will become more evident for Mexico in the discussion below.

Much of the production for North America was increasingly transferred to Canada and Mexico, just as significant production in the core European countries was transferred to Spain, which joined the European Economic Community in the 1980s. Canada's production grew from 1.3 million units in the early 1980s to over 2.2 million in 1983. Mexico's fell from about 0.5 million in the early 1980s due to the collapse of the domestic market, but recovered by 1988, ultimately rising to almost 1.1 million in 1993. Over 40 percent of that production was exported, mostly to the United States and Canada. In the Far East, South Korea grew at a stunning and uninterrupted pace from only 123 thousand in the mid-1970s to over 2 million in 1993. South Korea's development is not related to Japanese stagnation in the same way as Mexico and Canada's is related to that of the United States, or Spain's to the rest of Western Europe. For although Korea's production often incorporated licensed Japanese motor and chassis designs, it did

Table 5.3

**Global Production of Passenger Vehicles, by Country, 1988–1994**
(thousands of units)

|  | 1988 | 1989 | 1990 | 1991 | 1992 | 1993 | 1994 |
|---|---|---|---|---|---|---|---|
| **Total** | **33,816** | **35,100** | **35,318** | **34,158** | **35,322** | **34,197** | **35,711** |
| Japan | 8,198 | 9,052 | 9,948 | 9,753 | 9,379 | 8,494 | 7,801 |
| United States | 7,113 | 6,823 | 6,077 | 5,439 | 5,663 | 5,981 | 6,614 |
| Germany | 4,346 | 4,564 | 4,661 | 4,677 | 4,864 | 3,794 | 4,094 |
| France | 3,224 | 3,409 | 3,295 | 3,188 | 3,329 | 2,836 | 3,175 |
| Italy | 1,884 | 1,972 | 1,875 | 1,633 | 1,477 | 1,117 | 1,341 |
| Spain | 1,722 | 1,897 | 1,916 | 1,943 | 1,972 | 1,622 | 1,974 |
| United Kingdom | 1,227 | 1,299 | 1,296 | 1,237 | 1,292 | 1,376 | 1,467 |
| Russian Federation | 1,262 | 1,217 | 1,259 | 1,308 | 1,287 | 1,065 | 868 |
| South Korea | 872 | 872 | 987 | 1,158 | 1,307 | 1,593 | 1,806 |
| Canada | 1,025 | 1,049 | 1,070 | 1,060 | 1,020 | 1,353 | 1,216 |
| Mexico | 354 | 439 | 598 | 720 | 778 | 835 | 856 |
| Brazil | 782 | 731 | 663 | 705 | 816 | 1,100 | 1,248 |
| Australia | 315 | 333 | 386 | 311 | 269 | 294 | 329 |
| Sweden | 287 | 281 | 248 | 189 | 209 | 279 | 353 |
| Argentina | 136 | 108 | 81 | 114 | 221 | 287 | 338 |

*Source:* American Automobile Manufacturers Association, *World Motor Vehicle Data*, 1994.

not become incorporated into Japan's production or distribution network. In fact, with the help of state subsidies and protective tariffs, the Korean companies have become much more independent of Japanese designs and production technology, and Korean motor vehicles have competed directly with Japanese cars in the United States and elsewhere.

The global diffusion of automobile production to countries on the near periphery of the traditional auto centers highlights the temporal and geographical dimensions of the transformation of automotive production and distribution. These processes already had been set in motion before the Presidential Decree of 1989 and long before NAFTA was even proposed. Furthermore, this process was truly global, even though the effects were to consolidate only regional production and distribution systems. The global nature of this pursuit of larger markets and geographically more extensive systems of production reinforces the perception that automotive production was following at least in part a logic inherent to the industry itself.[5] That is, by the mid-1980s (more likely since the mid-1970s), changes in the nature and location of automotive production were largely independent of government policies, whether in Mexico, Japan, or Italy. Clearly, government policy has been important in supporting this process, but the era of strictly national automotive markets had begun to be replaced by regional systems, and there was much less room to maneuver for governments wishing to attract new direct investment by the automotive multinationals. By the mid-1980s, countries wishing to produce automobiles found it difficult to resist industry dynamics, often choosing to reinforce these dynamics rather than attempting to fundamentally redirect them. Such was the case in Mexico.

## The Transformation and Growth of the Mexican Automotive Industry

The transformation of the Mexican industry has produced impressive results in terms of production, export earnings, employment, labor productivity, and regional development within Mexico. Still, the effects of the reindustrialization of the automotive industry are not unambiguously positive for Mexico. The Mexican automotive industry still confronts continuing balance-of-payments difficulties, continues to rely on imported capital goods, has failed to diversify its limited range of automotive trading partners, and has failed to bring real wealth or opportunities to the working class.

As many have noted, automobile production in Mexico began in the 1920s in the form of assembling so-called "complete knockdown kits," and remained that way, with little development of supporting auto parts companies until the 1960s, when the administration of Adolfo López Mateos attempted to overcome some of the limitations of import-substitution industrialization (Roxborough 1984). With the 1962 automotive decree the Mexican industry received the first major push to produce complete vehicles with significant domestic parts content. By 1968 it had doubled production from almost 67 thousand to over 143 thousand, and it doubled production again in 1973. Except for declines in 1976 and 1977, production rose steadily through 1981, when it had more than doubled again, reaching 597 thousand. The "golden age" of populist, and then petroleum, growth in the 1970s, during which production tripled, came to an abrupt and brutal end in 1982, the year the foreign debt crisis crippled many Latin American economies. Production plunged to 285 thousand in 1983, recovered partially to 459 thousand before falling back to 341 thousand in 1985 and 1986. It was not until 1989 that the Mexican automobile industry overtook 1981 levels, when it produced 641 thousand motor vehicles. Since then Mexico produced steadily increasing numbers of vehicles through 1992 and 1993, when production leveled off at 1.08 million units.

Although the crisis of the 1980s profoundly impacted the sector, the foundations for the reorientation of the national automotive industry toward greater integration into the North American auto complex was already being constructed. Tables 5.4a and b show that the value of Mexican automotive exports (measured in current U.S. dollars) rose steadily from 1980 through 1992, more than tripling from 1980 to 1984, and quadrupling from 1980 to 1986. In 1988, the year before Carlos Salinas assumed the presidency, the nominal dollar value of

Table 5.4a

**Value of Mexican Automotive Exports, by Product, 1980–1986** (thousands of US$)

| | 1980 | 1981 | 1982 | 1983 | 1984 | 1985 | 1986 |
|---|---|---|---|---|---|---|---|
| **Total** | **415,402** | **456,113** | **530,967** | **717,037** | **1,445,649** | **1,470,855** | **2,153,204** |
| Passenger vehicles | 98,528 | 70,063 | 66,924 | 72,446 | 119,140 | 116,367 | 516,448 |
| Trucks | 30,116 | 39,454 | 14,305 | 11,743 | 26,747 | 24,383 | 29,387 |
| Chassis with engines (all classes) | 1,012 | 1,464 | 372 | 54 | n.a. | n.a. | n.a. |
| Engines for automobiles | 30,458 | 61,489 | 214,162 | 395,426 | 932,684 | 1,039,729 | 1,152,716 |
| Springs | 14,484 | 18,443 | 28,508 | 7,036 | n.a. | n.a. | n.a. |
| Loose auto parts | 209,437 | 165,028 | 131,422 | 152,236 | 270,222 | 240,743 | 373,780 |
| Engine components | 20,337 | 21,855 | 27,402 | 35,936 | 46,856 | 49,633 | 80,873 |
| Other | 11,030 | 78,317 | 47,872 | 42,160 | n.a. | n.a. | n.a. |

*Sources:* Mexico, Instituto Nacional de Estadística, Geografía, e Informática, *La Industria Automotriz en México, 1994.* CEPAL, *Reestructuración y Desarrollo de la Industria Automotriz Mexicana en los Años Ochenta,* 1992.

Table 5.4b

**Value of Mexican Automotive Exports, by Product, 1987–1993** (thousands of US$)

| | 1987 | 1988 | 1989 | 1990 | 1991 | 1992 | 1993 |
|---|---|---|---|---|---|---|---|
| **Total** | **3,158,225** | **3,540,256** | **3,804,427** | **4,837,740** | **5,769,254** | **9,297,207** | **8,900,093** |
| Passenger vehicles | 1,301,037 | 1,397,604 | 1,534,092 | 2,663,040 | 3,629,748 | 3,378,022 | 4,251,463 |
| Trucks | 23,525 | 95,618 | 32,724 | 27,973 | 171,264 | 588,386 | 670,480 |
| Chassis with engines (all classes) | n.a. | 8,564 | 17,491 | 31,573 | 44,897 | 80,982 | 134,313 |
| Automobile engines | 1,290,875 | 1,366,516 | 1,366,302 | 1,478,359 | 1,186,898 | 1,202,724 | 1,302,174 |
| Springs | n.a. | 49,304 | 53,156 | 46,209 | 56,444 | 63,015 | 106,036 |
| Loose auto parts | 444,398 | 443,484 | 396,759 | 337,523 | 445,053 | 1,524,715 | 1,888,961 |
| Engine components | 98,390 | 97,765 | 107,645 | 81,960 | 105,024 | 271,530 | 316,752 |
| Other | n.a. | 81,405 | 296,262 | 171,108 | 119,925 | 187,833 | 229,914 |

*Sources:* Mexico, Instituto Nacional de Estadística, Geografía, e Informática, *La Industria Automotriz en México, 1994.* CEPAL, *Reestructuración y Desarrollo de la Industria Automotriz Mexicana en los Años Ochenta,* 1992.

Mexican automotive exports was more than 8 times the 1980 level and more than 6.5 times the 1982 level. As Mortimore (1995, 62) has noted, "[b]etween 1983 and 1989, the automotive industry thrived while the domestic economy shriveled." Exports continued their fantastic growth through 1992, two years before NAFTA took effect, when the nominal value of Mexican automotive exports was over US $9 billion, or more than 20 times the 1980 level.

The early integration of the Mexican industry into a more comprehensive North American auto complex is revealed in the pattern of growth of Mexico's automotive exports. Automobile motors led the initial expansion of the sector's exports from 1980 through 1985. The nominal value of exported motors in 1980 of US $30.5 million doubled in 1981, tripled in 1982, doubled again in 1983, and more than doubled once more in 1984 to US $982.7 million. Exports of motors continued to expand at strong but reduced rates through 1990, when they were valued at almost US $1.5 billion.

In contrast, growth in exports of passenger vehicles returned only in 1986, but at a rate that far exceeded the growth in exports of motors. In 1986 alone, exports of passenger vehicles jumped 344 percent to US $516.5 million. The following year exports of passenger vehicles more than doubled in 1987 to US $1.3 billion, surpassing exports of motors for the first time since 1982. Growth in the value of passenger vehicle exports subsequently advanced in a series of two-year spurts followed by a year or two of stabilization. In 1988 and 1989, growth slowed significantly, but was followed in 1990 and 1991 by renewed fantastic rates of growth. In just two years from 1989 to 1991, the nominal value of vehicle exports more than doubled to US $3.6 billion. After a mild contraction in 1992, exports of passenger vehicles soared to almost US $4.3 billion, and accounted for almost half of the total value of Mexico's rapidly expanding automotive exports.

**Flying Geese or Caged Tigers? The Mexican Automotive Industry in the World Economy**

A recent study published by the United Nations Economic Commission for Latin American (Mortimore 1995) suggests that the companies constituting the Mexican terminal automobile industry have experienced a transformation from being weak targets of international automotive predators ("sitting ducks") to high flyers in the international skies of global competition ("flying geese"). Although the Mexican automobile industry has experienced profound transformations and growth since 1980, resulting in increased international competitiveness in both price and quality, the prospects for the automobile industry contributing positively to Mexico's economy and society are limited. Beyond domestic issues, the very image of individual companies as flying geese misrepresents the nature of global restructuring of the automotive industry in general, especially with regard to Mexico. That country has been assigned a role in the consolidation of a regional automotive complex whose primary focus is an expanded North American market primarily composed of Mexico, Canada, and the United States. The industry in Mexico is, in fact, producing vehicles and components that meet international price and quality standards, but this is required for consolidation of the regional complex, just as it would be required for broad-based international competition.

Because of the Mexican industry's reliance on both the national and the regional North American market, it is more useful to understand the whole Mexican automotive industry as a single "caged tiger" (competitive but restricted) than to focus on the leading automotive multinational companies as individual "flying geese." The data in Tables 5.5 through 5.7 reveal that in terms of balance of automotive trade and patterns of foreign trade, Mexico is unlikely to reap the potentially huge benefits that countries like South Korea enjoy. Instead, because of geography and a relatively long process (almost two full decades) of gradual consolidation into the North American regional auto complex, Mexico is likely to gain only minor benefits for at least a generation from auto related industrial growth. Mexico's automotive development is unique among Latin American countries, having more in common with Canada than with neighbors to the south. Consequently, Mexico does not provide a useful model for the development of automotive industries elsewhere in the region. Instead it points to the limitations for automotive growth elsewhere.

### Balance of Trade in the Mexican Automobile Industry

While Mexico's automotive exports grew at a high rates, so too did its automotive imports (see Table 5.5). In fact, they grew at such a rapid rate that for most of the 1990s the industry registered significant negative balances of trade. It was not until the currency crisis of 1995, during which the peso lost more than 60 percent of its value to the dollar, that domestic demand for consumer durables was reduced and the cost of exports fell, restoring a strongly positive trade balance.

The effects of domestic recession and currency devaluation in achieving positive automotive trade balances is evident from 1980 forward. Between 1980 and 1982, Mexico's automotive sector registered strong negative trade balances that averaged almost US $1.5 billion annually. These trade deficits were followed by a seven-year period of continuous automotive trade surpluses, a period of severe economic recession. But these recessionary years were characterized by partial recovery in 1985, followed by renewed sharp contraction in 1986. Notably, the automotive trade balance turned positive in 1983, and grew to US $673 million 1984. In 1985, however, the automotive surplus declined significantly, but reached successive new high levels in 1986 and 1987 at US $1.3 billion and US $1.8 billion, respectively. As the Mexican economy recovered since 1987, the trade surplus eventually became a deficit of almost US $1 billion in 1990 and US

$1.8 billion in 1991. In 1992 the sector recorded a modest trade surplus, but again in 1993 the trade balance turned sharply negative.

In each year of the entire fourteen-year period summarized in Table 5.5, the single category responsible for the highest value of imports was automobile assembly materials, which reached almost US $4 billion in 1990 and rose to over US $6 billion in 1992 and 1993. So, Mexico's impressive exports of almost US $4.3 billion in passenger vehicles and US $1.3 billion in motors in 1993 were dwarfed by over US $6.4 billion in auto assembly materials. Some optimism in the industry's performance can be found in the diversification of products in Mexico's automotive trade. Exports of auto parts expanded dramatically since 1992, from approximately US $1 billion to US $1.5 billion in 1992, subsequently rising to almost US $1.9 billion in 1993. Still, the industry's trade performance indicates continuing struggles with balances of trade.

### Destination of Exports

By 1993 Mexico was exporting almost half a million motor vehicles to over twenty countries; but closer examination of the countries of destination of these exports demonstrates the extremely concentrated nature of this trade. Instead of broad-based trade of significant numbers of vehicles to countries throughout the world, Mexico's automotive exports have been sent primarily to three countries: the United States, Canada, and Chile (and even Chile accounts for very few of those exports). Most of the rest have been sent to countries in Central America and the Caribbean. Indeed, as Mexican automobile production surged after 1989, the relative importance of its third most important recipient of automobiles, Chile, was reduced significantly. Table 5.6 summarizes Mexico's exports of motor vehicles from 1988 to 1993, by country of destination. It shows that the three highest ranked destinations of Mexican motor vehicles were the United States, which accounted for no less than 72.85 percent over the six-year period. Canada actually ranked well below Chile as a destination of Mexico's motor vehicle exports in 1988 and 1989, but surpassed Chile in 1990, when Canada's share of Mexican exports almost doubled, while Chile's diminished by about one-fourth. For the final three years recorded in Table 5.6, Canada's imports of vehicles from Mexico surged to about 60,000 units or more. Chile's, in contrast, stagnated at about 11,600 from 1991 to 1993.

Canada's rising share of Mexican vehicle exports coincided with a relative decline for the United States (see Table 5.7). From 1991 through 1993, when Canada's share jumped to over 15 percent from 3 to 4 percent, the U.S. share fell correspondingly from about 85 percent to about 74 percent. Over the entire six-year period, the United States and Canada accounted for no less than 86.88 percent in 1989, and as much as 91.54 percent in 1991. Despite the recession in the automobile market in 1992 and 1993, the United States still accounted for over 89 percent of Mexico's rapidly growing numbers of exported motor vehi-

Table 5.5

**Value of Automotive Imports to Mexico, by Product, 1980–1993** (thousands of US$)

| | 1980 | 1981 | 1982 | 1983 | 1984 | 1985 | 1986 |
|---|---|---|---|---|---|---|---|
| **Total** | **1,942,559** | **2,576,269** | **1,252,161** | **375,371** | **772,241** | **1,022,929** | **839,252** |
| Passenger vehicles | 155,293 | 182,245 | 93,681 | 13,398 | 17,890 | 40,891 | 37,156 |
| Special use automobiles | 108,425 | 148,610 | 58,379 | 7,339 | n.a. | n.a. | n.a. |
| Trucks (except dump trucks) | 118,892 | 184,065 | 59,483 | 6,252 | 22,924 | 55,077 | 27,795 |
| Dump trucks | 8,434 | 10,574 | 4,630 | 164 | 1,808 | 428 | 808 |
| Automobile chassis | 1,281 | 6,746 | 1,565 | 149 | n.a. | n.a. | n.a. |
| Assembly materials | 949,134 | 1,003,525 | 583,196 | 194,304 | 264,974 | 329,109 | 285,719 |
| Engines/engine components | 144,964 | 176,987 | 109,153 | 50,514 | 111,891 | 146,565 | 112,667 |
| Car and truck parts | 373,864 | 552,437 | 296,118 | 77,606 | 210,014 | 292,098 | 239,337 |
| Trailers | 22,400 | 241,964 | 7,084 | 198 | n.a. | n.a. | n.a. |
| Other | 59,872 | 69,116 | 38,872 | 25,447 | 143,040 | 158,761 | 135,770 |

| | 1987 | 1988 | 1989 | 1990 | 1991 | 1992 | 1993 |
|---|---|---|---|---|---|---|---|
| **Total** | **1,331,896** | **2,421,038** | **2,373,355** | **5,778,014** | **7,565,824** | **9,160,640** | **9,467,746** |
| Passenger vehicles | 41,709 | 65,721 | 85,727 | 254,117 | 297,282 | 384,289 | 404,575 |
| Special use automobiles | 47,158 | 66,708 | 45,618 | 44,546 | 84,408 | 122,667 | 86,571 |
| Trucks (except dump trucks) | 33,536 | 66,810 | 25,935 | 43,192 | 24,429 | 55,445 | 27,830 |
| Dump trucks | 521 | 26,549 | 4,546 | 3,478 | 5,438 | 3,166 | 4,778 |
| Automobile chassis | n.a. | 1,859 | 1,256 | 2,086 | 2,859 | 24,861 | 9,382 |
| Assembly materials | 752,505 | 978,826 | 949,793 | 3,891,053 | 5,197,934 | 6,007,099 | 6,439,689 |
| Engines/engine components | 102,671 | 148,017 | 170,918 | 177,561 | 250,547 | 376,917 | 394,219 |
| Car and truck parts | 243,104 | 552,431 | 639,713 | 520,809 | 816,237 | 1,337,861 | 1,377,121 |
| Trailers | n.a. | 40,193 | 14,207 | 24,003 | 15,205 | 41,606 | 22,456 |
| Other | 110,692 | 473,923 | 435,642 | 817,164 | 871,419 | 806,729 | 701,125 |

*Sources:* Mexico, Instituto Nacional de Estadística, Geografía, e Informática, *La Industria Automotriz en México, 1994.* CEPAL, *Reestructuración y Desarrollo de la Industria Automotriz Mexicana en los Años Ochenta,* 1992.

Table 5.6

**Annual Exports of Mexican-made Vehicles, by Continent and Country of Destination, 1988–1993** (units)

|  | 1988 | 1989 | 1990 | 1991 | 1992 | 1993 |
|---|---|---|---|---|---|---|
| **Total** | **173,147** | **195,999** | **276,869** | **358,666** | **383,374** | **471,912** |
| AMERICAS | 172,740 | 194,411 | 274,736 | 357,620 | 382,183 | 466,192 |
| Bahamas | 1,607 | 1,114 | 531 | 291 | 757 | 591 |
| Bolivia | 452 | 642 | 955 | 103 | 1,167 | 316 |
| Canada | 5,023 | 7,283 | 13,079 | 67,041 | 59,260 | 69,934 |
| Costa Rica | 799 | 847 | 1,037 | 369 | 699 | 651 |
| Cuba | 247 | 149 | 371 | 483 | 275 | 1,232 |
| Curacao | 617 | 827 | 655 | 347 | 585 | 453 |
| Chile | 7,520 | 13,229 | 9,664 | 11,597 | 11,632 | 11,562 |
| Dominican Rep. | 1,240 | 150 | 478 | — | — | — |
| El Salvador | 1,210 | 978 | 522 | 866 | 2,364 | 1,170 |
| Guatemala | 1,266 | 598 | 662 | 829 | 1,835 | 1,308 |
| Honduras | 432 | 206 | 348 | 317 | 656 | 281 |
| Panama | 297 | 979 | 2,507 | 1,810 | 1,671 | 1,126 |
| Paraguay | — | 347 | 1,007 | 1,160 | 1,315 | 1,081 |
| Peru | 252 | — | 477 | 4,561 | 3,608 | 3,018 |
| Puerto Rico | 2,295 | 2,532 | 2,718 | 1,727 | 1,166 | 2,120 |
| United States | 148,017 | 162,987 | 238,281 | 261,280 | 282,853 | 352,772 |
| Uruguay | 119 | 135 | 631 | 1,614 | 2,892 | 3,470 |
| Others | 1,347 | 1,408 | 813 | 3,225 | 9,448 | 15,107 |
| AFRICA | 92 | 125 | 289 | 121 | 50 | 0 |
| ASIA | 4 | 717 | 1,201 | 803 | 885 | 5,432 |
| EUROPE | 311 | 746 | 399 | 55 | 156 | 20 |

*Source:* Mexico, Instituto Nacional de Estadística, Geografía, e Informática, *La Industria Automotriz en México, 1994.*

cles. Importantly, in every year reported, the total number of units exported to the United States rose steadily, jumping in 1993, the last year reported, by almost 70,000 units to a level more than twice that of 1989.

Correspondingly, negligible numbers of vehicles, and decreasing shares of Mexico's vehicle exports, were sent to countries outside of the Western Hemisphere, or even to the South American continent. This concentration of Mexico's trade in vehicles to the United States and Canada, even as the number of units rose precipitously, provides some important lessons for other Latin American countries that are developing their own automotive industries. First, Mexico's foreign trade in automobiles indicates that a particular pattern of "globalization" (or better stated, "internationalization") of the automotive industry is occurring. As noted above, this process might better be referred to as "glocalization,"

Table 5.7

**Annual Exports of Mexican-made Vehicles to the United States, Canada, and Chile, 1988–1993**
(percentage of all vehicles exported)

|  | 1988 | 1989 | 1990 | 1991 | 1992 | 1993 |
|---|---|---|---|---|---|---|
| United States | 85.49 | 83.16 | 86.06 | 72.85 | 73.78 | 74.75 |
| Canada | 2.90 | 3.72 | 4.72 | 18.69 | 15.46 | 14.82 |
| Chile | 4.34 | 6.75 | 3.49 | 3.23 | 3.03 | 2.45 |

*Source:* Derived from Table 5.6.

whereby regional auto "complexes" are being consolidated. Second, the consolidation of these complexes began well before formal free-trade agreements were even imagined, never mind negotiated. Consequently, inclusion of additional countries into NAFTA should not be understood to be the necessary precursor to inclusion into the North American automotive complex, or the foundation for an expanded Western Hemisphere automotive complex. Third, even if inclusion into such a regional system of production and distribution were probable, it would not be favorable because of the dominance of the U.S. market and the consequent dependence of national production on the cycles of demand in the United States. Fourth, given the general maturity of the automobile industry, the relative stagnation of growth in the U.S. market, and the newly expanded installed capacity in Mexico, there is relatively little demand to absorb additional imports from other countries.

The fifth lesson derives from the data in Table 5.1, which show that much of Mexico's new export-oriented capacity has been located in its northern states, geographically closer to the U.S. market. This facilitates importation of materials for assembly as well as exportation of complete vehicles and vehicle subsystems such as motors. This spatial relocation within Mexico, the most proximate of the larger Latin American countries, to sites even closer to the United States indicates that there are limits to the "globalization" of automotive production. In spite of exports of Brazilian-made body panels for small pickups to Louisiana, for example, the integration of other countries on the South American continent into the North American automotive complex will be more difficult to achieve than was the integration of Mexico.

## Labor Relations and Industrial Transformation in the Automotive Industry

Examination of recent data on employment, wages, training, and labor productivity indicates that the automotive industry has been enjoying dynamic growth,

Table 5.8

**Daily Wages of Mexican Automobile Workers, Selected Plants, 1994**

| Plant | Wage* |
|---|---|
| Chrysler Saltillo | 47.51 |
| Chrysler Toluca | 58.30 |
| Ford Chihuahua | 67.86 |
| Ford Hermosillo | 70.32 |
| Ford Cuautitlán | 68.97 |
| Nissan Aguascalientes | 43.72 |
| Nissan Cuernavaca | 60.91 |
| Volkswagen | 73.04 |

*Total new pesos per day (as of September 1).
*Source*: JFCA and STPS-CGCFC Archives, as cited in Tuman (1996c, Table 7).

simultaneously achieving gains for both employers and workers. However, a longer view reveals that the effects of industrial restructuring and economic liberalization have had mixed results for workers. The relatively early initiation of the process of integrating the Mexican automotive industry into the larger North American automotive complex (beginning in the early 1980s *at the latest*), suggests that any effects on the organization of production, working conditions, and labor relations began well before the liberalization program of Mexican president Carlos Salinas (1988–94) and free trade negotiations with the United States and Canada.

Compounding the efforts by multinational corporations to reorient automotive production toward greater international competitiveness was the drastic contraction of the domestic market during the 1980s, giving greater impetus to the restructuring process. Consequently, there was even greater pressure either to close or to reorganize operations in the old industrial heartland in central Mexico, while simultaneously establishing new productive centers in northern areas. Within this context, the automobile companies proceeded rapidly with the construction of new productive units in areas outside of central Mexico, while attempting to restructure their older productive units.

*Industrial Restructuring and the Labor Force during the 1980s*

The profound changes occurring domestically and internationally for the Mexican automotive industry during the 1980s impacted workers in ways that were unavoidable and, at times, devastating. Automotive wages declined dramatically during the 1980s; employment dropped in central Mexico, but increased sharply in the northern states; the average age of the industrial work force dropped significantly as older workers were laid off and younger workers were hired to replace them as demand returned; and perhaps most importantly, traditional protections for seniority-based hiring and promotion were undermined. Parallel to these developments in the terminal industry, the auto parts industry relied to ever greater degrees on the use of maquiladoras to supply plants based in the United States.

Two effects of industrial restructuring stand out among the many that impacted workers: a reduction in wages, and the loss of worker autonomy. The reduction in wages was partly accomplished by opening new plants in the north with lower wages than those prevailing in the center. As capacity expanded in the new sites, plants in the center were either pressured to accept significant decreases in real wages or were ultimately closed (Carrillo V. 1990b; Middlebrook 1991a). Table 5.8 shows average wages as of September 1994 in the main productive units operated by the automobile assemblers. The oldest sites, inaugurated before the restructuring of the late 1970s and early 1980s, are located in the Federal District (General Motors, Chrysler, and Ford-Cuautitlán), Cuernavaca (Nissan), and Puebla (Volkswagen). With some notable exceptions, the older sites paid the best wages. This is strongly the case for General Motors and Nissan.

Chrysler generally follows the same pattern, except that the highest wages paid at the Toluca site were slightly higher than those paid in the Federal District. Ford deviates even more from the general pattern, with higher wages in its Hermosillo assembly plant instead of its assembly plant in the Mexico City suburb of Cuautitlán. The Cuautitlán site might be exceptional, because there is evidence that the company had already begun a campaign to break worker resistance to changes in wages and working conditions there (Morris 1994). Still, wages in the Cuautitlán plant were among the highest in the industry.

The very highest wages were paid by Volkswagen, in one of the oldest sites in the industry. This case might suggest that many other variables impact wage levels. The Volkswagen plant had a long history of worker combativeness and union democracy that is traced back to the Unidad Obrera Independiente (UOI), an "independent" union confederation that began to make significant advances organizing the automotive sector and other industries during President Luis Echeverría's administration in the early and mid-1970s (Aguilar 1982). Roxborough (1984) has argued strongly that a central determinant of wages and working conditions for auto workers is the degree of union democracy enjoyed by the union local representing the plant. This may be true, but it should not obscure the relative ease of instituting a new collective contract in a new plant, compared to the difficulty of fundamentally rewriting existing collective contracts. Politically and legally, it has proven much easier to build new plants with new collective contracts in areas that maximize the benefits of "greenfield" sites: hiring a new, young work force that is less likely to be injured or ill, and that has little or no tradition of union struggle and few preconceptions of how work should be organized.

Table 5.9

**Average Annual Remuneration in the Mexican Automotive Industry, by Sector, 1988–1992** (current new pesos per wage earner)

|      | Total     | Automobiles | Chassis, auto parts, engines, etc. | Rubber products |
|------|-----------|-------------|------------------------------------|-----------------|
| 1988 | 13,987.95 | 17,933.96   | 11,501.97                          | 14,747.96       |
| 1989 | 17,415.29 | 21,932.56   | 14,700.10                          | 17,718.87       |
| 1990 | 23,629.31 | 30,075.70   | 19,330.69                          | 22,784.95       |
| 1991 | 30,128.11 | 38,592.63   | 24,647.45                          | 29,282.26       |
| 1992 | 39,479.79 | 53,805.44   | 30,965.85                          | 37,858.52       |

Source: Mexico, Instituto Nacional de Estadística, Geografía e Informática, *La Industria Automotriz en México, 1994.*
Note: 3.478 new peso = US $1.00.

## Wages, Employment, Productivity, and Technology since 1988

Despite the use of industrial relocation toward northern greenfield sites to suppress wages in the automobile sector in the 1980s, workers throughout the broader automotive industry enjoyed notable real wage increases since 1988. Table 5.9 shows that workers have enjoyed rapidly rising nominal wages in each of the three major subsectors of the industry from 1988 to 1992: automobiles, auto parts and components, and tire and rubber products. Workers in the automobile sector earned the highest increase over the five-year period, with slightly more than a tripling of nominal wages and an increase of over 80 percent in real terms. In the auto parts and rubber products sectors, workers earned significant increases in both nominal and real wages, but at levels much lower than in the terminal automobile industry.

Interestingly, although workers in the rubber products sector enjoyed a slightly lower percentage increase than the auto parts workers between 1988 and 1992 (approximately 58 versus 65 percent), their wages remained at levels much higher. This appears to be a result of the phenomenon described above regarding the growth and relocation of the core automotive industry. The new northern sites producing chassis and motors, among other components, have paid wages significantly below those in central Mexico. Additionally, the automotive industry has increasingly relied on maquiladoras to supply both the national industry and to assembly plants in the United States. This is part of the phenomenon that Carrillo (1990b) refers to as the "maquilization" of the automotive industry in Mexico.

In spite of the significant increases in wages in the automotive industry,

Table 5.10

**Hourly Compensation for Workers in Motor Vehicle Production, by Country, 1975 and 1982–1992** (current US$)

|  | 1975 | 1982 | 1983 | 1984 | 1985 | 1986 |
|---|---|---|---|---|---|---|
| **Global Average** | **4.97** | **7.83** | **7.59** | **7.42** | **7.48** | **9.72** |
| Japan | 3.56 | 7.21 | 7.83 | 7.90 | 8.09 | 11.80 |
| United States | 9.55 | 18.15 | 18.32 | 19.02 | 19.71 | 20.09 |
| Germany | 7.89 | 13.03 | 13.16 | 11.92 | 12.11 | 16.96 |
| France | 5.10 | 8.85 | 8.79 | 8.20 | 8.31 | 11.06 |
| Spain | — | 6.69 | 5.69 | 5.35 | 5.54 | 7.74 |
| Canada | 7.25 | 12.30 | 12.85 | 13.03 | 12.99 | 13.35 |
| South Korea | 0.14 | 1.34 | 1.45 | 1.50 | 1.62 | 1.80 |
| Italy | 5.16 | 8.06 | 8.32 | 8.00 | 8.19 | 11.02 |
| United Kingdom | 4.12 | 7.86 | 7.32 | 6.86 | 7.17 | 8.77 |
| Taiwan | 0.64 | 1.86 | 1.66 | 2.09 | 1.85 | 2.23 |
| Brazil | 1.29 | 2.47 | 1.79 | 1.60 | 1.64 | — |
| Mexico | 2.94 | 3.56 | 2.61 | 2.55 | 2.34 | 1.93 |
| Australia | 5.79 | 9.78 | 9.33 | 9.87 | 8.24 | 8.71 |
|  | 1987 | 1988 | 1989 | 1990 | 1991 | 1992 |
| **Global Average** | **11.52** | **12.59** | **12.75** | **15.53** | **16.47** | **17.81** |
| Japan | 13.83 | 16.36 | 15.60 | 15.68 | 17.99 | 19.97 |
| United States | 20.40 | 20.80 | 21.39 | 22.48 | 24.28 | 25.12 |
| Germany | 21.47 | 23.05 | 22.36 | 28.01 | 29.12 | 32.61 |
| France | 12.93 | 13.54 | 13.11 | 15.94 | 15.89 | 17.42 |
| Spain | 9.54 | 10.85 | 11.74 | 15.00 | 15.93 | 17.52 |
| Canada | 14.49 | 16.41 | 17.88 | 19.14 | 21.01 | 20.92 |
| South Korea | 2.04 | 3.07 | 4.54 | 5.48 | 6.47 | 7.05 |
| Italy | 13.65 | 14.51 | 15.00 | 18.38 | 19.55 | 20.48 |
| United Kingdom | 10.61 | 12.08 | 12.12 | 14.58 | 16.10 | 16.80 |
| Taiwan | 2.83 | 3.50 | 4.16 | 4.76 | 5.72 | 6.57 |
| Brazil | — | — | — | — | — | — |
| Mexico | 1.61 | 1.96 | 2.31 | 2.79 | 3.36 | 4.35 |
| Australia | 9.60 | 11.28 | 12.15 | 12.93 | 13.27 | 13.25 |

*Source:* Ward's Communications, *Ward's Automotive Yearbook, 56th Edition*, 1994.

workers received very low wages in absolute terms, especially in comparison to their counterparts in other countries. According to the data in Table 5.10, workers in the automobile sector, the most advanced and highest paying sector of the automotive industry, saw their compensation, measured in nominal U.S. dollars, fall without interruption from 1982 through 1987. Only in 1988 did compensation rise again, but nominal compensation remained below 1982 levels through 1991. In 1992 compensation rose dramatically, but it was only 22 percent higher than in 1982, fully ten years later.

While it is true that measuring compensation in U.S. dollars might exaggerate

Table 5.11

**Number of Workers in the Mexican Automotive Industry, by Sector of Activity, 1988–1992** (annual average)

|      | Total   | Automobiles | Chassis, parts, engines, etc. | Rubber products |
|------|---------|-------------|-------------------------------|-----------------|
| 1988 | 156,793 | 44,400      | 80,291                        | 32,102          |
| 1989 | 170,300 | 50,164      | 87,142                        | 32,994          |
| 1990 | 180,742 | 59,640      | 88,015                        | 33,087          |
| 1991 | 189,511 | 63,303      | 93,008                        | 33,200          |
| 1992 | 185,095 | 62,717      | 89,877                        | 32,501          |

*Source:* Mexico, Instituto Nacional de Estadística, Geografía, e Informática, *La Industria Automotriz en México, 1994.*

the impact on buying power, it nevertheless provides a good estimate. Also, it facilitates comparison across countries. Here, again, the impact of industrial restructuring on Mexican workers is shown to be negative. The gap between compensation for Mexican workers and those of the advanced industrial countries grew wider throughout the 1980s. In 1991 and 1992 it narrowed as Mexican workers enjoyed significant percentage increases, but this narrowing was slight. Furthermore, because of inflation compensation in 1992 is likely to be even lower than in 1975. Compensation has remained so low in Mexico that Taiwan and South Korea, two "Asian tigers" famous for their low industrial wages, surpassed it in 1986 and 1987, respectively. In 1992, automobile workers in Taiwan and Korea were paid respectively US $2.22 and US $2.70 per hour more than workers in Mexico. Excluding Brazil, for which more recent data were unavailable, Mexico had the lowest levels of compensation of any of the countries listed in Table 5.10.

The real wage gains in the 1988–92 period were accompanied by steady increases in employment and productivity, again mostly concentrated in the terminal automobile sector (see Table 5.11). This sector experienced a 41 percent increase in employment, while the auto parts sector experienced employment growth of approximately 12 percent over the five-year period. The rubber products industry remained remarkably constant over the entire period, with an increase of just over 1 percent.

In spite of the increased employment and wages in the late 1980s and early 1990s, labor productivity increased dramatically (see Table 5.12). Interestingly, the biggest increases were achieved in the very sector of the automotive industry that experienced the greatest increases in wages and employment: the terminal automobile industry. While the index (based on 1980 levels) for the automotive industry overall rose strongly from 112.3 in 1988 to 163.0 in 1992, representing an increase of 45 percent, the terminal automobile sector rose from 125.6 to

Table 5.12

**Index of Productivity in the Mexican Automotive Industry, by Sector of Activity, 1988–1992** (base 1980 = 100.0)

|  | Total | Automobiles | Chassis, parts, engines, etc. | Rubber Products |
|---|---|---|---|---|
| 1988 | 112.3 | 125.6 | 111.1 | 102.0 |
| 1989 | 119.8 | 136.6 | 115.9 | 104.1 |
| 1990 | 130.3 | 149.9 | 116.5 | 106.3 |
| 1991 | 148.5 | 179.2 | 126.8 | 109.7 |
| 1992 | 163.0 | 202.4 | 130.9 | 115.5 |

*Source:* Mexico, Instituto Nacional de Estadística, Geografía e Informática, *La Industria Automotriz en México, 1994.*

202.4, an increase of 61 percent. In contrast, the auto parts and rubber products industries experienced increases in labor productivity of only 18 and 13 percent, respectively.

### *Technology, Flexibility, and Labor Relations*

Essential to the restructuring of the automotive industry in Mexico have been managerial and production innovations intended to introduce greater efficiency and quality by increasing the "flexibility" in the use of labor power and minimizing inventories. Generically these innovations are broadly classified under the rubrics of "post-Fordism" or "flexible specialization," and are contrasted with the rigidities of so-called "Fordist" mass production.[6] The initial optimism of early non-Marxist commentators, notably Piore and Sabel (1984), for the "possibilities for prosperity" offered by flexible specialization has been replaced by significant skepticism on the part of researchers of labor processes. Understandably, in the mid-1980s the increase in worker participation in shop-floor decision making and quality control was expected to liberate workers from the repressive rhythms of the mass production assembly line, and even to erode the power of traditional bureaucratic unions, as workers and managers cooperated more closely on production issues.

The theoretical and empirical connections between flexibility and worker participation, however, were never well established. Nor were such links well established between worker participation and either liberation from managerial authority, the rhythms of production, or repressive unions. In their survey of firms in the United States, Shaiken et al. (1986) showed that firms using flexible techniques and computer-controlled machinery had tended to *reduce* worker autonomy and participation in shop-floor decision making. In fact, managers overwhelmingly expressed distrust of granting workers greater autonomy and decision-making authority. The 1993 and 1994 discussions from a working group on "flexible specialization" concluded that improved working conditions are not a necessary result of flexible production. Instead, such improvements result from complex processes of negotiation and gradually increasing trust between workers and managers (Doner 1991). Shaiken et al. recommended that instead of positing necessary conditions of flexible specialization, it was more useful to examine concrete cases in which flexible specialization is pursued by either or both management and workers.

In Mexico, in addition to suffering a long-term decline of real wages, workers in the automotive industry experienced neither enhanced worker autonomy nor union democracy as a result of industrial restructuring and the institutionalization of flexible production. The process of industrial restructuring and relocation of the Mexican automotive industry was based on reducing or eliminating many of the traditional preferences for promotion and hiring ("job access rights") that Mexican automobile workers enjoyed. Middlebrook's (1991a) examination of the collective contracts of the terminal automobile industry (including Chrysler, Ford, General Motors, Nissan, and Volkswagen) demonstrated considerable loss of the provisions that protected workers from the unilateral decision making of management. Middlebrook identified three specific categories in which labor relations were fundamentally altered as the industry restructured and relocated: (1) promotion and employment security, (2) participation and fairness in production process decisions, and (3) specificity of conflict resolution procedures. In general, workers enjoyed significantly lower levels of security and participation in each category in the newer plants than in the older plants in the greater Mexico City area. Chrysler was the sole, and only partial, exception to the overall degradation of traditional worker and union rights and privileges sanctified in longstanding collective contracts. But Chrysler workers in the Federal District (the oldest site) enjoyed only extremely low levels of rights and privileges, negating the possibility of lower levels in the newer plants. This is the weak exception, then, that proves the rule.

At the Ford plant in Cuautitlán, the company and the national CTM-affiliated Ford workers' union attempted to impose, in strongly authoritarian fashion, the innovations in labor relations introduced in other Ford plants in the north. Initially, there was an attempt in 1987 to use inflation to erode wages in the Cuautitlán plant to levels similar to those in the north. When the workers resisted, a protracted struggle ensued, lasting through 1991 and involving extended wage strikes, unilateral replacement of the local executive committee, hunger strikes, dissolution of the union, road blockades, individual firings, and liquidation of the entire work force, as well as the existing collective contract. The conflict reached a crescendo in January 1990, after almost three years of intense struggle, when some 400 men dressed in Ford uniforms disembarked from CTM buses and brutally assaulted the workers of the first shift shortly after the start of the morning's operations. In addition to numerous beatings, several workers suffered gunshot wounds and one later died. This only heightened the intensity of the conflict, which required another two years to fully resolve. During the struggle the company and the union, acting in concert against the workers, were able to impose a new collective contract with many of the new restrictions on worker autonomy and security introduced in the northern plants (Arteaga 1990).

As the industry has restructured, a great effort and significant resources have been dedicated to education and training, which perhaps partially offsets the losses of earning power, worker autonomy, job security, and participation in decision making. Carrillo (1990b) observes that some 50 percent of the workers that inaugurated the Ford assembly plant in Hermosillo spent six months abroad for training. Additionally, a large national survey of technological change in Mexican manufacturing commissioned by the Ministry of Labor confirms that significant resources are being dedicated to education and training in the automotive sector (Secretaría del Trabajo y Previsión Social 1995). The data reported in the study demonstrate extensive training at all levels in the larger plants of the automobile industry. For instance, the study reports that over 74,000 workers in the automotive industry received training in 1991 (Secretaría del Trabajo y Previsión Social 1995, 531–32). This represents a significant increase over the 70,494 who received training in 1989 (Secretaría del Trabajo y Previsión Social 1995, 529–30). Interestingly, this increase in training in 1991 occurred exclusively in the large firms, while the medium, small, and micro firms showed declines in the number of workers receiving training.

In spite of extensive training, Carrillo observes that the dramatic increase in education and training of the work force has been accompanied by a general devaluation of skill (1990b, 93). Carrillo argues that the reduction of the number of job categories and levels from about twenty or thirty in the old contracts to about six to ten in the new contracts has created a situation in which previously highly ranked skill levels have been ranked much lower. This "devaluation" of skills is compounded by the tendency of workers in the northern plants to work between 45 and 48 hours in northern plants, compared to about 40 in the center. Additionally, the workers in the northern plants achieve greater levels of productivity. In sum, workers in the north are better trained, paid less, work longer hours, and are more productive, relative to their counterparts in the center. These results, combined with the shift in the balance of installed capacity to the north, have created what Carrillo refers to as the *maquilization* of the automobile industry in Mexico.

## Conclusions

The dynamism of the Mexican automotive industry has resulted mostly from its proximity to the United States and from its integration into the North American automotive complex. This process of integration began as early as the late 1970s, certainly before the 1982 debt crisis and the subsequent economic crisis in Mexico and the rest of the Latin American region. Mexico's accession to the General Agreement on Tariffs and Trade (GATT) in the late 1980s, and its participation in the North American Free Trade Agreement (NAFTA), only ratified officially a process of industrial restructuring that had long been unfolding in Mexico. The major impetus for restructuring and integration into the larger regional automotive complex came from within the industry itself, not just regionally, but globally. The Japanese "invasion" of the U.S. market had begun in the 1970s, forcing the relatively weak domestic manufacturers to develop new strategies for meeting the challenge. One component of the response of the "Big Three" and others selling in the U.S. market was to reconfigure the Mexican industry to serve better the needs of the markets in the United States and Canada. Eventually, fuller integration of the Mexican market into the regional market became a logical extension of the integration of North American production.

The domestic impacts of industrial restructuring in Mexico have included massive relocation north of the former industrial heartland around Mexico City, particularly to states along the border with the United States. In addition to proximity to the U.S. market and to supplies from the United States, this relocation has been predicated on the ability to create "greenfield" work sites with a new, young work force in excellent health, and with little tradition of labor struggle. Such conditions have permitted the general lowering of real wages in the industry, and their maintenance at extremely low levels compared to other countries, even South Korea and Taiwan. Indeed, wages in the Mexican automotive industry are among the lowest in the world. Additionally, workers have experienced a general erosion of traditional job security provisions and worker autonomy in the collective contracts for the new plants.

The preponderance of the evidence, then, indicates that the Mexican automotive industry is simultaneously an improbable and undesirable model for the national and subregional automotive industries developing in other parts of Latin America. It is improbable because of the special circumstances that prompted Mexico's integration into the North American complex, a process of restructuring that began almost two decades ago and that continues to tie it closely to the North American market. It is an undesirable model because of significant domestic social costs, as well as continuing concerns with balance of automotive trade associated with integration in the North American automotive complex.

**Notes**

1. Because of the extraordinarily high interest rates required to stabilize the Mexican peso in 1995, large consumer durables like automobiles have become prohibitively expensive. In response, the Mexican government exempted autos from the value-added tax (VAT), which was increased from 10 percent to 15 percent.
2. The regional character of the Mexican automobile industry (or, the Mexican component of the North American complex) is evident in the data on Mexico's automotive trade.

3. Shaiken and Herzenberg (1987) show that machine efficiency, labor productivity, and quality standards for a Mexican engine plant in a northern state were comparable to those of a U.S. and Canadian plant operated by the same U.S.-based multinational.

4. The annual growth estimates are considered to be less than 2.0 percent on a compound basis.

5. Ironically, the extension of the U.S. auto complex into a truly continental North American system has pulled Mexican production into closer proximity to the geographical center of the industry, as all of the important new sites have been created in northern states.

6. Piore and Sabel provide an excellent discussion of flexible production in *The Second Industrial Divide* (1984). Jessop (1990) provides a more elaborated discussion of "Fordism" and "post-Fordism," and the role of production technology and labor relations within a larger national and international political economy.

John P. Tuman

# 6 | The Political Economy of Restructuring in Mexico's "Brownfield" Plants: A Comparative Analysis

## Introduction

Over the course of the 1980s, a transformation occurred in the Mexican automobile industry. Prompted by a severe recession in the aftermath of the crisis of 1982,[1] transnational firms operating in Mexico were forced to slash production, reduce employment, and to limit the growth in real wages and benefits (AMIA 1988, 7; Arteaga 1993). By 1987, several older plants oriented toward the domestic market had been closed (e.g., Ford-Tlanepantla and Renault-Sahagún), while a number of other ones had been extensively reorganized. Yet even as the economic crisis threatened certain segments of the terminal sector, the globalization of automobile production simultaneously led to dramatic growth in Mexico's parts and vehicle export industries (Acevedo 1990; Hinojosa-Ojeda and Morales 1992). Indeed, Ford, General Motors, Chrysler, and Nissan opened five new export plants throughout the decade, generating a 2,317 percent increase in finished vehicle exports between 1982 and 1994 (Figure 6.1).[2] According to recent studies of the impact of trade liberalization, small- and medium-size vehicle production in the Mexican export sector will continue to grow in response to the opportunities created by the North American Free Trade Agree-

Some material in this chapter has been reprinted with permission from *Industrial Relations Journal,* volume 27, no.1 (December 1996), pp. 317–30, Blackwell Publishers, UK.

Figure 6.1. **Production, Sales, and Exports of Finished Vehicles, Mexico, 1980–1994**

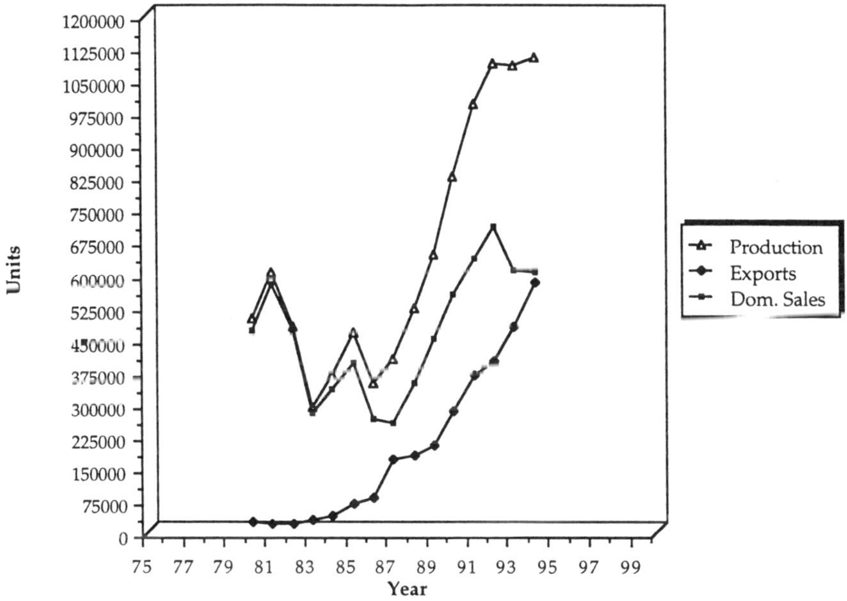

*Source:* Asociación Mexicana de la Industria Automotriz (AMIA), *Boletín*, various years/issues.

ment (NAFTA) (Hunter, Markusen, and Rutherford 1992; Berry, Grilli, and López de Silanes 1992).

The process of restructuring has produced important challenges for Mexican automobile unions. In the majority of new export plants, union elites associated with the Confederación de Trabajadores de México (Confederation of Mexican Workers, or CTM) pressured local union leaders into acquiescing to a wide range of company demands, thus facilitating the introduction of work teams, quality circles, broadly defined job descriptions, and below-average wages and benefits.[3] Having won these concessions from unions organized in the export plants, managers sought to use disparities in wages and working conditions to force union leaders in *older* plants (producing for the domestic market) to acquiesce to layoffs, automation, and the introduction of "flexible" labor processes.[4] To date, however, the results of restructuring initiatives in the older segment of the industry have produced mixed results. In some cases, the introduction of work rule changes and production flexibility has been achieved with relatively little resistance from workers and unions. At the same time, in other cases, workers have engaged in strikes, protests, and other forms of militant political action in order to resist restructuring. Given the variation in union responses in the terminal sector, the analyst of Mexican labor is presented with a (deceptively) simple question: Why have some unions adopted accommodative bargaining strategies to restructuring, while others have responded with more militant tactics?

An analysis of the variation of union responses to restructuring programs in the Mexican automobile industry can contribute to a broadly comparative assessment of economic reform in Latin America. In the first place, a study of the Mexican case can generate insight into the factors that determine the success (or failure) of reform efforts. Indeed, an emerging body of comparative literature suggests that within the developing world, the strategies adopted by unions often affect the timing and extent of restructuring and adjustment programs (Nelson 1992; Tuman 1994a; Towers 1996). In addition, a focus on labor's responses to the crisis can contribute to our understanding of the process of political liberalization in Mexico. State–labor relations have often been implicated in the logic of political legitimation for the Mexican regime. Since at least 1940, a principal source of stability for the Mexican state has been its historic pact with unions organized in the official labor sector. By securing a number of important social and political benefits for the organized labor movement, the dominant political party (the Partido Revolucionario Institucional, or PRI) has been able to draw a link between itself and the ideological goals and symbols associated with the Mexican Revolution. The distribution of government patronage to members of official unions also created a large electoral base for the PRI, ultimately helping to stabilize its rule as the dominant party in the arena of Mexican politics (Grayson 1989; Middlebrook 1995). Nevertheless, to the degree that privatization, fiscal reform, and export promotion have undermined the material basis of Mexico's social pact, it seems likely that rank-and-file union support for the party may have diminished in recent years.[5] Viewed from this angle, even when workers' strike movements have failed to halt changes occurring at the plant level, the incidence of highly publicized protests concerning restructuring (e.g., Ford-Cuautitlán strikes, 1987–90; Volkswagen strike, 1992) has demonstrated that the regime's neoliberal policies may be jeopardizing the basic arrangements in its inherited institutions of political legitimation and control (Laurell 1992, 49; Luna 1991, 17–27).[6]

This chapter seeks to explain the variation in union responses to restructuring in the Mexican automobile industry, focusing principally on the period of 1980 to 1994. It begins with a brief survey of the recent theoretical literature on Mexican industrial relations and a discussion of the methodology used in the analysis. The second and third parts discuss the origins, and outcomes, of union democratization movements in the Mexican automobile industry, and examine the relationship between union government and militancy for six unions. In the concluding section, I outline the broader implications of the findings.

## Theoretical Approach and Methodology

Analyses of unions in Mexico and other Latin American countries are usually informed by the framework of state corporatism (Spalding 1977, 5, 280–82; Collier and Collier 1991, 48–99). This theory emphasizes the legacies of the historic pact made between labor and the state, in which organized workers (and other social actors) gave up political autonomy in exchange for access to social and economic benefits. While the pact granted organized labor formal representation within the governing coalition, it simultaneously gave the regime considerable opportunities to influence the political behavior and bargaining postures of organized workers (Collier and Collier 1991; Zapata 1992).

When applied to the case of Mexico, the theory of corporatism suggests that the pattern of state–labor relations is reproduced through three mechanisms. The first concerns the imposition of state controls over the structure of interest representation within the labor movement. In order to form a union, workers must comply with certain registration requirements, which are based partly on political criteria. These legal controls are used both to make it more difficult to join independent unions, and to discourage changes in affiliation (Bensusán 1994, 54). Indeed, a number of studies claim that the regime encourages the growth and maintenance of the official labor sector by applying registration rules to benefit unions that are incorporated into the PRI (Collier and Collier 1991, 407–20, 575–601; Zapata 1992, 148–51; Bizberg 1990, 109–30; Grayson 1989, 49–63; Bensusán 1994, 54–56). As a result, while some autonomous unions have managed to gain recognition during periods of political liberalization, the vast majority of organized workers remain affiliated to the CTM and other official confederations.

The second mechanism concerns the use of institutional constraints to shape decision-making processes in incorporated unions. In particular, the state corporatist perspective suggests that the regime sanctions electoral rules that insulate union elites from possible democratic challengers.[7] Elections in CTM unions often are irregular, uncontested, and do not afford workers the right to a secret ballot (Roxborough and Bizberg 1983; La Botz 1992, 44–54; Middlebrook 1995, 67). At the same time, officials in the Ministry of Labor and Social Welfare have tacitly encouraged unions to coordinate bargaining with government mediators, and to employ centralized decision-making processes as a standard feature of union government (Zapata 1992, 154; Bizberg 1993, 301–4; Middlebrook 1995, 67).

Finally, the theory of state corporatism underscores the impact of the selective distribution of political and economic benefits to union leaders.[8] For example, the PRI often has set aside seats in the Chamber of Deputies and positions in the bureaucracy for representatives from the labor delegation (Grayson 1989, 49–51, Table 4; Zapata 1992, 180; Middlebrook 1995, 101–5). In addition, the regime has promoted (and protected) membership for the CTM, and has made a variety of other economic resources available to union leaders through the organs of the dominant party (Grayson 1989, 49–63, Table 4; Collier and Collier 1991; Samstad and Collier 1995, 4; Middlebrook 1995, 98–101). In exchange for being guaranteed access to political and economic resources, leaders in the official labor sector have been expected to conform their bargaining demands to the terms of government policy, and to mobilize support for the PRI during elections.

Analysts who apply the state-corporatist perspective to the Mexican automobile industry have generally focused on the degree of union integration into, or autonomy from, Mexico's official labor confederations. In general, the hypothesis advanced is that incorporated unions have been more likely to adopt accommodative responses toward restructuring than "independent" unions (Carrillo V. and García 1987, 305, 336–38; Middlebrook 1991a, 277, 281–92).[9] On the one hand, because the regime structures and controls the internal political life of corporatist unions through the use of various inducements, powerful incentives exist for labor elites to be more responsive to the demands of the government than to the rank and file. Consequently, as the government embraced a neoliberal model of economic development grounded in export promotion and industrial restructuring, union leaders came under strong pressure to facilitate the process of modernization and restructuring at the plant level. On the other hand, because decision-making processes in incorporated unions are centralized and nondemocratic, the rank and file lack the political space to contest accommodative responses to restructuring. At the same time, unions that are autonomous from corporatist institutions have generally enjoyed the capacity and associational freedom to mount militant campaigns against restructuring with varying levels of success.

The analysis presented in this study is grounded in the state-corporatist framework. I argue that the outcome and legacies of union democratization movements in the automobile industry best explain the variation in workers' responses to restructuring. In those cases where democratization movements were successful, workers severed (or substantially changed) their relationship to the CTM, democratized internal decision-making processes, increased their level of participation, and made frequent demands for stronger work rules, control over the production process, and higher wages and benefits. In the absence of corporatist controls over the associational life of the union, workers forged new alliances with regional and national groups of the left. Democratic unions tended to perpetuate militant bargaining positions once restructuring emerged. In particular, democratic unions were unwilling to make concessions because neither the Mexican state, nor transnational employers, would guarantee future employment, modest real wage growth, or assistance to unemployed workers in exchange for union accommodation.[10]

By contrast, in those cases where union democratization movements were defeated, labor elites representing the CTM increased the level of centralization and control over decision making and the internal life of their unions, and also helped to restore conflict-free labor relations at the plant level. In the aftermath of the 1982 debt crisis, the regime placed strong pressures on these elites to help firms shift to export production through comprehensive modernization and restructuring initiatives. While these policies increased the level of tension among workers at the plant level, the rank and file often lacked the autonomy and institutional capacity to act against the CTM.

In order to examine the validity of the incorporation hypothesis, I engage in a systematic, comparative analysis of six cases in the industry. The independent variable for the study is "union government"; it is operationalized to capture governing practices that range from incorporation and internal democracy, to autonomy and internal democracy. Three principal measures are utilized in the analysis of union autonomy and democracy: (1) the frequency of union elections, and the ratio of contested to uncontested elections, (2) turnover in union leadership, and (3) workers' participation in bargaining and contract negotiations.[11] When the measures show the presence of electoral contestation, frequent rotation in leadership, and workers' participation in decision making, I situate the union at the democratic and autonomous end of the continuum; alternatively, the absence of turnover, participation, and electoral contestation are taken as an indication that the union is moving toward incorporation and oligarchy. The dependent variable, "union response," is operationalized to include both accommodative and militant bargaining strategies. Here I employ measures that focus on demand making and the outcomes of bargaining, including: (1) union proposals over wages and work rule changes, (2) the frequency of industrial conflict, and (3) relative changes in nominal and real average wages. I assume union militancy is present when workers reject flexible work rules, engage in more frequent strikes and protests, and enjoy higher rates of growth in average wages and benefits.

The study focuses on six plants and unions in the older "brownfield" segment of the Mexican automobile industry: Chrysler-Toluca, Ford-Cuautitlán, General Motors-DF, General Motors-Toluca, Nissan-Cuernavaca, and Volkswagen-Puebla (see Table 6.1). These cases were selected because of their historical variation in union organization. The data for the measures were collected from government labor archives,[12] from private company and union files, and from confidential interviews with company industrial relations officials and union members.

## Union Democratization in the Mexican Automobile Industry: An Historical Overview

### The Emergence of Union Democratization Movements in ISI Plants, 1968–77

The CTM has been the dominant actor in the Mexican labor movement since the 1940s. As the largest and most politically influential union confederation, the

Table 6.1

**General Characteristics of ISI Plants, Mexico**

| Plant (Year founded) | Union | Affiliation | Type | No. Workers (1993) | Production* |
|---|---|---|---|---|---|
| Chrysler-Toluca (1964) | Sindicato Nacional de la Industria Automotriz Integrada, Similares y Conexos | CTM | Enterprise | 3,600 | Passenger cars K-Frame Engines |
| Ford-Cuautitlán (1964) | Sindicato de Trabajadores de Ford Motor Company, CTM | CTM | Enterprise | 5,100 | Light trucks Passenger cars Engines Forge |
| General Motors-DF** 1936 | Sindicato de Obreros y Empleados de la Planta de Montaje de General Motors de México | CROC† | Plant | 2,514 | Light trucks P–30 Chassis |
| General Motors-Toluca (1966) | Sindicato Nacional de Trabajadores de la Industria Metalúrgica, Sección 9 | CTM | Sectoral | 1,260 | Engines Forge |
| Nissan-Cuernavaca (1966) | Sindicato Independiente de Trabajadores de Nissan Mexicana | Independent | Plant | 4,250 | Utility vehicles Engines |
| Volkswagen-Puebla (1964) | Sindicato Independiente de la Industria Automotriz, Similares y Conexos "Volkswagen de México" | FESEBES† | Plant | 17,880 | Passenger cars Engines Parts |

\* Production during 1993–94. Since NAFTA became effective, some changes in product lines have taken place.

\*\* Closed on 9 September 1995.

† The CROC is the Revolutionary Confederation of Workers and Peasants. FESEBES is the Federation of Goods and Services Unions.

*Sources:* JFCA and STPS-CGCFC Archives, and unpublished company and union records.

CTM brought a considerable measure of stability to the industrial relations system in Mexico. Indeed, with the exception of more pronounced strike activity surrounding the labor crisis of the late 1950s, the CTM limited strike actions, with the result that the aggregate number of strikes remained low during the period of 1940–72 (Zapata 1989, Table 7.4). The leadership of the CTM also facilitated the process of capital accumulation by restraining the wage demands of rank-and-file workers. Nevertheless, in spite of several decades of social peace, by the end of the 1960s both the CTM and the regime were faced with a severe legitimacy crisis. Indeed, after 1968, organized workers in a number of strategic sectors of the economy demanded internal reform and autonomy from the CTM and the PRI. The nature of this crisis, and the manner in which it was resolved, led to important changes in the structure and organization of the Mexican labor movement.

The emergence of popular protests and democratization movements during the late 1960s can be attributed to the conjuncture of two processes. The first involved the breakdown of the CTM's traditional control structures at the plant level. In the late 1960s, the Mexican state deepened import-substitution industrialization within the automobile sector, resulting in rapid growth throughout the industry (Bennett and Sharpe 1985, 94–154; Jenkins 1987, 58–62). In the absence of adequate work rules concerning health and safety issues, the growth of production often led to serious labor–management conflicts on the shopfloor. In this context, the ad hoc system of conflict resolution employed by CTM plant delegates proved to be largely ineffective. As Middlebrook (1989a, 81–82) has observed:

> sharply increasing worker concentrations per firm posed special challenges for the informal, paternalistic labor-relations arrangements that had long prevailed in the industry. . . . [L]arge worker concentrations in manufacturing activities such as the automobile industry require institutionalized procedures for conflict resolution that are capable of resolving the day-to-day grievances arising from a complex, closely integrated production process. Paternalistic responses to workplace problems based on the supervisor's personal relationship with the worker are no longer adequate in a modern manufacturing environment. . . . Because labor leaders affiliated with the CTM were often closely identified with company management, grievances arising from a more conflictive industrial environment frequently produced demands for more democratic union representation.

At the same time, government responses to the political crises of the late 1960s created an enabling environment for reform and liberalization in the labor movement. The idea of liberalization gained currency in the aftermath of repression of the 1968 student protests. In the wake of this event, criticisms of the PRI and the political system rose sharply, prompting the administration of Echeverría (1970–76) to initiate a process of controlled political liberalization. By allowing some unions to democratize and change their relationship to the CTM, the regime hoped to preempt the emergence of a radicalized working-class movement, and also sought to demonstrate to opposition parties that it could tolerate dissent (Basurto 1983, 9–12, 20, 32–34, 236–44; Coleman and Davis 1983, 5–8; Roxborough 1984, 161–63). In general, reform movements succeeded in those unions where state-level CTM federations lacked the capacity to defeat dissident leaders, or where government policy makers talked CTM elites into acquiescing to a limited number of defeats (Aguilar García 1982, 54–64; Roxborough 1984, 163).

By the early 1980s, however, developments in Mexico's political economy forced the state to abandon its commitment to liberalization of the official labor sector. In particular, the effects of the 1977 electoral reforms, coupled with the impact of the 1982 debt crisis, prompted leaders to defend the hegemonic position of the PRI within the party system. In this context, the regime came to rely upon the CTM to relegitimate the PRI with Mexico's popular sectors.[13] Labor's accommodation to restructuring policies also was required to facilitate economic reform. In rewarding the loyalty of the confederation, the regime guaranteed the CTM new members. Indeed, the CTM was allowed to regain its monopoly on union representation in the strategic sectors of the economy, including the automobile industry (Tuman and Greenway 1997, Table 1).[14] Thus, while some unions implemented internal reforms and gained autonomy from the CTM between 1968 and 1977, patterns of political bargaining since 1980 have placed significant limits on the opportunities for union democratization in the export segments of the industry.

The outcomes of democratization movements changed the political practices of organized workers in the Mexican automobile industry. In those cases where unions gained autonomy from the CTM, workers democratized internal decision-making processes and reorganized union structures in a way that maximized rank-and-file participation (e.g., by encouraging participation in union assemblies and departmental organizations). Emphasizing solidarity and unity in the labor movement, the democratic unions also formed new alliances with socialist political parties and groups, often with the aim of constructing a democratic socialist political project from below.[15] This trajectory occurred in two cases, Nissan-Cuernavaca and Volkswagen-Puebla. In a third case, General Motors-DF, reform movements in the 1970s strengthened internal democracy, but did not lead to the creation of ties to external parties and groups.[16]

On the other hand, where union democratization movements were defeated or failed to develop, a different pattern emerged. In the aftermath of such conflicts, leaders in the official labor sector maintained centralized control over negotiations and union government. Moreover, to insulate themselves from rank-and-file opposition, labor elites often excluded dissident workers from the work place and the union by employing the *cláusula de exclusión*.[17] The presence of such centralized, authoritarian practices perpetuated the sense that internal revolts were costly, dangerous, and potentially self-defeating. Cases following this pattern included Chrysler-Toluca and General Motors-Toluca.

Finally, Ford-Cuautitlán experienced a movement for trade union democracy that failed to be consolidated. Under the terms of a 1977 reorganization plan, Ford workers were integrated into a national enterprise union (SITRAFORD) that remained affiliated to the CTM. The statutes adopted in 1977 provided for a two-tiered structure of government in which democratically elected local executive committees coexisted under a national executive committee. The formal institutional arrangements of SITRAFORD granted the national general secretary of the union final control over contracts and strike movements, and also made the national general secretary directly accountable to the executive committee of the CTM. Furthermore, since the new union statutes made it difficult to recall the national leadership, workers at the local level had few means at their disposal to challenge the national executive committee (Sindicato de Trabajadores de Ford Motor Company–CTM 1977, Articles 26, 29, 103, and 104; Talavera and Muñoz 1991; von Bülow 1995).[18] Between 1987 and 1994, workers in Cuautitlán fought continuously with the national executive committee for control over collective bargaining and union affairs. In general, then, the two-tiered structure of SITRAFORD has not functioned well within the structure and confines of corporatist relations with the CTM.

The types of union governments institutionalized in the 1970s are still present today. One central legacy of the democracy movements was the emergence of electoral contestation in some of the cases. The data in Table 6.2 indicate that the unions in Nissan-Cuernavaca, Volkswagen-Puebla, and General Motors-DF have had frequent contested elections for the general secretary in both periods. Since 1970, there has been a high ratio of contested to uncontested elections in these three cases. The data also suggest that in Nissan and Volkswagen, a significant degree of leadership turnover has occurred for the post of the general secretary and the executive committees. The one partial exception to this trend emerged in General Motors-DF, where a popular and aggressive general secretary managed to be reelected four times between 1981 and 1991. Ford-Cuautitlán initially moved toward electoral contestation after the 1977 reorganization plan was adopted. Nevertheless, because of continuing conflicts between the union base and the national leadership, the two most recent national general secretaries of SITRAFORD were imposed by the CTM. As a result, despite frequent protests from workers in Cuautitlán, the rank and file have been largely unable to exercise effective control over the national executive committee (Arteaga 1990, 153–54; Talavera and Muñoz 1991, 24–26; Comité de Observadores Independientes 1991).

The cases of Chrysler-Toluca and General Motors-Toluca show strong signs of incorporation and oligarchy. In both of these unions, workers are forced to vote by acclamation in the presence of union officials. Perhaps more importantly, elections in both unions are uncontested: the incumbent general secretaries are

Table 6.2

**Union Democracy and Worker Participation**

| | Elections | Contested Elections | Turnover in Office | Revisions[*] | Frequency of Participation[**] | Average Size of Delegation[†] |
|---|---|---|---|---|---|---|
| **Chrysler (CTM)** | | | | | | |
| 1970–76 | 2 | 0 | 0 | — | — | — |
| 1981–95 | 2 | 0 | 1 | 8 | 0 | 0 |
| **Ford (CTM)** | | | | | | |
| 1985–95 | 4 | 3 | 5 | 7 | 4 | 12 |
| **GM-DF (CROC)[††]** | | | | | | |
| 1937–77 | 28 | 22 | 21 | — | — | — |
| 1980–95 | 8 | 8 | 4 | 8 | 8 | 5 |
| **GM-Toluca (CTM)** | | | | | | |
| 1966–78 | 5 | 0 | 0 | — | — | — |
| 1982–93 | 2 | 0 | 0 | 7 | 1 | 8 |
| **Nissan (Independent)** | | | | | | |
| 1966–77 | 9 | 6 | 7 | — | — | — |
| 1982–94 | 6 | 6 | 6 | 7 | 7 | 30 |
| **VW (FESEBES)[††]** | | | | | | |
| 1972–78 | 2 | 2 | 2 | — | — | — |
| 1981–95 | 7 | 7 | 8 | 9 | 6 | 20 |

[*]Total number of contract negotiations.

[**]Frequency of participation by workers' delegations in contract negotiations.

[†]Average size of the workers' delegation in contract negotiations.

[††]The CROC is the Revolutionary Confederation of Workers and Peasants. FESEBES is the Federation of Goods and Services Unions.

*Sources:* Roxborough (1984,Table 7.1) for data before 1980. Data for second period are from STPS-CGCFC and JFCA Archives, and unpublished company and union records.

listed as the only candidates eligible for election. These practices have led to the perpetuation of union oligarchy. For example, the general secretary of Chrysler, a former production manager, was in power continuously between 1970 and 1993. With the help of the company and the CTM, he defeated emerging democracy movements in 1970 and 1975 by applying the exclusion clause against dissident workers. Because of his loyalty to the CTM, the general secretary of the Chrysler union was made a PRI labor sector representative in the Chamber of Deputies in the 1970s. Retiring from office in 1993, he appointed his son as the new general secretary of the Chrysler union. Similarly, the general secretary of General Motors-Toluca has served in that office since 1966, the year that the union was first formed and incorporated into the CTM. Working with other members of his immediate family, the general secretary of General Motors-Toluca has controlled the executive committees of the metalworkers' union and several other CTM affiliates located in Toluca for many years.[19]

Table 6.2 provides a measure of workers' participation in the bargaining process. The data show that between 1980 and 1992, workers' delegations in General Motors-DF, Nissan-Cuernavaca, and Volkswagen frequently played a role in contract and wage negotiations. Furthermore, union records suggest that the rank and file in these three unions met regularly in order to vote on bargaining proposals.[20]

In contrast, Ford-Cuautitlán shows signs of intermediate levels of participation. As a result of continuing struggles between the Cuautitlán local and the national general secretary of SITRAFORD, in 1989 the national executive committee consented to create a local workers' delegation in order to defuse tensions in the plant. However, in 1993, members from the Cuautitlán delegation were refused access to contract negotiations (*La Jornada,* 26 March 1993, 14; 6 April 1993, 14; Interview 3A, Mexico City, 1993). Finally, workers in General Motors-Toluca and Chrysler-Toluca are virtually excluded from negotiations. While a five-person delegation was present during the 1982 contract negotiations in General Motors-Toluca, the delegation was not given any formal decision-making powers. Instead, the executive committee and a legal assistant from the CTM have been the only union participants in bargaining. Similarly, in the case of Chrysler, negotiations are handled exclusively by the general secretary and a CTM legal adviser.

To summarize, the process of union democratization emerged in three cases (General Motors-DF, Nissan-Cuernavaca, and Volkswagen) and remained unconsolidated in a fourth (Ford-Cuautitlán). At the same time, Chrysler and General Motors-Toluca continued to show indications of incorporation and union oligarchy.

While union democracy was consolidated in some cases, attempts at forming a single, national automobile union repeatedly failed. This outcome probably reflected the influence exerted by rival political groups associated with two of the cases (Nissan and Volkswagen), as well as the CTM's refusal to cooperate with locals who had broken ties with the official labor sector. Nevertheless, despite the persistence of organizational fragmentation, democratic unions were able to maintain some leverage over firms during the period in question. Prior to the ratification of NAFTA, tariffs and quantitative import restrictions limited the entry of automobile imports; therefore, nearly all firms relied upon a single plant to produce several different product lines for the Mexican market. Since strikes cost firms a tangible loss of sales in a closed market, managers had powerful incentives to come to the bargaining table.

## Contrasting Union Responses to Restructuring

### Strike Movements

An examination of the strike data from the industry is revealing about the contrasts in union bargaining responses to industrial restructuring. If the hypothesis

Table 6.3

**Strikes in the Terminal Industry, 1970–1995**

|  | 1970–80 | | 1981–95 | |
| --- | --- | --- | --- | --- |
| Union | Number | Days | Number | Days |
| Chrysler-Toluca | 0 | 0 | 0 | 0 |
| Ford-Cuautitlán | 3 | 43 | 3 | 122 |
| GM-DF | 6 | 227 | 1 | 2 |
| GM-Toluca | 0 | 0 | 0 | 0 |
| Nissan-Cuernavaca | 6 | 74 | 5 | 35 |
| VW | 4 | 31 | 7 | 131 |

*Sources:* Data for the period of 1970–80 are drawn from Roxborough (1984, Table 2.4). Data for the period of 1981–95 are from unpublished records in STPS-CGAPL Archive.

advanced by the state-corporatist perspective is valid, then the democratic and autonomous unions should be more strike-prone.[21]

Table 6.3 summarizes the frequency and duration of industrial conflict occurring in each plant for the periods of 1970 to 1980, and 1981 to 1995. In general, the strike evidence reveals three important tendencies. First, the data lend support to the claim that industrial conflict is strongly related to the emergence and consolidation of democratic and autonomous trade union organization. The majority of democracy movements in the Mexican automobile industry occurred between 1969 and 1975. Before 1969, strikes in the industry were practically nonexistent, with only three conflicts taking place between 1938 and 1969. Yet once union democratization swept through the industry, a different pattern emerged. Between 1970 and 1980, the democratic unions in General Motors-DF, Nissan-Cuernavaca, and Volkswagen-Puebla struck between four and six times. In addition, the democratic unions continued to be strike prone after restructuring plans were introduced into the sector between 1980 and 1994. At the same time, however, the perpetuation of incorporation and union oligarchy gave rise to a different tendency in strike behavior. As noted previously, union democratization movements were defeated at both General Motors-Toluca and Chrysler. Since 1970, leaders in both of these cases have not permitted a single strike to break out. Indeed, the Chrysler union is the only union that has not registered a strike petition in over twenty-six years.[22]

Second, the pattern of strike activity in the sector is correlated to the incidence of high inflation and the imposition of austerity measures. The overall level of strikes for the democratic unions peaked between 1976 and 1978, and 1986 and 1988. In the former period, strikes followed the introduction of austerity measures and a currency devaluation implemented by the government of Echeverría. Similarly, industrial conflict during the period of 1986–88 was triggered by severe inflation, which diminished the purchasing power of real wages. In response, there were democratic-initiated strike movements to protect workers' real wages.

Strike movements over wage issues had varying levels of success. In 1987, for example, workers in Ford-Cuautitlán struck for sixty-two days in order to force the company to implement a 23 percent emergency wage increase (Garza and Méndez 1987a, 384). For its part, Ford had insisted that labor costs in Cuautitlán were too high, and had offered only a 6 percent increase in wages and a 10 percent increase in benefits. After it became clear that the union was losing the support of the national CTM leadership, the national general secretary of the union (SITRAFORD) ended the strike by acquiescing to layoffs, a wage reduction for entry-level workers, and a new contract with more flexible work rules (Garza and Méndez 1987a; Arteaga 1990).[23] During the same year, however, workers at Volkswagen struck for fifty-seven days, won a wage increase of 78 percent, and also succeeded in blocking a restructuring plan that would have imposed a wage freeze and layoffs. The success of the Volkswagen strike was partly due to the solidarity actions taken by Volkswagen workers in West Germany and the United States (Garza and Méndez 1987b, 381–83; Montiel 1991, 183–207).

In addition to striking for higher-than-average wage increases and employment guarantees, democratic and autonomous unions in the sector were also more likely to initiate strikes over work rules and plant modernization. An analysis of strike negotiations in Nissan-Cuernavaca, General Motors-DF, Ford-Cuautitlán, and Volkswagen indicates that workers sought to protect seniority and job classifications, controls over job rotation and the use of temporary workers, and union input in the process of plant modernization. In several cases, workers initiated strike movements to resist contract changes that would have facilitated the introduction of quality circles and team concepts. In 1992, for example, Volkswagen workers stopped work after the general secretary of the union ratified an agreement introducing work teams into the plant. In this case, however, the company and government labor authorities backed the incumbent union leadership, resulting in the dismissal of some dissident workers and the retention of the new work teams (Othón Quiroz and Méndez 1992; Tuman 1994a, 155–60).[24]

Because government policy explicitly sanctioned industrial restructuring throughout this period, strike movements in the incorporated unions had a more narrow focus. As noted previously, the general secretary of the Chrysler union has not filed any strike petitions since 1970. Similarly, while leaders in General Motors-Toluca registered six strike petitions between 1980 and 1994, the scope of their demands was limited primarily to wage and benefit issues.

### Work Rules and the Lean Production Model

The reorientation of the terminal sector was accompanied by a sweeping initiative to redefine labor relations on the shopfloor. However, there were important differences in union responses to such initiatives; in particular, democratic and autonomous unions were more likely to resist the use of team concepts and flexible production by bargaining for the maintenance of strong work rules. The analysis presented here is based upon a content analysis of collective contracts and contract revision agreements[25] and interviews with union and company officials.

The drive to implement teamworking in the older segments of the sector gained momentum in the mid-1980s. Managers often insisted that wage increases be conditioned upon union acceptance of work teams. Despite these threats, team concepts were introduced successfully in only two of the six cases: General Motors-Toluca and Chrysler-Toluca. In both plants, union leaders had already acquiesced in the early 1980s to major contract changes that yielded plant managers broad powers over labor relations on the shopfloor; as a result, managers were able to rapidly organize production departments into teams, implement pay-by-knowledge schemes, reduce the number of skilled job classifications, and begin the process of job rotation (particularly in the sub-assembly areas).[26]

Acting against the preferences of union members, leaders at Ford-Cuautitlán and Volkswagen acquiesced to the creation of work teams and a reduction in the number of skilled job classifications. Nevertheless, because of strong rank-and-file resistance, the new teams failed to achieve the desired production performance, defect levels, operator proficiencies, and "morale" levels.[27] Similarly, in General Motors-DF and Nissan-Cuernavaca, union members established (and maintained) strong work rules that effectively preempted the introduction of team concepts. In both plants, union contracts restricted the power of managers to move workers within (and between) departments, maintained strictly defined job classifications and seniority criteria for promotions, and granted union officials the right to establish jointly plant production rhythms. Workers in General Motors-DF and Nissan also consistently rejected team concepts as a company strategy intended to diminish the internal solidarity of the union (Navarro Delgado 1989; Shaiken and Browne 1991, 33–48; Guzmán 1993, 133; Interview 4B, Mexico, 1993).[28] There were important parallels here with regard to the use of quality circles. By 1993, for example, only two plants in the older parts of the sector had functioning quality circles, General Motors-Toluca and Chrysler Toluca. In the other four plants, the evidence gleaned from interviews and official records suggests that attempts to form and maintain quality circles were unsuccessful.

There has also been considerable variation in the degree of recuperation of "dead time" on the shopfloor. In Chrysler-Toluca and General Motors-Toluca, union leaders have cooperated with managers in disciplining workers who refuse to obtain permission to use the bathroom, and for those who are tardy returning to work stations. Work rules in both plants give plant managers the power to determine the appropriate penalties for tardiness. Similarly, Ford implemented a bell-to-bell operating procedure in Cuautitlán in 1988. The new process included use of sirens in each production department and the relocation of toilets to lessen the travel time from the production line. While the program was effective in its early stages, workers eventually refused to cooperate, demanding termination of the system during the 1990 strike. A combination of union control over internal discipline and work rules led to different outcomes in General Motors-DF and Nissan. In both of these cases, managers were unable to combat absenteeism and tardiness on the line.

Finally, democratic and autonomous unions were also more likely to negotiate (and maintain) important employment guarantees. First, in General Motors-DF, Nissan, and Volkswagen, union leaders have been granted formal decision-making power with respect to all employment adjustments (including those resulting from technological change) and the use of temporary workers. In fact, in these three cases, the contracts force firms to promote temporary workers to full-time status after a specified period (eighteen months at General Motors) or as a result of layoffs (two promotions for every one full-time worker laid off at Volkswagen); in addition, temporary workers are often guaranteed generous severance benefits. In Ford-Cuautitlán, some of the rules governing temporary employees were lifted when the new contract was imposed in 1987. Nevertheless, management is still obligated to negotiate with the union over the entry and placement of temporary workers, and the contract (clause 7) grants temporary workers the same rights as full-time employees. Second, in General Motors-DF, Volkswagen, Nissan, and Ford, severance payments for full-time (*planta*) employees laid off due to automation or downturns have consistently exceeded the legal minimum required by Federal Labor Law. Third, employees in the democratic cases are guaranteed full pay and benefits regardless of whether the plant is operating at full capacity. Thus, while the devaluation crisis has forced Volkswagen to reduce its operating capacity between January and April 1995, workers in the Puebla plant have been remunerated at full-time pay levels.[29]

In contrast, the contracts for Chrysler and General Motors-Toluca provide workers with the minimum level of protection mandated by the Federal Labor Law, and there are few (if any) restrictions concerning the use of temporary workers or adjustments caused by automation.[30] Managers in both plants have the prerogative to assign temporary workers without prior union approval or negotiation. In addition, the overall level of severance payments in both plants has remained below the other four cases.

## *Wages and Wage Trends*

### *Methodological Caveats*

The evidence suggests that the degree of union autonomy and democracy influenced bargaining over work rules and the overall level of strike proneness. In this section, we examine the impact of union incorporation on wage trends in the sector. The government traditionally has pressured official unions to limit wage demands, and to respect wage ceilings established under anti-inflation pacts. If there is a relationship between incorporation and wage demands, then one would expect to see some difference in wage revision proposals among these six cases. The wage revision records lend support to this argument. Between 1986 and 1992, workers in the democratic and autonomous unions (e.g., Nissan-Cuernavaca, Volkswagen and General Motors-DF, and Ford-Cuautitlán) consistently made the highest wage demands in the sector. Furthermore, in 1992 and 1993, the democratic cases sought wage increases exceeding the ceilings established under the government's inflation programs (e.g., *Pacto de Estabilidad y Crecimiento Económico,* or PECE).[31] However, leaders in Chrysler and General Motors-Toluca, the two strongly incorporated and oligarchic unions, made wage demands that complied with the PECE.

To examine the relationship between union incorporation and the outcomes of wage bargaining, it will be necessary to look at wage trends in the sector. However, the wage data present a number of methodological problems. First, since governmental authorities can intervene to establish contract wage levels, it is possible that the outcomes of wage bargaining do not necessarily reflect union demand making. Although Federal Labor Law theoretically gives the government some latitude in regulating wage increases, in practice, federal labor authorities have tended to refrain from altering the outcomes of wage bargaining. Rather, in influencing wage determination, the government has relied upon official union elites to limit demands during the initial stages of negotiations. The linchpin of Mexican corporatism is government control over the structure of union representation; therefore, we have good reason to suppose that the degree of autonomy and democracy should affect wage trends in the sector.

A second problem is that the data set is not complete. Wage data for General Motors-Toluca are available only from 1986 to 1991. As a result, it is possible only to make a biennial comparison of wage changes in five of the cases for the period of 1984 to 1994. Nevertheless, a complete set of average annual wage data are available for four cases—Ford-Cuautitlán, General Motors-DF, Chrysler-Toluca, and Volkswagen. Since these four unions exhibit strong degrees of variation in their governance practices, a comparison of their annual average wage trends should help to strengthen the overall analysis.

A third issue concerns the type of measure used in the comparison. Ideally, we would want to compare changes in the wage of the average worker. In order to estimate wages in this manner, it is necessary to know the distribution of workers, and the corresponding wage, in each step of the scale. Unfortunately, this information was not always accessible. As an alternative, I employ the average of the wage scale (*tabulador de salarios*).

Table 6.4

## Wage Trends*

| | Chrysler-Toluca | Ford-Cuautitlán | GM-DF | GM-Toluca | Nissan-Cuernavaca | VW |
|---|---|---|---|---|---|---|
| 1984 | 2,053 | 2,739 | 2,305 | — | 2,147 | 2,039 |
| 1986 | 5,434 | 4,445 | 5,855 | 4,813 | 5,235 | 9,007 |
| 1988 | 20,010 | 20,228 | 25,041 | 25,437 | 22,291 | 28,757 |
| 1990 | 30,330 | 29,620 | 36,433 | 35,188 | 36,649 | 45,220 |
| 1992 | 45,970 | 40,848 | 53,010 | — | 50,303 | 62,139 |
| 1994** | 58,070 | 55,177 | 65,640 | — | 60,914 | 73,045 |
| 1995 | 73,870 | 68,971 | — | — | — | 82,872 |
| Change 1984–94 | +2,728% | +1,914% | +2,747% | — | +2,737% | +3,482% |

*Average of the wage scale (as of September 1), expressed as total old pesos per day.
**Data for 1994 and 1995 are given in old pesos (1,000 old pesos = 1 new peso).
*Source*: Collective contracts and wage revision agreements in JFCA and STPS-CGCFC Archives.

*Changes in Nominal Wages*

Table 6.4 presents data on the cumulative change in nominal wages. These data reflect the September 1 average of wage scales for the even years in the series.[32] In general, the data show that the cumulative change in average nominal wages was greatest in the democratic and autonomous cases. Between 1984 and 1994, nominal average wages in Volkswagen-Puebla, General Motors-DF, and Nissan-Cuernavaca grew by 3,482, 2,747, and 2,737 percent, respectively. During this same period, however, Chrysler-Toluca and Ford-Cuautitlán showed growth of only 2,728 and 1,914 percent.[33]

A more complete set of annual data for nominal wages strengthens these findings. Despite gaps in the files for General Motors-Toluca and Nissan, the archival records do show the annual growth (December–December) of nominal wages in four cases: Chrysler, Ford-Cuautitlán, General Motors-DF, and Volkswagen. Once again, higher levels of average annual growth are associated with union democracy. Between 1985 and 1994, the average annual change in nominal wages for Volkswagen and General Motors-DF was 56 and 49 percent, respectively, followed by Chrysler and Ford, who showed an annual average growth of 46 and 41 percent.

On the whole, these results show a fair degree of continuity with the wage trends of the 1970s. Based upon a review of nominal wages for the periods of 1969–77 and 1972–80, Roxborough (1984, 57–8) found that average wages grew faster in General Motors-DF, Ford, Volkswagen, and Nissan-Cuernavaca when compared to General Motors-Toluca and Chrysler. In a separate survey of the industry from 1975 to 1980, Ford Motor Company (as reported in Roxborough 1984, Table 3.5) also reported the highest rates of growth in average annual nominal wages among General Motors, Volkswagen, and Nissan. While this comparison to previous studies of wage trends in the ISI plants is neither systematic nor conclusive, the evidence does suggest that two tendencies were at work. First, wage militancy in the 1970s followed the emergence and consolidation of democratic and autonomous union organization; and second, despite the onset of the debt crisis in the 1980s, democratic unions were able to protect the real wage gains made during the previous decade.

*Changes in Fringe Benefits*

Transnational automobile firms also offer workers and unions various types of benefits. One type of benefit, which can be defined as "collective benefits," includes payments and subsidies made to the union to support sports programs, festivals for workers and their families, transportation, educational and cultural events, and children's scholarships. In providing for these activities, the firm usually makes a cash payment to the union on an annual or biennial basis. Since the distribution of collective benefits is mediated by each union's budgetary process, the monetary value for each union member varies and is difficult to estimate. At the same time, collective contracts provide workers with individual fringe benefits. Because these payments affect directly the incomes of individual members, most workers tend to focus on fringe benefits. For these reasons, the comparison that follows is limited to trends in individual fringe benefits.

   Table 6.5 shows the evolution and growth of the Christmas bonus (*aguinaldo*), paid holidays, and coupons for food and other essential items.[34] Between 1983 and 1994, the number of paid holidays remained constant across the sector, with Chrysler granting workers 18 days' pay, and the rest of the plants offering 17 days. However, there is considerable variation with respect to the Christmas bonus payment. Nissan and General Motors-DF each gained 13 and 12 days' pay, respectively, in the *aguinaldo*. Volkswagen workers, who have consistently enjoyed the highest Christmas bonus, showed an increase of 11 days.[35] Nevertheless, the size of the bonus, and the gain in days' paid, lagged in Chrysler and Ford. In both of these cases, the number of days increased by only 4 and 6, respectively, throughout this period.

   An examination of the cumulative change in the monetary value of the Christmas bonus, paid holidays, and coupons for essential items shows that democratic and autonomous unions outperformed the incorporated ones by a significant margin.[36] Between 1984 and 1994, the growth in the nominal value of these three benefits increased by 4,670, 3,799 and 3,537 percent, respectively, in Volkswagen, General Motors-DF, and Nissan. At the same time, the cumulative change in Chrysler was 3,260 percent. Similarly, in Ford, the national

Table 6.5

## Fringe Benefits in Mexican Automobile Plants, 1983–1994

| | Christmas Bonus (Days) | Paid Holidays | Cost of Living* | Savings Fund* | Vacation** | | | |
|---|---|---|---|---|---|---|---|---|
| | | | | | 1yr | 5yr | 10yr | 20yr |
| **Chrysler** | | | | | | | | |
| 1983–85 | 26 | 18 | $1,200 | $1,800 | 7+143% | 13+115% | 15+120% | 21+119% |
| 1991–93 | 30 | 18 | $64,383 | 13% | 7+200% | 13+177% | 15+166% | 18+166% |
| **Ford** | | | | | | | | |
| 1983–85 | 27 | 17 | $1,750 | $1,950 | 10+207% | 12+263% | 14+361% | 18+361% |
| 1991–93 | 33 | 17 | 7% | 1% | 7+205% | 9+286% | None | None |
| **GM-DF** | | | | | | | | |
| 1983–85 | 29 | 17 | $1,900 | Voluntary | 10+165% | 17+ 65% | 19+165% | 19+165% |
| 1991–93 | 41 | 17 | $101,695 | $36,000 | 10+187% | 17+187% | 19+187% | 20+187% |
| **GM-Toluca** | | | | | | | | |
| 1984–86 | 28 | 17 | By agreement | Voluntary | 10+156% | 17+156% | 18+156% | 20+156% |
| 1992–94 | 45 | 17 | $70,044† | Voluntary | 10+190% | 17+190% | 18+190% | 20+190% |
| **Nissan** | | | | | | | | |
| 1984–86 | 29 | 17 | 1% | $240 | 6+233% | 12+167% | 16+156% | 16+156% |
| 1992–94 | 40 | 17 | 1% | 6% | 6+367% | 12+237% | 16+216% | 18+197% |
| **Volkswagen** | | | | | | | | |
| 1984–86 | 44 | 17 | n.a | n.a | 14+107% | 14+107% | 17+107% | 20+107% |
| 1992–94 | 54 | 17 | $53,000 | $150,000 | 14+100% | 14+193% | 17+170% | 20+145% |

*Monthly payments, in total old pesos, or as a percentage of monthly salary.

**For vacation data, the first number refers to the total number vacation days; the second is the size of the bonus (as a percentage of number of vacation days).

†Average of benefit scale, as stipulated in special agreements for General Motors-DF and Toluca.

*Sources:* Collective Contracts and Contract Revision Agreements, JFCA and STPS-CGCFC Archives.

Table 6.6

**Annual Variation of Real Wages, 1985–1994**

| Year | Chrysler-Toluca | Chrysler-Saltillo | Ford-Cuautitlán | GM–DF | Volkswagen |
|---|---|---|---|---|---|
| 1985 | −4.29 | −3.46 | −32.09 | −15.6 | −26.07 |
| 1986 | −38 | −30.3 | −60.66 | −0.42 | 112.93 |
| 1987 | 32.01 | −64.2 | 44.91 | −48.99 | −56.26 |
| 1988 | −23.22 | 34.61 | −21.47 | 62 | 31.43 |
| 1989 | 4.57 | 1.61 | −0.36 | 1.06 | −6.12 |
| 1990 | −6.89 | −10.84 | −8.43 | −10.61 | 7.01 |
| 1991 | 4.89 | 8.6 | −0.23 | 3.72 | −4.27 |
| 1992 | 5.23 | 8.24 | 11.76 | 10.39 | 8.33 |
| 1993 | 1.71 | 11.94 | 12.15 | 2.05 | 0.84 |
| 1994 | 7.5 | 2.94 | −1.43 | 3.17 | −1.9 |
| Real Average Annual Change | −1.649 | −4.086 | −5.585 | 0.677 | 6.592 |

*Sources:* Wage data from JFCA and STPS-CGCFC Archives, and city-level inflation data from INEGI.

leadership's acceptance of cost-cutting measures in 1987 reduced the growth in wages and benefits. Although workers in Ford-Cuautitlán had the highest benefits in the sector in 1984, this trend quickly reversed itself, as the union posted a gain of only 1988 percent in the nominal benefits between 1984 and 1994.

*Changes in Real Wages and Benefits*

To summarize the findings thus far, the data on nominal wage and benefits support the hypothesis regarding the effects of union incorporation on wage militancy. In general, democratic and autonomous unions in the sector have had the strongest growth in nominal wages and benefits. However, as noted previously, the regime's stabilization policies during this period sought to control inflation by producing wage flexibility, and elites placed strong pressures on leaders in the CTM to adhere to this policy. Therefore, if union incorporation is linked to real wage flexibility, then strongly incorporated unions can also be expected to post wage gains that lag slightly behind inflation.

Table 6.6 shows the average annual change in real wages between 1985 and 1994. To control for the variation in the cost-of-living levels between different metropolitan areas, the deflator for the series is based upon the *local* consumer price indices for Toluca, Puebla, Cuernavaca, and Mexico City, the cities where each automobile plant is located.[37] The data in Table 6.6 suggest that union incorporation had a significant and negative effect on real wage growth. Between

1985 and 1994, the average annual variations in real wages in Chrysler and Ford-Cuautitlán, the two incorporated unions, were –1.65 and –5.59 percent, respectively. By contrast, while the rate of growth in the democratic cases slowed somewhat after 1990, they nonetheless exhibit moderate to strong average change throughout this period. Indeed, in General Motors-DF and Volkswagen, the average annual change in real wages was 0.68 and 6.6 percent, respectively.

Unfortunately, gaps in the benefit data prevent us from examining the average annual growth in real wages and benefits. However, the cumulative change[38] in real wages and benefits shows a similar pattern. If we add average nominal wages with benefits and deflate them with the city-level price data, the following picture emerges. Between 1984 and 1994, the real change in wages and benefits in Chrysler and Ford was –9.17 and –35.62 percent, respectively. The contraction in General Motors-DF was somewhat less severe, as workers experienced an overall decline in real wages and benefits of –5 percent. The only case where the tendency was positive was Volkswagen, which posted a 7.9 percent gain in real terms. The pattern in wage and benefit trends is illustrative of two tendencies. One is that gains in benefits did help to offset some of the losses in real wages. Indeed, as we saw above, if benefits are excluded from the analysis, then the contraction in real wages is slightly worse in most of cases. A second tendency is that union organization does appear to make a difference in the performance of real wages and benefits. With the exception of Nissan, democratic and autonomous unions do a better job of protecting the purchasing power of their workers' real incomes.

*Rival Explanations of Wage Determination*

Competing explanations of wage bargaining have not been compared in a systematic way to the state-corporatist framework advanced in this chapter. While a more rigorous investigation might attempt to assess the effects of other independent variables on wage bargaining, the paucity of the data on institutional factors, productivity, labor market conditions, and firm performance create strong barriers to the completion of a more sophisticated statistical analysis. In spite of these problems, it is still possible to assess the major rival explanations on the basis of the limited available evidence.

*State Intervention.* One alternative explanation suggests that the differences in wage performance are due to the intervention of government labor authorities. According to this argument, government intervention during collective bargaining has a negative impact on the process of wage determination (Shaiken 1994, 58–9). Certainly, this is a plausible hypothesis. Nevertheless, while the Federal Labor Law does provide for government involvement in collective bargaining, the available evidence does not suggest that government mediation has produced wage restraint throughout the sector.

More frequent government involvement in negotiations and mediations[39] is actually associated with higher levels of nominal and real wage growth in the ISI plants. According to data provided by the Junta Federal de Conciliación y Arbitraje and the Secretaría del Trabajo y Previsión, between 1982 and 1994, 16 government mediations occurred in contract and wage revision talks at Volkswagen, followed by 12 and 10 mediations in Nissan and General Motors-DF during the same period. However, as we have seen, these cases have consistently enjoyed the greatest cumulative change and average growth in wages and benefits. At the same time, in Chrysler-Toluca, a case demonstrating very low growth in wages and benefits, no government mediations have occurred.[40] The only case that might support this argument is Ford-Cuautitlán, where a strongly negative average change in real wages is associated with frequent mediations (a total of 16). Yet, even here, the relationship is a rather weak one, since in former periods (1975–80) Ford was a leader in wage growth and had the second-highest number of mediations in the sector.

*Unemployment.* In a perfectly competitive labor market, wages are determined by the supply of and demand for labor. Therefore, it is possible that the variation in wage trends between plants may reflect higher levels of unemployment in the geographical areas where each plant is located. Putting aside the methodological problems associated with the Mexican unemployment statistics, the data on local rates of open unemployment do not seem to bear much relationship to the wage trends in the sector. For example, between 1987 and 1994, the average annual unemployment rates in Mexico City and Toluca were 3.71 and 2.32 percent, respectively. Yet, despite the fact that the labor market in Toluca was somewhat tighter, the growth in nominal and real wages at Chrysler lagged behind General Motors-DF. The inclusion of data for Cuernavaca and Puebla for a shorter period (1991 to 1994) also suggests no clear relationship between unemployment rates and wage growth.

Employment levels may have a limited impact on wages in the sector partly because of the density of union organization in the terminal sector and entrance requirements for new employees. All of the engine and finished vehicle plants in the terminal sector are organized. In this context, unions maintain a closed shop and create entry barriers that limit access from external labor markets. In addition, auto firms increasingly have sought workers who possess reading and basic math skills (Shaiken and Herzenberg 1987, 53–58; Shaiken 1994, 39–71, Covarrubias 1995, 13–16). Since many potential job-seekers lack the minimum skills required for employment in the auto industry (Zapata 1996, 73), the supply of labor to firms has tended to be somewhat inelastic.[41]

*Productivity.* The variation in real wage performance may also be related to increases in the productivity of labor. In the standard neoclassical explanation of wage determination, an overall rise in the productivity of labor implies a larger quantity of goods (or services) per worker, and, consequently, the potential for higher real income for employees of the firm.

The validity of this explanation is open to question on both theoretical and empirical grounds. In the first place, even if we assume that labor productivity plays a role in wage determination, its effects are likely to be mediated (and shaped) by the character and strength of union organization existing at the plant level. Indeed, if firms are conceived as profit maximizers, they may have little (or no) incentive to pass along the benefits of productivity growth in the absence of union pressures for such a proposal. Moreover, in Mexico, incorporated unions generally were unable to link productivity and wages until 1992, when the regime passed the National Accord on Increasing Quality and Productivity (ANEPC).[42] By contrast, the democratic and autonomous unions have possessed the strength and capacity to bargain aggressively over wages and productivity.

Second, the fragmentary evidence does not support the supposition that real wages move in the same direction as the productivity of labor. Unfortunately, the data used for calculating the standard measure of productivity, net value added per worker, are not available for all firms in the sector. An alternative measure that can be used is the volume of production per worker. Viewed from this angle, the data suggest that at the plant level, there is no clear relationship between productivity and real wages. Indeed, plants exhibiting strong growth in productivity also seem to have among the lowest growth in real wages. In a study of North American automobile plants, for example, Harbour and Associates found that Chrysler-Toluca had the best performance in terms of the number of workers per vehicle in 1993 and 1995, followed by Ford-Cuautitlán and General Motors-DF for the same period (Harbour and Associates 1994, 19; 1996, 32–33).[43]

The growth of productivity at the firm level also illustrates a negative relationship between productivity growth and wages. The growth of production per worker between 1985 and 1993 was highest in Chrysler and Volkswagen, followed closely by Ford.[44] Yet throughout this same period, Chrysler posted weak growth in real wages, while Volkswagen showed the strongest gains in wages. This evidence is supported by intra-firm data. For example, according to internal reports completed by Ford Motor Company, since approximately 1987, productivity growth and quality levels have been highest in its export plants in Chihuahua and Hermosillo. However, wage and benefit growth in these two plants have lagged behind Ford-Cuautitlán. A similar pattern is evident among Chrysler's Toluca and Saltillo installations.[45]

## Conclusion

The outcomes of democratization movements shaped union responses to restructuring in the older segments of the Mexican automobile industry. The emergence and consolidation of union democracy in the 1970s led to a sharp rise of rank-and-file participation, with important consequences for internal solidarity and workers' political efficacy. In this context, restructuring plans were seen as a threat to the hard-won gains these unions had made during the previous decade; moreover, the general unwillingness of transnationals (and the Mexican state) to negotiate the terms of restructuring forced the democratic cases to adopt militant stances. These unions were more strike prone, and enjoyed stronger worker rules and a higher level of growth in average wages and benefits. However, the defeat of democracy movements led to different outcomes. In these cases, stable union oligarchies remained under the CTM. Consequently, leaders had incentives to facilitate change, and the process of restructuring occurred with little union resistance.

The six cases reveal the limitations of plant- and enterprise-level bargaining in the era of NAFTA. The fragmentation of union organization in the sector ultimately limited the range of options that democratic unions could muster in the face of capital mobility. The present trade regime permits transnational producers to replace certain product lines produced in Mexico with imports and to relocate production *within* Mexico to new greenfield sites. Managers have therefore gained new leverage over democratic unions in older parts of the sector. Indeed, the perpetuation of militancy in the DF plant led General Motors to relocate to Guanajuato. There are indications that Nissan is contemplating a similar move for its plant in Cuernavaca.

While stronger links between the automobile workers in Canada, Mexico, and the United States could help to form viable strategy with respect to regional integration and restructuring, efforts at cross-border organizing have been undermined by a number of different factors. The majority of automobile plants in Mexico are now controlled by the CTM.[46] Because the current regime has viewed links between American and Mexican labor as a threat to direct foreign investment, political elites have placed pressures on the CTM to limit the scope of talks with their counterparts in Canada and the United States (Williams and Passé-Smith 1992, 98–100; Cook 1994, 148–49, 152–55). Thus, while Canadian and U.S. locals have shown an ongoing interest in Mexico, no overall bargaining platform has been established among the CAW, the UAW, and Mexican automobile unions. At the same time, groups who have been most receptive to American cross-border initiatives—such as the FAT—are relatively small, loosely organized associations with few members in the automobile industry or other strategic sectors of the economy. Given the hegemony of the CTM in the auto industry, these initiatives are likely to be unsuccessful unless state–labor relations within the Mexican regime are first transformed. What this would imply, then, is that the fate of transnational bargaining will be tied to the process of democratization in Mexico.

### Notes

1. Calculated from Nacional Financiera (1990, Table 7.32) and AMIA (1994).
2. Calculated from Instituto Nacional de Estadística, Geografía, e Informática

(INEGI) (1990, Table 4.1), INEGI (1992, Table 3.18), and AMIA (1995, 1).

3. On this point, see Carrillo V. and García (1987), Arteaga (1988 and 1993), de la Garza Toledo (1990), Carrillo V. (1990a), and Middlebrook (1991a). See also Interviews 1A, 3A–3B, and 16, Mexico City, 1993 and 1996.

4. Middlebrook (1991a, 284), Arteaga (1993), Tuman (1994b, 111–61, 191–204), and Interviews 3A, 3F, Mexico City, 1993.

5. Between 1983 and 1988, the cumulative change in social spending per capita was –40.2 percent. See Lustig (1992, Table 3.7), and González Tiburcio and de Alba (1992, 25–63). Concerning the impact of adjustment on voting patterns, see Pacheco Méndez (1991), Klesner (1994), Davis (1994), Domínguez and McCann, (1995), and Dieter (1995).

6. This point was not lost upon the Office of the Presidency, which monitored the Ford and Volkswagen strikes closely. Regarding the Ford strike, for example, see letters from the Office of the President to the Ministry of Labor and Social Welfare, in STPS-CGCFC Archive, Expediente No. 2.1/(12)"83"/3504, 11 August 1989, 22 August 1990.

7. In addition, state-corporatist analyses point out that Mexican labor law permits union leaders to use the "exclusion clause" (cláusula de exlcusión) to remove dissident workers from the unions and the workplace. In addition, the state has resorted to the use of intimidation, force, and other extra-legal means to defend incumbent leaders in the CTM against independent unions (de la Garza 1991; La Botz 1992).

8. Particularly during the 1970s, the regime extended benefits to the rank and file in incorporated unions. However, since austerity and restructuring policies have forced dramatic cuts in social spending, many of the subsidies and benefits offered to workers have been eliminated. As a result, most state-corporatist theorists focus only on the benefits granted to union elites in order to explain labor's accommodation to economic reform.

9. While advancing our understanding of union behavior in Mexico, this work has tended to suffer from three methodological problems. First, investigators have neglected to make use of systematic, overtime measures of the independent and dependent variables. Rather than operationalizing the concept of incorporation, for example, analysts frequently assert that CTM unions are necessarily undemocratic and centralized by virtue of their affiliation. Second, these studies often classify union responses as "accommodative" or "militant" on the basis of data given for only one point in time. Third, most studies have not been sufficiently comparative across unions in the sector.

10. That is to say, when workers do not receive sufficient guarantees that sacrifices in the present will be rewarded with future gains in employment or real wages, then they will usually adopt shortened time horizons and engage in militant responses. For a discussion, see Lange (1984) and Przeworski (1987).

11. In developing these measures, I have drawn upon the work of Roxborough (1984, 132–44).

12. The data for this project were collected from private company and union files, and from the Junta Federal de Conciliacíon y Arbitraje (JFCA Archive); Coordinación General del Cuerpo de Funcionarios Conciliadoras, Secretaría del Trabajo y Previsión Social (STPS-CGCFC Archive); Coordinación General de Análisis y Política Laboral, Secretaría del Trabajo y Previsión Social (STPS-CGAPL Archive).

13. Ultimately, the restructuring policies introduced after 1982 undercut the capacity of the CTM to relegitimate the PRI with its popular sectors (Klesner 1994). Nevertheless, at the outset of the crisis, state elites perceived that it was important to safeguard the regime's relationship to the CTM. Thus, in contrast to the manner in which the 1968 crisis was resolved, in the 1980s the regime refused to allow unions to become autonomous from the CTM. In particular, the Salinas government secured labor's support for neoliberal policies by using state resources to promote and protect union membership in the

official labor sector. Of course, protection of membership was part of the old corporatist exchange. By the end of the 1980s, however, this became the primary (indeed, virtually the only) inducement offered to organized labor. The revised bargain was made primarily with the CTM, the largest and most important labor confederation. As a result of the revised bargain, the CTM has maintained its position as the dominant labor confederation in Mexico. Indeed, official data show that in industries under federal jurisdiction, the proportion of unionized workers affiliated to the CTM increased from 29.76 percent in 1978 to 41.23 percent in June 1997 (calculated from data from the Secretaría del Trabajo y Previsión Social, as cited in Zazueta and de la Peña, 1984, Table 8.12; and unpublished data from the Registro de Asociaciones, Secretaría del Trabajo y Previsión Social, 11 August 1997).

The terms of this reconstructed relationship between state and labor elites reflected a convergence of interests on the part of both sets of actors. From the point of view of state elites committed to neoliberal reform, cooperation with labor leaders offered advantages over confrontation during the critical period of economic transition. Despite the labor sector's diminished capacity to deliver workers' votes, liberalizers feared that a confrontational strategy would have raised the costs of implementing industrial reforms. Since Mexico's new model of development is dependent upon securing high levels of foreign direct investment, state technocrats had a strong interest in reducing the possible threat of union militancy in order to protect the investment climate. For an analysis of the revised bargain, see Tuman and Greenway (1997).

14. The CTM has organized all of the finished vehicle export plants opened since 1980 (Secretaría del Trabajo y Previsión Social, Dirección General de Registro de Asociaciones, 1993). The confederation and firms have also cooperated to control the structure of interest representation in the unions organized in these new plants (Middlebrook 1991a). Thus, while the CTM has allowed workers from different groups to contest elections for positions on the executive committees of unions in the export plants, bargaining has remained somewhat centralized and controlled by legal advisers working for the CTM. In Ford-Chihuahua, Ford-Hermosillo, and Nissan-Aguascalientes, workers and union officials who have advocated more control and autonomy from the CTM have been promptly fired and thrown out of the union.

15. Volkswagen-Puebla and Nissan-Cuernavaca broke off relations with the CTM in 1972 and 1973, respectively. Until the early 1980s, both unions were affiliated to the Unidad Obrera Independiente (Independent Worker Unit, UOI), a leftist trade union association. The Frente Auténtico del Trabajo (Authentic Labor Front, FAT)—another independent and leftist labor association—also enjoyed the support of a number of workers in Nissan. For more on the history of these two cases, see Montiel (1991) and Tuman (1994b, 69–76, 92–98, 130–34, 144–60), Rodríguez L. (1993) and López (1989).

16. Owing partly to the history surrounding the formation of the Revolutionary Confederation of Workers and Peasants (CROC), the union in General Motors-DF enjoyed a long period of internal democracy and autonomy from the confederation (Roxborough 1984; López 1989). Nevertheless, amid controversies surrounding the practices of the executive committee, in 1975 union members approved a reform creating positions for elected departmental delegates. See Sindicato de Obreros y Empleados de la Planta de Montaje de la General Motors de México (1990, Articles 5, 2.13, 26, and 36), and Interviews 8A-B, 15A, 15C, 15F, Mexico City, 1993.

17. Intended originally as a legal mechanism to protect the closed shop, this rule compels employers to fire any employee who loses his or her union membership. Although democratic union leaders have also used the *cláusula* to sanction some workers, it is applied with less frequency in the democratic unions.

18. Some of these points were also made by former union officials in Cuautitlán. See

Interviews 3A, 3F, 9C, Mexico City, 1993. For more on recent conflicts between the local in Cuautitlán and the national executive committee of SITRAFORD, see *La Jornada* (15 April 1993, 10; 4 June 1993, 15; 22 June 1993, 15), and *Unomásuno* (23 September 1993, 1).

19. For documentation concerning the composition of the executive committee of General Motors-Toluca, see records in STPS-CGCFC Archive, Expediente 2.1/(12)- "82"/3321, JFCA Archive, Expediente CC–133-XII-J15. For evidence that the general secretary of General Motors-Toluca also controls other CTM affiliates in Toluca, see Secretaría del Trabajo y Previsión Social, Dirección General de Registro de Asociaciones (1993, 88–89). Indeed, in 1993 the general secretary of General Motors-Toluca also served as the general secretary for textile and chemical unions in Toluca.

20. In the cases of Nissan and Volkswagen, proposals formulated by each department or section in the plant were presented for debate and voting in union assemblies. In addition, the institutional arrangements in General Motors-DF and Nissan do not permit representatives from either official or independent trade union confederations to intervene in contract negotiations. Although some analysts have asserted that changes in Volkswagen's union statutes permitted legal advisers from FESEBES some control over decision making, a review of the union's collective bargaining proposals does not indicate that external officials have exercised any direct power in negotiations with the firm. On this point, see records concerning the 1994–96 contract revision, in STPS-CGCFC Archive, Expediente 2.1/313(29)/2579, 23 June 1994, 26 July 1994, 8 August 1994.

21. Mexican strike statistics present certain methodological problems. Because the Federal Labor Law places different industrial sectors under both local and federal jurisdiction, separate lists are compiled for strikes in industries that are under federal and state control. A related problem is that strikes declared "nonexistent" or "illegal" by government labor officials are not counted in official strike statistics. Fortunately, most of these problems do not apply to the data from the automobile industry. Since the 1970s, the sector has been under federal control; as a result, one can obtain a complete data set by consulting authorities who regulate industries under federal jurisdiction. In addition, because of the high visibility of the sector, "illegal" strikes often receive coverage in the press, and can therefore be added to the official data set.

22. In the case of Chrysler, wildcat strikes (against the union) occurred in 1970 and 1975. Because of the special nature of these conflicts, they are excluded from the analysis.

23. For changes in the pre- and post-1987 strike contracts and wage scales in Ford-Cuautitlán, see JFCA Archive, Expediente No. CC–260/87-XII-J15, 1 April 1987, 21 October 1987. It should be noted that Ford realized a significant cost savings after this strike because workers were "terminated" and then rehired without seniority, and because the value of most key fringe benefits was reduced in the new contract.

24. While the outcome of the 1992 strike did result in the introduction of work teams and other flexible work rules, the union maintained employment guarantees and also negotiated a large increase in wages and benefits. Since 1992, the union also has introduced new work rules that have placed strong union controls over the role, function, and power of work teams on the shopfloor. In addition, some scholars have asserted that changes in the union by-laws in the aftermath of the 1992 strike vitiated internal democracy and worker participation (e.g., Othón Quiroz and Méndez 1992; Bensusán and García 1993, 249–52). It should be noted that the archival records show that general assemblies have continued to be held since 1992, and that workers have participated in decision making through their departmental organizations. See documents in STPS-CGCFC Archive, Expediente 2.1/313(29)/2579, 26 July 1994, 8 August 1994, 13 November 1995, 24 November 1995, and 3 January 1996.

25. For previous analyses of some of the older contracts reviewed in this section, see

Roxborough (1984, 120–31), Dombois (1985/86, 40–72, 91–95), and Middlebrook (1991a, 287–91, Table 2). The contracts and wage revision agreements discussed in this section generally cover the period between 1980 and 1995.

Some analysts might argue that the content of collective bargaining agreements is a poor indicator of the continuities (or changes) in work organization. From this perspective, the organization of production is continuously reproduced (and contested) informally through the everyday forms of conflict and cooperation among managers, workers, and union representatives. Without denying the significance of informal bargaining and contestation, it would appear that the work rules incorporated in collective contracts do, in fact, play a primary role in structuring union power on the shopfloor. Indeed, both companies and unions pay close attention to the wording and content of contract clauses during each revision; moreover, the parties often make explicit reference to contract clauses when they are engaged in disputes or are appealing for the intervention of government labor authorities.

26. Chrysler-Toluca, *Contrato Colectivo de Trabajo,* 1981–95, clauses 6, 20 (1981–93 contracts), clauses 5, 20, 46–9 (1995 contract), in JFCA Archive, Expediente CC–6-XII-J15, CC–421/91-XII-J15; and General Motors-Toluca, *Contrato Colectivo de Trabajo,* 1982–94, clauses 6, 8, 27, and 28, in JFCA Archive, Expediente CC–133-XII-J15. For further discussion of work teams and quality circles in these plants, see Toledano (1993, 11–14), and Interviews 5A, 5C, Mexico City, 1993.

27. Interviews 4D, 5B, Mexico, 1993. Volkswagen, *Contrato Colectivo de Trabajo,* 1992–96, clauses 6, 7, 23, 25, 55, and proposal for union control over the size, function, and power of work teams (clause 25bis), in STPS-CGCFC Archive, File 2.1/313(290)/ 2579, 3 August 1994, 7 March 1995. See also Tuman (1994b) and Montiel (1991) on pre-1992 Volkswagen contract rules.

28. General Motors-DF, *Contrato Colectivo de Trabajo,* 1983–94, clauses 9, 16–19, in JFCA Archive, File CC–147-XII-J15; Nissan, *Contrato Colectivo de Trabajo,* 1984–94, clauses 1, 13–18, 48, in JFCA Archive, File CC–218-XII-Mor(1). On Nissan, see also Interview 4B, Mexico, 1993, and Shaiken and Browne (1991, 33–48). Indeed, at General Motors-DF, the contract specified that management had to maintain one meter between workers on the production line. In addition, management was obligated to notify the union before changes in production rhythms were introduced, and the contract limited the right of managers to move workers from one production area to another. Similarly, at Nissan, production rhythms are established by a joint union–management productivity commission; importantly, the contract obligates management to provide union members on this commission with training in time and motion studies.

29. Nissan, clauses 13–16, 19–24, 36; General Motors-DF, clauses 5, 12–18, 19bis, 33–34; Volkswagen, clauses 2, 5, 13, 22, 80. Concerning Volkswagen, see also special agreement on the temporary suspension of production during the 1995 crisis, in STPS-CGCFC Archive, 26 March 1995.

30. Chrysler-Toluca, clauses 13–17, 20 (1981–93 contracts), and clauses 5, 12–15, 18, 22 (1995 contract). General Motors-Toluca, clauses 6, 8, 10, 21–3. However, clause 44 of the General Motors-Toluca contract specifies that temporary workers will be granted permanent status after a period of twelve months.

31. For discussions of the PECE and other wage and price agreements, see Navarrete (1990, 35–42), Roxborough (1992, 639–64), and Zapata (1995, 150–51).

32. Wage revisions in these six cases occur between the beginning of February and the end of August. Nearly all unions in the sector follow this pattern, with the exception of Nissan-Lerma, where negotiations take place around the first week in October.

33. It is important to note that the inclusion of General Motors-Toluca in a shorter series does not alter the outcome of the analysis. Between 1985 and 1990, Volkswagen

and General Motors-DF's nominal wages (as of September 1) grew by 1,255 and 959 percent, respectively, followed by General Motors-Toluca (901 percent), Chrysler (833 percent), and Ford (720 percent).

34. These three benefits represent the largest share of direct monetary payments. Both incorporated and democratic unions negotiated benefits that exceed the minimums mandated by the Federal Labor Law. In 1994, for example, the law guaranteed workers at least seven paid holidays and a Christmas bonus equivalent to a minimum of fifteen days' wages.

In addition, some companies also pay a portion of the cost of workers' lunches, health insurance premiums to IMSS, and offer transportation subsidies. Since the rules governing these benefits tend to vary, and the data on these benefits were not always complete, they are not included in this analysis. In any case, the fragmentary evidence suggests that insurance and transportation payments were higher in the democratic unions.

35. Volkswagen officials have consistently put forward proposals to cut the number of days in the Christmas bonus payment. At the same time, the union has pushed for an increase in the size of the bonus. For example, in its initial proposal for the 1994–96 contract, the union proposed increasing the *aguinaldo* from 54 to 72 days. Management balked at this demand, and both sides settled for an increase of only one day, the smallest increase in the Volkswagen *aguinaldo* in over 25 years. See "Convenio" and "Estado comparativo de pliegos petitorios—Revisión Contractual 1994–96," in STPS-CGCFC Archive, Expediente 2.1/313(29)2579, 8 August 1994, August 1994, p. 73.

36. To calculate the monetary values of these benefits, I have employed the average wage for 1984 and 1994. This measure is used in the absence of data on the actual value of cash payments made by each firm.

37. The data are generated by the Banco de México, and were obtained from INEGI, Banco de Información Económica, "Índice Nacional de Precios al Consumidor por Areas Metropolitanas y Principales Ciudades," unpublished data.

38. The analysis here presents the cumulative change between 1984 and 1994. In addition, it should be noted that the cumulative change in real wages and benefits for Nissan was −11.88 percent during this period. As noted in this section, Nissan's performance is somewhat exceptional among the democratic cases.

39. Government mediation is the best—and the only—measure of state intervention. Under the Federal Labor Law, the only time that government authorities may become involved in contract negotiations is during a strike or in a dispute where the parties request mediation. In all other circumstances, unions and employers are free to negotiate wage and contract changes, with the stipulation that the new contract or wage scale must be filed with the appropriate federal or local Arbitration and Conciliation Board. (The filing of the wage scale or contract is a routine process that does not involve regulation of the substance of the agreement.)

40. Since the 1970s, the general secretary of the Chrysler union and the head of Human Resources have met privately to revise the wage scale and the collective contract. After they conclude their talks, the new scale and contract are filed with the Federal Arbitration and Conciliation Board. Because neither side has requested mediation, no (formal) opportunity has existed for the government to influence the outcomes of wage bargaining. Indeed, as noted above, when unions and employers negotiate privately, the government's involvement is limited to verifying that the agreements have been signed, notarized, and filed properly.

41. It is also worth noting that wage growth has tended to be *lower* in plants that employ more highly trained and educated workers. On this point, see Carrillo V. (1990).

42. That is to say, prior to 1992, incorporated unions were pressured into real wage flexibility, even during years when productivity may have been increasing.

43. The study found that Chrysler-Toluca employed 4.43 workers per vehicle in 1993, and 6.24 workers per vehicle in 1995. During the same period, Ford-Cuautitlán employed 6.38 and 8.08 workers per vehicle, respectively; for General Motors-DF, the figures were 9.69 and 10.56 (Harbour and Associates 1994, 19; 1996, 32–3). It is important to note that the study compiled separate figures for engine assembly in Chrysler and Ford; the figures on engine productivity are largely the same, however.

44. Calculated from data provided by Asociación Mexicana de la Industria Automotriz (AMIA), internal company records from Ford, General Motors, Nissan, housed in STPS-CGCFC Archive, and unpublished records from Chrysler.

45. This finding has been made in previous comparisons of ISI and export plants. See Carrillo V. (1991). Indeed, Carrillo V. (1991, 16) argues, "The results are seemingly contradictory, the most productive workers [in the automobile industry] have the lowest wages and the least productive workers enjoy the highest wages."

46. Between 1980 and 1994, the CTM organized every new export plant in the sector, gaining more than 10,000 new members. See Tuman and Greenway (1997, 19–20).

Héctor Lucena

7 | **Recent Development in the Venezuelan Automotive Industry: Implications for Labor Relations**

## Introduction

Venezuela embraced a new model of economic development toward the end of the 1980s. By this time, a number of Latin American countries had already begun to introduce structural reforms, dismantling import substitution industrialization (ISI) policies in favor of economic liberalization. From a comparative perspective, then, Venezuela could be viewed as a relative late-comer to the process of structural adjustment. Nevertheless, while the timing of economic reform in Venezuela was lagged somewhat, the adjustment process did result in a significant degree of economic restructuring.

Economic restructuring has had diverse consequences for the country's industrial establishments. In some cases, such as textiles, the shoe industry, and manufacturing, trade liberalization and restructuring have led to deindustrialization. In the automobile industry, however, although liberalization had a strong impact during the initial stages of reform, production in this sector eventually recovered. In adjusting to these new conditions, multinational firms in the automobile industry have sought to limit the size of the workforce, and they have also emphasized the continual improvement of productivity. However, the restructuring

---

Some sections in this chapter are reprinted with permission from *Los efectos laborales de la reestructuración productiva,* ed. Héctor Lucena (Venezuela: Universidad de Carabobo and Asociación de Relaciones de Trabajo, 1996).

policies of the automobile industry are also having an impact on manufacturing sector as a whole (e.g., chemicals, plastics, electrical parts, and electronics), despite the fact that only a small part of the labor force is employed in autos, and although restructuring has been concentrated primarily in vehicle assembly, metalworking, and spare parts production.

A transformation is occurring in the global automobile industry. In the comparative literature, attention has been focused on the Japanese because of the significant innovations they have introduced in the global industry (Womack, Jones, and Roos, 1990; Hoffman and Kaplinsky 1988). Throughout Latin America, those countries with large automobile industries—such as Mexico and Brazil—have been investigated widely in the literature as well (e.g., DIEESE 1995a; Rodríguez L. 1993; Humphrey 1992; Salgado 1993; Carrillo V. 1990b; Middlebrook 1989a; Arteaga 1990b; Herrera Lima 1993). By contrast, less research has been completed on countries such as Venezuela.1 By posing questions similar to the ones addressed in the comparative literature, we hope to highlight the contrasts between restructuring in Venezuela and other cases in Latin America.

This chapter analyzes the impact of liberalization and restructuring in the Venezuelan automobile industry, focusing on the implications for workers in that sector. After discussing the history of the industry during the period of ISI, this chapter examines trends in output, employment, wages, and conditions of work. We will then examine the industrial relations system in the sector, and the organization and structure of Venezuelan automobile unions. The final section assesses the most recent changes in the sector, including company efforts to improve productivity and quality, and to change the organization of production and technology.

**The Development of the Venezuelan Automobile Industry**

The development of the automobile industry in Venezuela during the ISI period can be attributed to three main factors. First, as a country endowed with oil resources, Venezuela's gasoline has been comparatively inexpensive. Second, partly as a result of the first factor, the government favored cars and trucks as the dominant mode of transportation for people and commodities. Third, the industry benefited from governmental protection.

The expansion of the automobile industry began in 1950 with the introduction of Chrysler and General Motors plants in Caracas. After 1960, Ford, Fiat, and Renault also established operations. Henceforth, the sector tended to develop in the Central Region, primarily in the states of Carabobo and Aragua.

In the early years of the industry, the state granted import licenses to firms to import and assemble completely knocked-down kits (CDKs). However, the deepening of import substitution after 1962 led to the formation of three subsectors in the automobile industry: finished vehicle assembly, stampings and

Table 7.1

**Production in the Venezuelan Automobile Industry, 1988–1994**

| Company | 1988 | 1989 | 1992 | 1993 | 1994 |
|---------|------|------|------|------|------|
| GM | 26.1% | 28.1% | 30.6% | 32% | 34.4% |
| Ford | 24.6% | 14.9% | 22.2% | 24.1% | 27.2% |
| Toyota | 15.3% | 18.2% | 18.1% | 18.5% | 13.9% |
| Fiat | 15.7% | 16.9% | 13% | 9.5% | 10.5% |
| Others | 18.3% | 22% | 16.1% | 15.9% | 14% |
| Total* | 113,915 | 27,637 | 92,179 | 93,041 | 71,924 |

*Total units produced.
*Source:* FAVENPA, various years.

body manufacturing,[2] and spare parts production. The finished vehicle sector has been poorly integrated with the other two subsectors. This was partly a consequence of the state's industrial policy, which failed to encourage sufficient foreign or domestic investment in the parts industries.

Since the 1970s, important changes have occurred in the industry. First, Japanese and Korean producers have established assembly operations, concentrated primarily in the eastern region of the country. During the 1970s, for example, Nissan initiated operations in Valencia through a partnership with the Mendoza Group.[3] Toward the end of the 1980s, Toyota and Mitsubishi also began assembly in Cumaná and Barcelona. Honda followed suit by opening an installation in Aragua in the 1990s. By 1995, Hyundai, a Korean producer, had arrived as well. With the exception of the Honda and Hyundai, however, the decision by Japanese producers to establish branch operations was influenced by the terms of the ISI policy, which had prohibited imports of assembled vehicles after 1962.

In addition, the recession of the 1980s had a severe impact on the production of finished vehicles (Table 7.1). Production peaked in 1978 at 170,000 units for the domestic market. Since then, however, the government's adjustment programs have led to a drop in production. In 1988, the year prior to liberalization, 113,915 finished vehicles were produced. Amid economic liberalization and the ensuing recession in 1989, however, production fell to only 27,637 units, while in 1990 approximately 43,000 vehicles were produced. Despite a minor recovery in the early 1990s, production in 1995 amounted to approximately 100,000 units—a high figure—but one still well below pre-liberalization production levels.

The Venezuelan automobile industry is, however, the fourth largest in the region, surpassed only by Brazil, Mexico, and Argentina. Despite the restrictions of ISI policies and the limitations inherent in a small market, the overvaluation of Venezuela's currency contributed to the growth of the market for automobiles. Within the Andean Pact countries, for example, Venezuela's automobile industry is considered as being among the most sophisticated and modernized, with an installed capacity of 240,000 vehicles per year. The automobile market is among the largest as well. The domestic market encompasses some 2,400,000 vehicles, or approximately 8.3 vehicles per person, which, along with Brazil, is one of the highest ratios in Latin America (Edgar Fiol, Executive Director of the National Association of Automobile Parts Distributors, CAINDRA, as cited in *El Universal,* 11 June 1994:1). However, due to the economic crisis, the Colombian market surpassed Venezuela's for the first time in 1993 (*Economia Hoy,* 23 May 1994, 10).

Assessing recent changes in the automobile parts market is more difficult because of the diversity of the subsector. In general, firms have produced for three markets: original equipment (i.e., parts for assembly plants); replacement markets; and the export market. With the opening of the market to imports, the market destination of parts production has changed somewhat. Between 1988 and 1993, the amount of domestic parts destined for the original equipment market decreased from 49.7 percent of production to 35.2 percent. During the same period, the proportion of domestic parts production for replacement markets increased from 41.2 percent to 46 percent, while the amount for exports increased from 9.1 percent to 18.8 percent. The replacement market overtook assembly firms as the main consumer of auto parts. In part, this was a consequence of the drop in finished vehicle production, as well as the freedom (and historical tendency) of the terminal firms to import parts from abroad.

**Employment in the Automobile Industry**

Economic liberalization has also had a strong impact on employment levels and the number of companies operating in the automobile industry. Between 1988 and 1992, total employment in the industry went from 22,041 to 19,098 workers, a 13 percent decrease. This parallels the contraction in formal sector employment, which declined annually at an average rate of 5.45 percent between 1989 and 1993, and which declined cumulatively by 20 percent during the same period.

In 1992, the number of establishments in the automobile industry fell from 251 to 221, a 12 percent decline. Most of this decrease was registered among medium-sized companies employing between 20 and 100 employees; indeed, in 1992, the number of medium-sized establishments contracted by 33 percent. The subsector most affected by these trends is the automobile parts industry. Between 1988 and 1992, the number of medium-sized parts establishments fell from 155 to 133. In part, this can be explained by the fact that downsizing and mergers have resulted in the reclassification of some companies to "small" or "large" establishments. In addition, part of the decline was due to the closing of some businesses. In any case, the number of large-sized plants registered an increase between 1988 and 1992, jumping by 23 percent. With regard to the number of assembly plants in operation, not much variation has occurred. While the reces-

Table 7.2

**Number of Workers in Different Branches of the Automobile Industry, by Size of Industrial Establishment, 1988–1992**

|  | 1988 | | | 1989 | | | 1992 | | |
|---|---|---|---|---|---|---|---|---|---|
|  | A | C | P | A | C | P | A | C | P |
| Large Industry | 9,920 | 804 | 6,668 | 5,652 | 482 | 4,862 | 7,067 | 881 | 7,175 |
| Medium "Superior" | 51 | 403 | 1,320 | 305 | 659 | 1,021 | 69 | 307 | 1,228 |
| Medium "Inferior" | 157 | 509 | 967 | 89 | 328 | 1,137 | 0 | 334 | 714 |
| Small | 49 | 520 | 1,083 | 29 | 484 | 1,086 | 75 | 516 | 732 |
| Total by Divisions | 10,177 | 2,236 | 10,038 | 6,075 | 1,953 | 8,106 | 7,211 | 2,038 | 9,849 |
| Total for year | 22,451 | | | 16,134 | | | 19,098 | | |

*Note:* A = terminal assembly.
C = body and chassis manufacturing.
P = automobile parts production.
*Source:* OCEI Industrial Survey (1992).

sion has reduced the size of the internal market, the shift toward export has partially compensated for the loss in domestic sales, motivating these firms to maintain their operations.

With respect to employment and the size of different establishments, it would appear that the labor force is concentrated in large industrial concerns. In the automobile industry, 80 percent of the workforce is concentrated in large-scale establishments, while in the manufacturing sector as a whole, the figure is 60 percent. After the adjustment "shock" of 1989, the proportion of workers in large industry fell to 68 percent. Nevertheless, with the gradual recovery in production, these figures returned to their historical levels. It should be noted that in absence of sectoral programs to mitigate the impact of unemployment, dismissed workers attempted to collect benefits through the Tripartite Law Commissions, a complicated administrative process designed to review unjustified dismissals.[4] In 1990, the government also began giving unemployment benefits initially for a period of twelve weeks, at a rate of 50 percent of the workers' latest salary.[5]

Table 7.2 gives data on the distribution of employment among assemblers, body manufacturers, and automobile parts producers. The data reveal several interesting tendencies. Both before and after the adjustment "shocks" introduced in 1989, 90 percent of employment in the sector has been concentrated in the assembly and automobile parts companies. However, between 1989 and 1992, the proportion of workers in the sector employed in final assembly went from 45 percent to 38 percent. At the same time, the proportion of workers in automobile parts increased from 45 percent to 52 percent.

For the entire automobile sector, the proportion of hourly workers in the labor force increased slightly from 72.5 percent of employment in 1988 to 74.2 percent in 1992. By contrast, the percentage of managers and white collar employees dropped from 27.4 percent to 25.8 percent of total employment in the same period. Thus, while studies of some sectors have documented an increase in white collar employees, caused mainly by the introduction of technological innovations, this tendency has not occurred in the automobile industry.

## Compensation and Productivity in the Industry

### Recent Trends

Between 1988 and 1992, national wages and salaries contracted by 10.46 percent, but increased by 3.43 percent per capita. However, manual labor costs increased by approximately 25 percent, and by 26.2 percent in large industrial establishments. What would account for the increase in manual labor costs?

A more refined analysis of the increase in manual labor costs suggests that the change is not necessarily a result of gains in wages and salaries, but instead a product of factors that do not directly affect take-home pay. Among the more significant factors here are: (1) social security contributions paid by employers, which have increased for several years now; (2) the promulgation of new laws requiring contributions (from employers and employees) for housing, unemployment, training, and other programs administered by governmental labor authorities; and (3) the impact of inflation, which has fluctuated between 80 percent in 1989 and a low of 35 percent in subsequent years. Inflation has created pressures for more frequent salary revisions; and since accrued unemployment benefits are partly recalculated on the basis of a worker's last salary, the revisions have increased the costs of severance benefits to employers.

With regard to individual labor costs for large companies in the Central Region, the average hourly wages (for companies with the best compensation) reached US $3.32 in 1992.

### International Comparisons of Wages

For the purposes of making international comparisons, we have some fragmentary data on wage rates in Venezuela and the Mexican and Argentine automobile industries. In January 1993, the average hourly wage in the Venezuelan automobile industry was US $2.61. In Ford-Hermosillo, an export plant located in Mexico, hourly wages (excluding benefits) in 1993 ranged from US $1.80 to US $2.15 per hour. In Argentina, the average hourly wage (excluding benefits) for automobile workers in 1993 was US $3.75 (El Monitor de la NAFTA y Comercio Latinoamericano 1994; INCE 1993, 40). These data would appear to show that labor costs of Venezuelan automobile workers are somewhat lower than the amount paid to workers in comparable countries.

*Productivity*

Productivity levels have improved in the automobile industry. The OCEI Industrial Survey, which is one of the only reliable sources on the subject, documents a significant increase in productivity for automobile workers. Between 1988 and 1992, the gross value of production (in constant 1988 Bolivars) increased by 48.4 percent. In large- and small-scale establishments, the increase in the gross value of production was 54.4 percent and 35 percent, respectively. During the same period, the gross value of production per worker increased by 71 percent in medium-size establishments, and by 77 percent in large-scale establishments.

The net value added in the industry increased by 96 percent between 1988 and 1992. The net value added per worker (in constant 1988 Bolivars) increased by 126 percent in the same period. Nevertheless, the cost of manual labor in relation to value added dropped from 28.7 percent in 1988 to 19.11 percent in 1992. In addition, manual labor costs in relation to the gross value of production have been reduced as well, both in the automobile industry and in other large firms. In 1988, manual labor costs represented 8.3 percent and 7.95 percent of the gross value of production in the automobile industry and in large firms, respectively; in 1992, these figures had dropped to 6.97 percent for the automobile industry and 6.12 percent for large industry.

Improvements in productivity have occurred mainly as a result of layoffs and changes in the work organization. While union elites and top-ranking managers have negotiated an agreement that recognizes the importance of improving productivity and product quality, this agreement lacks specific goals, and was negotiated at high levels in the absence of rank-and-file participation. At the firm level, productivity agreements are not common. In the state of Carabobo, the only firm that has signed such an agreement is Rualca, a producer of automobile rings.

## Organized Labor in Venezuela

### Overview: The Development of the Labor Movement in Venezuela

The Venezuelan labor movement can be characterized as a movement of *control and conciliation*. To control union affiliates, union leaders subject workers to internal discipline and authoritarianism. These practices can be traced to the origins and evolution of the labor movement. Before constituting themselves as a significant political force, the dominant actors in Venezuelan society adopted strategies to subordinate the labor movement to external influence, and these strategies evolved into a long-term system of labor control.

Two actors succeeded in dominating the labor movement and in securing its dependence upon external support. The first was the Venezuelan state. As a consequence of its control over oil rents, the Venezuelan state possessed the capacity to intervene and influence nearly all spheres of society. The other actor was the political party system, which, from the time that representative democracy was established in Venezuela, mediated the channels of interest articulation between state and society.

During the initial stages of industrialization, political parties played a significant role in the construction of the trade union movement. Dominated by the state and political parties, unions were placed in a subordinated position in relationship to employers. For their part, employers understood the control exercised by the state and parties, and used this as a means to resolve important issues.

From 1958 on, unions were influenced tremendously by Acción Democrática (AD) and COPEI, the two leading parties that shared power in the government and assumed the function of controlling the labor movement. A principal task given to unions was the consolidation of democracy, while the dominant parties enjoyed access to state resources in order to structure social organization. Through their control over public power and the administration of oil revenue, AD and COPEI were able to distribute patronage to unions and secure the organizational dependence of the labor movement.

The role and orientation of the labor movement in this system was functional for public and private investment. In particular, the control and discipline exercised by union leaders was compatible with Taylor-Fordism, the prevailing form of production during the stage of modernization and industrialization. The capital invested under this form of production did not require skilled labor, but did demand the submission of the workforce to the discipline typical of Taylor-Fordist work organization. It is for this reason that throughout the 1960s, 1970s, and part of the 1980s, the labor movement was an agent of control that responded to the directives of the state and parties in political power.

### Union Affiliation in the Labor Movement

Relations between political parties and trade unions have been modified somewhat over the past few years. The weakening of parties that had traditionally controlled the labor movement has translated into a loss of influence by parties within unions. With regard to the organization of the labor movement, there are four major labor confederations in Venezuela, although the growth in their membership has stagnated for some years now. The largest and most influential confederation is the Venezuelan Confederation of Labor (CTV). The CTV has a claimed membership of 2.5 million workers, and enjoys a presence (and influence) in every state of the republic and in all of the productive sectors of the economy. The other three confederations are notably smaller than the CTV. For example, the Unified Center of Venezuelan Workers (CUTV) has approximately 80,000 members but is slowly fading, although it maintains union affiliates in Caracas, Valencia, La Victoria, Barquisimeto, and Mérida.

Unions with a Christian Democratic orientation have only weak support in the labor movement, and are divided between two confederations, the General Confederation of Workers (CGT) and the Confederation of Autonomous Workers (CODESA). The region's Christian Democratic confederation (the Latin American Confederation of Workers) located its offices in Venezuela some time ago. Both the CGT and CODESA have received support from the Latin American Confederation of Workers, and its location in Venezuela has given them reason to be hopeful about the possibilities of growth.

Finally, there are some unions that are not affiliated with any confederations. These include the Workers' Press Union, diverse unions of university employees (representing professors, staff, and workers), and the Metro Workers' Union.

### Political Currents in the Labor Movement

Within the labor movement, one can observe several distinct political currents. In order to simplify the analysis, it is useful to compare unions according to the following classification of political behavior and bargaining.

#### Traditional Corporative Unionism

Traditional corporative unionism can be observed mainly among unions that are controlled by AD and COPEI and affiliated to the CTV. These unions have been the beneficiaries of government patronage, distributed through the medium of diverse governmental organizations. However, the economic policies implemented since 1989 have placed the leadership of corporative unions in an embarrassing (and untenable) situation. On the one side, government support for unions has been withdrawn. On the other side, leaders of the corporative unions have not defined a new way of responding to these important changes.

The leaders of corporative unions are maintained through the support of political parties, public entities, and large-scale companies that traditionally have cooperated with this sort of trade unionism. As a political current, traditional corporative unionism is located primarily in the manufacturing sector, and particularly in the states of Carabobo and Aragua.

#### Traditional Class Unionism

Left-wing organizations such as CUTV and some small groups in the CTV are located within this current. A few of these unions have achieved quite a degree of stability in their internal relations. Such is the case for the National Union of Journalists and the Trade Union of Textile Workers of the State of Carabobo. However, because this current is usually concerned with promoting internal democracy, the leaders of traditional class unionism sometimes come to power only to lose it later; in particular, by calling elections, the leaders permit opposition forces in the union to unite and defeat them.

*New Unionism*

Within this set of unions, two types of political currents can be recognized. One is related to the movement of Causa-R (Radical Cause). The other is somewhat heterogeneous in terms of the alternatives it proposes, and is related to the Movimiento al Socialismo (Movement Toward Socialism). Given the accusations these unions make against corporative organizations, the leaders of class unions often emphasize "transparency" in the handling of union resources and the need to carry out regular elections according to union regulations. This current can be observed in several important companies, including CANTV-Caracas, Caracas Metro, Electricidad de Caracas, and Cadafe. It is notable that most of these enterprises are located in the capital of the country. As for the new unionism associated with Causa-R, its epicenter is undoubtedly located in the southern part of the country, in the state of Bolivar.

*Employer-Dominated Unions*

In addition to the three categories mentioned above, one must add a fourth, referred to as "business" unions. In this case, employers encourage the constitution of trade unions. With the implementation of the Organic Labor Law (LOT), nonunionized workers were denied the right to negotiate collective bargaining agreements, including at those workplaces where collective bargaining had been established. As a result, some employers have been motivated to encourage "loyal" workers to organize themselves into a trade union, thus preempting or limiting the possibility of forming genuine trade unions Unsurprisingly, employer-dominated unions refrain from making public pronouncements about their politics.

## Unions in the Automobile Industry

The automobile sector has a high density of trade union membership. Between twelve and fifteen thousand workers in the sector are organized, which translates into a unionization rate of between 65 and 80 percent of the workforce.[6] This is one of the highest rates in the country. Although there is no federation that exists solely to organize automobile workers, nearly all automobile unions have been affiliated with the Federation of Metallurgical, Mining, Mechanical, and Similar Workers (FETRAMETAL) since its inception. Still, because a federation is considered legally to be a "second grade" union organization, collective bargaining is carried out directly between trade unions and management.

Created through the initiative of the CTV, FETRAMETAL was officially formed on May 31, 1964. Throughout its existence, this federation has been controlled by the AD party, a practitioner of corporativist conciliation and control. The second largest political force in FETRAMETAL is Christian Democratic in orientation, while leftists have been in the minority.

Nationally, there are twenty-two automobile unions, and most are medium-sized organizations. Eleven unions are located in the state of Carabobo. Although there are no national unions of automobile workers, regional unions organized at the sectoral level have the greatest possibility of reaching the most workers. The prevalence of enterprise- and local, sectoral-level unions is partly a result of the labor relations system in Venezuela, which makes the enterprise the focus of union action. In addition, these types of unions are favored by the integration of assembly firms in the automotive sector, which operate as suppliers for one another. Nevertheless, the automobile parts companies are not as well integrated with one another as the assembly plants.

As far as union bargaining styles are concerned, trade unions in the automobile industry tend to operate on the basis of control and conciliation. Conciliation is privileged above and beyond any other union strategy; at the same time, however, union leaders seek to control and discipline the rank and file through authoritarian internal governance practices. For members, union elites seem to have two functions. On the one side, members of the executive committee appear as bosses, while on the other they are leaders. The perception that union officers are bosses more than leaders is associated with the high degree of confidence that management invests in them to secure the consent of the workforce. However, this perception is also strengthened by the practice of everyday unionism, which throughout Venezuela's thirty-five years of democracy has been identified plainly with those who exercise power in government, and which sometimes rewards union leaders with political positions.

As noted previously, the disciplinary and control functions exercised by automobile unions have been compatible with Taylor-Fordism, the dominant form of production in the sector during the period of modernization and industrialization. Indeed, the labor process under Taylor-Fordism did not require skilled labor but instead a workforce that would submit to the organizational discipline of mass production in a developing country. To summarize, after the industrial "boom" of the 1960s and 1970s, the labor movement was an agent of control that responded not only to the exigencies of production, but also to political parties in power.

### Union Organization in the Assembly Plants

The rate of unionization in the assembly plants is higher than in the automobile parts plants. The assembly plants are controlled by the largest firms in the sector, and approximately 100 percent of their workers are organized. It should be noted that, from the outset, producers have been oriented only toward the assembly of finished vehicles and not manufacturing. As a result, the terminal firms tend to source more of their parts from abroad than from the local parts industry. This distinguishes Venezuela from other Latin American countries, such as Mexico and Brazil, where important parts of the vehicle are manufactured by the assemblers.

The terminal sector is dominated by eight multinational corporations, including Ford, General Motors, Chrysler, Fiat, Renault, Toyota, Mack-Honda, and Mitsubishi. Nearly all of the workers in these companies are unionized. In addition, there are five smaller, domestic companies in the sector that produce buses and cargo vehicles, including Encava, Fanabus, Talleres Gago, Ensamblaje Superior, and Fiav (with equity held by Italians). These latter firms are classified as small- and medium-sized establishments, and unionization rates in them are somewhat lower.

The high rate of unionization in the assembly plants is due to the fact that unions have the right to propose candidates when vacancies occur. The number of workers that the union can propose varies between 75 and 100 percent, depending on the rule stipulated in the collective bargaining agreement. In any case, this tradition allows unions to gain new members from the time they begin employment. For their part, the companies have cooperated with this practice. In particular, the companies know that employment in the automobile industry is in high demand because of the (comparatively) high level of remuneration and benefits paid to automobile workers. For this reason, the unions always have a large supply of prospective workers to meet the company's staffing requirements at any given moment. In addition, as noted below, the geographic concentration of firms in the sector creates favorable conditions for unionization.

### Union Organization in the Automobile Parts Plants

The rate of unionization in the automobile parts plants is somewhat lower than in the assemblers. There are a total of 133 parts companies, of which 30 are large-scale, employing more than one hundred workers, and with high rates of unionization. The rest of the small and medium-size automobile parts firms have lower rates of organization. It is also useful, however, to distinguish the auto parts companies from one another on the basis of firm ownership. Viewed from this angle, there are three distinct groups of companies, each with varying rates of union organization. The first is composed of multinational firms, operating with a fixed capacity given their market share or technology. A second group represents firms owned by domestic industrial groups, encompassing plants such as Procesa, Metalcon, Mancini, and Covenal. Finally, there are independent auto parts companies that operate a plant or several small installations. Of these three groups, unionization is high in the first two, but not in the third.

The trend in unionization in the automobile parts sector is a result of diverse factors. One central factor is the geographical dispersion of autoparts plants. For example, manufacturing companies tend to be concentrated in the central region and the "iron zone." Thus, whereas automobile parts unions can be found in fourteen distinct federal entities, the unions in the terminal sector are located in only four states: Carabobo, Aragua, Anzoategui, and Sucre. Moreover, it is rare to find unions in these states that are organized specifically for automobile parts workers, such as the cases of Falcon, Zulia, and Yaracuay. Rather, what often transpires is that parts workers are affiliated to metallurgical and metal-mechanical unions, becoming members with other workers who are not employed in the automotive sector (e.g., Miranda, Lara, Mérida, Tachira).

The level of union membership in the parts plants may also be related to the productive capacity of this sector. According to the 1992 OCEI Industrial Survey, of the 220 firms registered in the automobile sector (final assembly, automobile parts, and stampings), there were 171 establishments with fewer than one hundred workers. These are classified as small and medium-size companies. The OCEI Survey also documented the existence of 120 small establishments with fewer than twenty employees. However, as noted previously, although the automobile assembly companies are located in the large-size segment, the automobile parts firms are almost exclusively small and medium-size operations.

Finally, while the total number of unionized workers in final assembly has decreased, the proportion of the labor force that is organized has not. This is understandable if we recall that unions have control over applicants for vacant positions in the assembly firms, a practice that is reinforced by the LOT. However, because many automobile parts companies have closed or have been converted toward other product lines, there has been a net loss in the number of organized workers in the parts industry.[7]

## Collective Bargaining in the Automobile Industry

We now turn to an analysis of recent trends in collective bargaining. The analysis focuses on collective bargaining agreements for nearly all of the firms in the sector.[8] The comparison includes some contracts negotiated before (and after) liberalization so that the changes emanating from restructuring can be fully appreciated. To anticipate, although some changes have taken place, these are not as marked as what firms have stated publicly about the new industrial relations systems.

The analysis focuses on the following aspects of the contracts: (a) the collective bargaining unit, with special reference to the plants and workers covered by the scope of the agreement; (b) the organizational forms through which workers bargain, and the strategies workers adopt in the process of collective bargaining; (c) the fringe benefits guaranteed by collective bargaining agreements, and the costs that these benefits generate for the firm; (d) the administration and implementation of the contract, including its function in structuring the organization of production.

### The Collective Bargaining Unit and Scope of the Contracts

In the automobile industry, collective bargaining occurs at the company level, as is customary in the Venezuelan industrial relations system. Despite the existence of some important national industrial unions, there is no sectorwide bargaining in the automobile industry. Companies belonging to the same corporate group tend to have similar contracts; however, when workers are organized in an industrial union and a local section exists in each company in the sector, bargaining takes place separately on a company-by-company basis.

In any case, the workforce covered by automobile contracts includes weekly (i.e., full-time) wage workers. But in most cases the scope of the agreements is extended to cover other employees, with the exception of personnel of confidence and top managers. Provided that there is no union for white collar employees, the companies retain the prerogative to apply or deny benefits and work conditions (established in the contract) to other employees. In addition, the wage scales and job classifications included in contracts always apply to weekly payroll workers. Generally, skilled workers in special positions are not covered by the wage scales incorporated into the collective bargaining agreements.

### Organization of Workers in the Negotiation Process

Workers' bargaining delegations are organized through unions with a double affiliation, making them "second grade" organizations. On the one side, the unions serve as national organizations with a professional nature; on the other side, they function as regional, inter-professional organizations. Generally, three or four workers' representatives participate in the negotiation process. Nevertheless, these delegations are usually headed by the leaders of the union and the local section.

The development of the collective bargaining project usually is realized by workers of a specific section or union local, with the advice given by leaders of FETRAMETAL. One exception to this pattern has occurred within Toyota and Bundy, two unions that are not controlled by either AD or COPEI, and that operate with more autonomy from the Federation.

### Wages and Fringe Benefits

The collective bargaining agreements contain a large number of clauses. In the small companies, the contract clauses often repeat what is stipulated in the labor law. In addition, a fair amount of the content of the agreements concerns matters that are not directly related to production, but rather to the concession of benefits to workers and their relatives.

The overall level of wages and fringe benefits tends to be higher in the assembly firms than in the automobile parts companies. But among the assem-

Table 7.3

**Wage Increases in the Terminal and Automobile Parts Firms,  Various
Years** (percentage increase at ratification, and amount in total Bolivars)

| Terminal | 1986–89 | Bs | 1989–92 | Bs | 1992–95 | Bs |
|---|---|---|---|---|---|---|
| GM | 75% | 20 | 60% | 50 | 39% | 320 |
| Chrysler | 1985–88 79% | Bs 19 | 1988–91 58% | Bs 38 | 1991–94 35% | Bs 230 |
| Mack | 1986–89 79% | Bs 19 | 1992–95 39% | Bs 260 | | |
| Encava | 1988–91 56% | Bs 18 | 1994–97 33% | Bs 300 | | |
| **Auto Parts** | 1987–90 | Bs | 1990–93 | Bs | 1993–96 | Bs |
| Sidaven | 50% | 30 | n.a. | n.a. | 36% | 370 |
| SH Fundiciones | 62% | 16 | 39% | 56 | 38% | 320 |
| Ocimetalmecánica | 85% | 20 | n.a. | n.a. | 38% | 260 |
| Microtor | 1987–90 36% | Bs 34 | 1991–94 38% | Bs 80 | | |

*Note:* "Bs" is amount in total Bolivars.
*Source*: Wage revision agreements,  selected years and companies.

blers, one can observe a marked difference between transnational firms and ones
controlled by domestic capital. For example, the data in Table 7.3 show that,
between 1988 and 1992, the relative change (and absolute gain) in wages and
benefits was higher in General Motors and Chrysler than in Encava, a domestically owned company that produces buses. Table 7.3 reveals a similar pattern for
the automobile parts companies. Once again, the companies tied to large industrial conglomerates (e.g., Sidaven and S.H. Fundiciones, a subsidiary of the
Metalcon and Procesa Group) tend to grant larger increases than Ocimetalmecá-
nica, a smaller company with ties to the Mendoza Group, or independents like
Microtor that have less fixed capacity.

The clauses dealing with wage and benefit increases create the most friction
during collective bargaining. This is understandable, since this clause directly
affects the labor costs of employers. Traditionally, the large assembly firms used
to grant three salary increases—one per year—during the life of the contract.
However, it is now customary for the large firms to grant a salary increase every
six months.

Previously, the greatest portion of the salary increase was granted at the time
when the collective bargaining agreement was ratified. This pattern was more

prevalent among the assembly firms than the automobile parts companies. In particular, not only did the parts companies tend to grant smaller relative increases, they also tended to give a lower percentage increase when the contract was ratified. However, patterns of wage bargaining in the assembly and automobile parts firms have become more uniform. Previously, both assembly and parts companies used to grant a wage increase when the contracts were ratified, and then two more increases while the agreements were in effect. Currently, the norm is to grant an increase when the contract is ratified, and then give four to five increases during the life of the contract. In addition, the increases are usually granted in absolute values. Yet in two agreements reviewed from the Sivensa Group, the increases are expressed in relative terms.

With regard to inflation, the unions have not succeeded in reducing the time period of collective bargaining agreements in order to have more frequent negotiations over wages and benefits. The CTV had approved a policy to reduce the duration of contracts to two years at its IXth (1985) and Xth (1990) Congresses. In addition, the unions have not been effective in introducing revision clauses while the agreements are in effect. Nevertheless, there has been a change in Chrysler's 1995 contract, which compels the union and management to realize a wage revision every six months. It should be noted here that normally only employees in medium- and high-level positions were subject to a biannual salary revision and performance evaluation. However, it is now becoming more common to grant workers biannual wage revisions as well. In some of the large assembly and automobile parts firms, unscheduled "extra-contractual" wage increases are also granted from time to time. For example, in 1994, given the high level of annual inflation (70 percent), unscheduled wage increases were negotiated in most of the assembly and parts companies.

One point that is not fully appreciated is that wage increases do not always affect employee's severance payments. Article 138 of the LOT states that when unions and employers negotiate annual wage increases in excess of 20 percent, the additional amount above 20 percent need not be taken into account in the calculation of workers' seniority, salary history, and severance payments. While the government has tried to implement this policy through decrees, the unions have avoided inclusion of Article 138 into collective bargaining agreements; rather, unions have negotiated separate agreements that grant workers severance payments based upon the length of service and salary history.[9] In any case, wage increases exceeding 20 percent in the sector are infrequent. Based upon the agreements we have reviewed, the only cases exceeding 20 percent were Metalcar with a 30 percent increase in 1993, and Rudeveca, with an increase of 22 percent in 1991. The parties in Metalcar and Rudeveca did not, however, invoke the provisions of Article 138.

With the new LOT coming into force, firms are now required to pay workers up to 120 days as a profit-sharing bonus (see Table 7.4). Before this regulation went into effect, these values ranged from 70 to 90 days in the large companies,

Table 7.4

**Profit-Sharing Bonus** (number of days paid)

|  | 1987–88 | 1990–91 | 1992–93 | 1994–95 |
|---|---|---|---|---|
| GM | 74 | 75 | 120 | 120 |
| SH Fundiciones | 68 | 71 | 101 | n.a. |
| Metalcar | 72 | 72 | 100 | 110–120 |
| Rudeveca | 74 | 90 | 90 | 110–120 |
| Danaven | n.a. | n.a. | n.a. | 105–120 |
| Ocimetalmecánica | 74 | 74 | 90 | 90 |

*Source:* Collective bargaining agreements, various companies and years.

and a little less in the small companies. While not all companies increased the profit-sharing bonus to 120 days, substantial increases in the post LOT agreements have been observed. Some agreements maintained the number of days paid in the collective bargaining agreement, and subsequently added additional days through a special accord.

## Work Organization

The companies claim that the most complicated clauses for them to administer relate to permissions for absences, the dispensing of medicine, school stationery, and perfect attendance. But there are other administrative controls that are also necessary to make the agreements function properly.

Many different issues are often the subject of extra-contractual negotiations between the unions and employers; sometimes these negotiations result in accords that have the same impact as collective bargaining agreements. For example, Danaven negotiated a special side agreement with its union that implemented a fourth shift, new schedules, and compensation. Toyota and its unions used extra-contractual negotiations as a vehicle to establish a cafeteria for its workers. These side agreements are not always registered with the Labor Office, although some unions register the agreements to give them more legitimacy. However, it is likely that employers and unions assume that compromises will sustain these side agreements, making it unnecessary to appeal to governmental labor authorities for enforcement.

In addition, one of the most important clauses concerns personnel recruitment. The unions preserve their control over the workforce through this clause, avoiding competition from other unions, and acting together with the company as a filter for the recruitment of new personnel. Although the selection and retention procedure is carried out by the companies, the unions have the benefit of being guaranteed that a percentage of the candidates they recommend will be hired. As noted previously, this percentage ranges from 75 to 100 percent. This clause also allows unions to exclude "problem" workers once union officials have received references from other friendly unions. In this regard, the companies also share information about workers among themselves.

Firms that are introducing innovations in personnel administration and compensation systems have generally avoided incorporating these changes into collective contracts. For example, pay-by-knowledge systems, which have been observed in nearly a dozen automotive firms in the state of Carabobo, were hardly mentioned in the last agreement of Rudeveca (1995–98). In addition, very few companies have negotiated compensation systems grounded in productivity. Rualca is an exception here, although productivity bonuses for its workers operate outside the framework of collective bargaining.

With regard to personnel development, the collective bargaining agreements do not generally make provisions for training or employee development. In the few that do mention training, the relevant clauses only state that the unions will provide managers with the names of workers who are interested in courses. What is evident to most companies is that workers who become involved in union affairs are less likely to participate in employee development programs.

Another interesting trend that can be observed is a reduction in the number of job categories. While eliminating some categories, firms have also expanded job responsibilities for other positions so that workers may perform a variety of tasks; this constitutes a form of internal flexibility. The move to reduce job categories began in the late 1980s. For example, in its 1989 collective contract, General Motors reduced the number of categories from 95 to 75. Chrysler followed suit, going from 40 job classifications to a compacted list of 11 categories. In the case of Ford, the contract was modified from having 34 position types and 15 categories in 1989, to 16 positions and 6 categories in 1993 (see Table 7.5).

The changes in job classifications are being accompanied by modifications in the employment status of workers. Following the pattern established in the manufacturing sector, automobile firms traditionally have privileged the employment of full-time workers for an unspecified period. But one effect of the restructuring process has been the greater use of temporary workers for a fixed period of time. Indeed, the LOT has contributed to this trend by permitting companies to extend the probation period (for new workers) from 30 to 90 days, and by allowing the probation period to be renewed once, with the effect of creating a fixed period of employment of six months.

### Conflicts in the Automobile Industry: Toward Labor Peace?

The general perception about industrial relations in the automobile industry is that there is little conflict between workers and management.[10] Industrial relations in the manufacturing sector are often characterized in the same way. However, it is necessary to call attention to some important factors that explain this

Table 7.5

**Job Classifications at Ford, 1989 and 1993**

| 1989 | 1993 |
| --- | --- |
| 1. Warehouse worker | GROUP I |
| 2. General assistant | Shop Foreman |
| 3. 1$^{st}$ Foreman | GROUP II |
| 4. 2$^{nd}$ Foreman | Molder |
| 5. 1$^{st}$ Carpenter | Instrumentalist |
| 6. 2$^{nd}$ Carpenter | Plant Foreman |
| 7. Periodic inspector | GROUP III |
| 8. 1$^{st}$ Driver | Maintenance operator |
| 9. 2$^{nd}$ Driver | Process Auditor |
| 10. Instrument electrician | Specialist |
| 11. Specialist | GROUP IV |
| 12. Specialized electrician | Painter |
| 13. 1$^{st}$ Inspector | Sewing operator |
| 14. 2$^{nd}$ Inspector | Brassworker |
| 15. Welder/Brassworker | Welder |
| 16. 1$^{st}$ Brassworker | 1$^{st}$ Watchman |
| 17. 1$^{st}$ Molder | GROUP V |
| 18. 2$^{nd}$ Molder | Production operator |
| 19. Supply operator | Supply Workman |
| 20. Maintenance operator | 2$^{nd}$ Watchman |
| 21. 1$^{st}$ Maintenance operator | GROUP VI |
| 22. 2$^{nd}$ Maintenance operator | General Worker |
| 23. 1$^{st}$ Production operator | |
| 24. 2$^{nd}$ Production operator | |
| 25. 3$^{rd}$ Production operator | |
| 26. 4$^{th}$ Production operator | |
| 27. 1$^{st}$ Paint sprayer | |
| 28. 2$^{nd}$ Paint sprayer | |
| 29. 3$^{rd}$ Paint sprayer | |
| 30. 1$^{st}$ Welder | |
| 31. 2$^{nd}$ Welder | |
| 32. 3$^{rd}$ Welder | |
| 33. 1$^{st}$ Watchman | |
| 34. 2$^{nd}$ Watchman | |

*Source:* Ford Motor Company de Venezuela, unpublished records.

condition. Certainly, the practice of union conciliation and control in the sector has been effective in securing labor peace. In other words, the absence of conflict is a product of the maintenance and reproduction of control systems exercised by the unions, with strong support from the companies. What are the specific mechanisms that contribute to the maintenance of labor peace? How is union control strengthened?

First of all, unions function as the principal access point for employment in the automobile industry. The LOT allows unions to offer human resources to companies, a role unions have exercised for many years now. For their part, the companies trust unions to recruit personnel; for once unions engage in recruitment, they acquire a quasi-business character by disciplining workers recommended for employment. In addition, this system reduces the recruitment costs for companies and has prevented the employment of left-wing or "problem" workers. However, this process has also contributed to the socialization of workers within the dominant political currents of the unions.

Of course, what the companies are really interested in is having productive and submissive workers. When workers become absentee, take frequent leaves, or are uncooperative, then the union is called upon and informed about the situation, with the expectation that corrective action will be taken. If nothing is done, then the company warns the worker what actions will be taken, understood as "sanctions." Yet, usually in the interests of protecting labor peace, the union leadership recognizes that disciplinary actions are within their sphere of influence.[11] In this sense, then, one can see that there is a congruence between this style of trade unionism and the interests of the companies. Exercising disciplinary authority is sometimes a fundamental condition of the union's existence within the plant.

It is understandable that the unions assure the company that they act as genuine representatives of their members, as this is an indispensable condition that allows both parties to make agreements and commitments that are demanded on both sides. This normative framework requires that the unions provide rules for representation for union actors. When these rules do not materialize, then the forms of representation tend to be more arbitrary. This can be a delicate situation for the companies because, as a rule, the normative framework does not permit management to interfere in internal union affairs. As a result, the companies often must hide or ignore controversial situations involving union freedom and representativeness.

The level of socioeconomic benefits that workers receive is also implicated in the logic of labor quiescence. Workers in the automobile parts and assembly firms generally enjoy average benefits above those in other productive activities in Venezuela. With the economic opening, this sector also has actively contributed to nontraditional exports, thus compensating for the deterioration of the domestic market for automobiles, and allowing workers to preserve their social and economic conditions. The situation is quite different for small companies (with fewer exports) who are independent from transnational corporations or the large domestic groups; in particular, given the predominance of company-level bargaining in the sector, workers in small firms suffer from a greater differentiation in their salary and working conditions than those in larger companies.

Finally, despite the strength and economic importance of the automobile industry, the unions lack financial and organizational capacity. Although Article 441 of the LOT requires unions to provide an annual report and accounting of their finances, and prohibits the reelection of union officers who fail to comply with this regulation, most unions do not provide information about their finances. The law is not enforced by public officials in the labor ministry. For their part, the companies feign ignorance about union finances.[12]

Given the lack of economic resources for union organization in the sector, workers have not been in a position to support conflicts and strike actions. In the event that a strike were to develop, the union would provide necessities for its affiliates and the striking members. However, no one knows the true amount of resources that unions have to support such actions. This is true even in the case of FETRAMETAL, which operates some businesses in the iron zone of Guayana.

To summarize, what occurs in the industry is a form of safety-valve conflict—that is to say, conflict that externalizes everyday problems in the employment relationship. For example, the union base often claims that there are discrepancies and mistakes in their pay, and attempts to have them corrected. Generally, these problems occur because information concerning overtime and other points (e.g., food, transportation, paid leave, temporary changes in category, substitutions) are not provided in a timely manner to payroll officials. This obligates union officials to be on the premises every Friday, which is payday. Conflict over payroll is one of the most prominent examples of "everyday" conflict, which serves as a safety-valve to release tension. However, the growth in forms of everyday conflict typically leads all of the concerned parties to resolve these matters promptly. Workers' complaints are usually handled by officials at the lowest level in the union organization, who in turn work with the lowest-ranking industrial relations representative of the company. In the large firms, however, a small number of complaints are channeled directly to the highest levels of the management and union hierarchy. The small and medium-sized companies only have one, or at most two, levels of staff who deal with complaints. When complaints make their way to the highest-ranking officials, an attempt is usually made to resolve the problem. By contrast, at the lower levels of organization, the parties threaten to take matters to the next level as a way of holding each other in check.

## Conclusions

What conclusions can we draw from this analysis? The brief period of expansion and restructuring that has taken place during the 1990s has already had a profound impact on the workforce and operation of the automobile industry. Although this study has been concerned more with the repercussions of changes in labor relations, one finding of the research is that in the area of human resources, the increase in personnel policy innovations—which are often implemented through unilateral management decisions—appears to have been more effective than the traditional mode of decision making, which involved joint implementation with unions. Indeed, everyday forms of organizational innovation at the company and sectoral level are not being generated by concerted action between unions and management. Rather, organization innovation is being driven by management experiments of a moderate scope, implemented with the aid of a conservative trade unionism that is supportive of changes proposed by the most aggressive companies.

Union leaders were strongly influenced by the fact that trade unionism performed a stabilizing role in the sector during the period of ISI. Partly as a consequence of their previous role, union leaders have been ill suited for the task of adapting to the demands of industrial restructuring. Lacking a complete understanding of the changes taking place, automobile union leaders have been unable to articulate an alternative as they have been confronted by the processes of restructuring and labor flexibility. As a result, they have been largely unable to formulate a response that would provide workers with a greater role in these changes, a strategy that would translate into higher levels of well-being for the workforce.

For their part, the companies have accepted the status quo since it has reinforced the capacity of managers to implement reforms unilaterally. In many cases, the unions working in the midst of restructuring end up legitimating processes that have not been sufficiently explained to the union base. For workers, this often amounts to a form of empty union representation.

Given the recent trends in the industry, one can envisage two scenarios of future change. In the first scenario, companies would perform well as a result of the transformation and renovation in work organization; but these companies might also recognize that in modern enterprises, it is important to have stable industrial relations, since doing so helps to legitimate modifications in the organization of work. Therefore, companies would not assume an anti-union position while union leaders were adapting and renewing their roles. In a second scenario, companies will continue to transform work organization and personnel administration unilaterally, taking advantage of the weaknesses of unions and their slow response in adapting to change. An excess of this type of strategy runs the risk of compromising the larger goal of providing workers with more opportunities for involvement and participation under the leadership of management.

## Notes

1. For examples of recent work on Venezuela, see Villalba (1995) and Sánchez (1993). Perhaps the most complete study of the sector is found in Iranzo, Betencourt, Lucena, and Sandoval (1995).
2. The body manufacturing division for commercial vehicles is limited. This subsector consists primarily of metallurgical shops controlled by domestic capital, producing commercial vehicle bodies. According to the Central Office of Information and Statistics, the typical firm is small to medium-size, employing less than 100 workers.
3. This same group also assembled American Motors vehicles, and for a two-year period worked with General Motors as well.
4. These courts were dismantled with the passage of the Organic Labor Law (LOT)

in 1991, which established new labor courts for the purposes of reviewing claims for severance benefits, and which were ultimately merged with the Labor Court of First Instance.

5. Subsequently, the eligibility period was extended to sixteen weeks. However, evaluations of this system indicate that workers have to wait for long periods before receiving their benefits.

6. The Ministry of Labor does not collect data on union affiliation. In addition, most unions do not present annual reports with information on the number of members. The figures on union membership for the automobile sector come from an author's interview with Andrés Mercau, general secretary of FETRAMETAL, 5 April 1995.

7. The fieldwork for this project documented a high corporate "mortality rate" for the small companies. In some cases, small companies have merged with larger ones. Others have dedicated themselves to other product lines, have relocated, or have simply ceased producing.

8. The study examines collective bargaining agreements for eight assembly plants, representing half of the total in the sector, and twenty-five automobile parts firms of diverse sizes.

9. In the aftermath of liberalization, managers have renewed their efforts to modify workers' severance payments, arguing that these benefits place firms at a disadvantage in relationship to global competitors. The current system gives workers one month of salary for each year of service. Payment is given when the employment relation is terminated, and is based upon the most recent salary of the worker. In recent years, however, the labor movement has expressed its willingness to review this system. For example, in a recent agreement negotiated by the Unions of Workers of Torcar (Tornillos Carabobo), the leadership agreed that part of the salary increase would not be taken into account in the calculation of severance benefits.

10. This section analyzes collective conflicts. The way that individual conflicts are expressed is diverse and does not always respond to collective organization but instead to dissatisfaction that generates individual responses. Examples of individual conflicts include absenteeism, tardiness, lack of cooperation, being accident prone, sabotage, loss of material or tools, complaints, and individual administrative or judicial actions. Generally, more frequent individual conflict is a sign of deficient human resource management, or the presence of arbitrary or abusive management styles at high, intermediary, or supervisory levels in the organization. Regardless of the causes of the conflict, top managers have a responsibility to correct this situation.

11. One expression of this has been observed in the contractual clauses that demand the authorization or signature of a union representative for paid leaves. See clause 24 of the collective bargaining agreement between Ford and Sutramotriz.

12. Recently, however, the National Telephone Company and Pepsi Cola demanded that their unions comply with the legal regulations concerning financial reporting. However, it would appear that the companies' motivations were derived more from poor union–management relations than from a genuine preoccupation with union democracy and accounting practices.

# Bibliography

Acevedo, Jorge. 1990. "El nuevo papel de México en la región norteamericana: El caso de la industria automotriz." In Anguiano 1990a, 30–63.

Agosin, Manuel R. 1995. "Foreign Direct Investment in Latin America." In *Foreign Direct Investment in Latin America,* ed. Manuel Agosin. Washington: Inter-American Development Bank.

Aguilar García, Javier. 1980. "Historia sindical de General Motors y la huelga de 1980." *Revista A* 1, no. 1: 3–16.

———. 1982. *La política sindical en México: Industria del automóvil.* México: Ediciones Era.

———, ed. 1990. *Historia de la CTM 1936–1990.* Volumes I and II. México, DF: UNAM.

Aguilar García, Javier, and Lorenzo Arrieta. 1990. "En la fase más aguada de la crisis y en el inicio de la reestructuración o modernización 1982–88." In Aguilar García 1990, 157–204.

Álvarez Béjar, Alejandro. 1991. "Economic Crisis and the Labor Movement in Mexico." In Middlebrook 1991c, 27–55.

American Automobile Manufacturers Association. 1996. *World Motor Vehicle Data, 1996 Edition.* Detroit: American Automobile Manufacturers Association.

Anguiano, Arturo, ed. 1990a. *La modernización de México.* México: Universidad Autónoma Metropolitana.

———. 1990b. "Crisis politica, modernizacíon y democracia." In Anguiano 1990a, 387–405.

Arbix, Glauco. 1995. *Uma aposta no futuro. Os três primeiros anos da câmara do setor automobilístico.* São Paulo: Scritta.

Arteaga, Arnulfo. 1985. "Innovación tecnológica y clase obrera en la industria automotriz." In *Reestructuración productiva y la clase obrera (Testimonios de la crisis, No. 1),* ed. Esthela Gutiérrez Garza, 146–69. México, DF: Siglo Veintiuno Editores.

———. 1988. "Reconversión industrial y flexibilidad en la industria automotriz en México." In *Austeridad y reconversión (Testimonios de la crisis, No. 2),* ed. Esthela Gutiérrez Garza, 166–188. México, DF: Siglo Veintiuno Editores.

———. 1990. "Ford: Un largo y sinuouso conflicto." In *Negociación y conflicto laboral en México,* ed. Graciela Bensusán y Samuel León, 141–170. Mexico, DF: Flasco and Fundación Friedrich Ebert.

———, ed. 1993a. *Proceso de trabajo y relaciones el la industria automotriz en México.* México, DF: Friedrich Ebert Stiftung.

———. 1993b. "La reestructuración de la industria automotriz en México y sus repercusiones en el viejo núcleo fabril." In Arteaga 1993a, 1–54.

Ashby, Joe. 1967. *Organized Labor and the Mexican Revolution under Lázaro Cárdenas.* Chapel Hill: University of North Carolina Press.

———. 1985. "The Dilemma of the Mexican Trade Union Movement." *Mexican Studies/Estudios Mexicanos* 1, no. 2: 277–301.

Asociación de Fábricas de Automotores (ADEFA). 1993. *Anuario.* Buenos Aires, Argentina: ADEFA.

———. 1995. *Boletín 351,* March: 1.

———. 1995. *Boletines mensuales.* March–July.

Asociación Mexicana de la Industria Automotriz (AMIA). 1988. *La industria automotriz en México en cifras.* México, DF: AMIA

———. n.d. *Boletín.* Various years/issues.

Associação Nacional dos Fabricantes de Veículos Automotores (ANFAVEA). 1994. *Anuário Estatístico.* Brazil: ANFAVEA.

*Avance.* 1994. No. 9.

Bailey, John, and Leopoldo Gómez. 1990. "The PRI and Political Liberalization." *Journal of International Affairs* 43, no. 2: 291–312.

Bartolomé, Maria, and Mariana Buceta. 1995. "Nuevas formas de relaciones interfirmas y calificaciones emergentes en el escenario de la reconversión del complejo automotriz argentino." In *Educación, eslabonamientos productivos y formación profesional,* ed. Marta Novick. Buenos Aires, Argentina: Convenio Ministerio de Cultura y Educación, Confederación General de Trabajo.

Basurto, Jorge. 1983. *En el régimen de Echeverría, rebelión e independencia.* México, DF: Siglo Veintiuno Editores.

Bennett, Douglas C., and Kenneth E. Sharpe. 1979. "Agenda Setting and Bargaining Power: The Mexican State versus Transnational Automobile Corporations." *World Politics* 32, no. 1: 57–89.

———. 1985. *Transnational Corporations versus the State: The Political Economy of the Mexican Auto Industry.* Princeton: Princeton University Press.

Bensusán Areous, Graciela. 1994. "The Mexican Model of Labor Regulation and Competitive Strategies." In Cook and Katz 1994, 52–66.

Bensusán, Graciela, and Carlos García. 1993. "Entre la estabilidad y el conflicto: Relaciones laborales en Volkswagen de México." In Arteaga 1993a, 211–253.

Berry, Steven, Vittorio Grilli, and Florencio López de Silanes. 1992. "The Automobile Industry and the Mexico-US Free Trade Agreement." Working Paper No. 4152. Cambridge, MA: National Bureau of Economic Research.

Bizberg, Ilán. 1990. *Estado y sindicalismo en México.* México: El Colegio de México.

———. 1993. "Modernization and Corporatism in Government–Labour Relations." In *Mexico: Dilemmas of Transition,* ed. Neil Harvey, 299–317. London and New York: University of London and British Academic Press.

*Business Week.* 1997. "Autos: Stuck in First Gear." 3 February: 54 and 56.

Cámara Automotriz de Venezuela (CAVENEZ). n.d. *Informe.* Valencia, Venezuela: CAVENEZ, various issues.

———. 1992. *Memoria y cuenta.* Valencia, Venezuela: CAVENEZ.

Cano, Fabio B. 1990. "La renovación programática de la CTM, 1977–82." In Aguilar García 1990, 579–637.

Carrillo V., Jorge, ed. 1990a. *La nueva era de la industria automotriz en México.* Tijuana: El Colegio de la Frontera Norte.

———. 1990b. "Maquilización de la industria automotriz en México: de la industria terminal a la industria de ensamble." In Carrillo V. 1990a, 62–116.

———. 1991. "Restructuring in the Mexican Automobile Industry: Trends and Labor Implications." Working Paper no. 42, Center for Latin American Studies, University of Texas, Austin.

Carrillo V., Jorge, and P. García. 1987. "Etapas industriales y conflictos laborales en la industria automotriz en México." *Estudios Sociológicos* 5, no. 4: 20–45.

Cedrola Spremolla, Gerardo. 1992. "Calidad total como nueva forma de 'management' y sus efectos sobre las relaciones laborales." *Revista Relasur* (Venezuela) no. 3: 95–115.

CIOSL, ORIT, FITIM, and CISL. 1990. "Industria automotriz y nuevas tecnologias." Seminar paper at the CIOSL, ORIT, FITIM, and CISL conference, Saint Louis, MO, November.

Clemente, Lino. 1993. "Evolución y perspectivas de la industria automotriz." Caracas, Venezuela: Ministerio de Fomento, Venezuela.

Cockroft, James D. 1990a. *Mexico: Class Formation, Capital Accumulation and the State.* Revised Edition. New York: Monthly Review Press.

Coleman, Kenneth, and Charles Davis. 1983. "Preemptive Reform and the Mexican Working Class." *Latin American Research Review* 18, no. 1: 3–31.

Collier, Ruth Berins, and David Collier. 1979. "Inducements versus Constraints: Disaggregating Corporatism." *American Political Science Review* 73, no. 4: 967–986.

———. 1991. *Shaping the Political Arena: Critical Junctures, the Labor Movement, and Regime Dynamics in Latin America.* Princeton: Princeton University Press.

Comisión Económica para America Latina y el Caribe, Naciones Unidas (CEPAL). 1987. *Reestructuración de la industria automotriz mundial y perspectivas para America Latina.* Santiago, Chile: United Nations, Economic Commission on Latin America and the Caribbean.

———. 1992. *Reestructuración y desarrollo de la industria automotriz mexicana en los años ochenta.* Santiago, Chile: United Nations, Economic Commission on Latin America and the Caribbean.

———. 1995. *La inversión extranjera en América Latina y el Caribe, Informe 1995.* Santiago, Chile: United Nations, Economic Commission on Latin America and the Caribbean.

———. n.d. "Código de productos acabados." Programa Estadísticas Industriales, Documento Técnico no. 4. Santiago, Chile: United Nations, Economic Commission on Latin America and the Caribbean.

———. n.d. *Informes Estadísticos.* Series M, No. 4, (CIIU). Santiago, Chile: United Nations, Economic Commission on Latin America and the Caribbean.

Comisión Económica para America Latina y el Caribe, Naciones Unidas (CEPAL), and CIID. 1994. *Reconversión industrial y cambio estratégico en el bloque automotriz argentino, 1980–1993.* Santiago, Chile: United Nations, Economic Commission on Latin America and the Caribbean.

Comité de Observadores Independientes. 1991. *Ford Motor Company: Recuento 3 junio 1991, Informe resultivo COI.* México, DF: Centro de Derechos Humanos Miguel Agustín Pro Juárez.

Cook, Maria Lorena. 1990. "Restructuring and Democracy in Mexico: Twenty Years of Trade Union Strategies (1970–90)." Paper presented at the XVIth International Congress of the Latin American Studies Association, April 4–6, Washington, DC.

———. 1994. "Regional Integration and Transnational Labor Strategies under NAFTA." In Cook and Katz 1994, 148–55.

Cook, Maria Lorena, and Harry C. Katz, eds. 1994. *Regional Integration and Industrial Relations in North America.* Ithaca, NY: ILR Press, Cornell University.

Cook, Maria Lorena, Kevin J. Middlebrook, and Juan Molinar Horcasitas, eds. 1994. *The Politics of Economic Restructuring: State–Society Relations and Regime Change in Mexico.* San Diego: Center for U.S.-Mexican Studies, UCSD.

Coutinho, Luciano, and João Carlos Ferraz, eds. 1994. *Estudo da competitividade da indústria brasileira.* Campinas, Brazil: Papirus/Editora Unicamp.

Covarrubias, Alex. 1995. "Actitudes obreras y compromiso organizacional en la industria automotriz mexicana: Transformaciones bajo sistemas de producción flexibles." Paper presented to Seminário Internacional de Globalização, Restructuração Productiva e Tranformação nas Relações Capital-Trabalho no Complexo Automobilístico, August 26–28, São Paulo, Brazil.

Covarrubias V., Alejandro, and Vicente Solís Granados, eds. 1993. *Sindicalismo, relaciones laborales y libre comercio.* Hermosillo, México: El Colegio de Sonora, Instituto Sonorese de Cultura, and Centro Nacional de Promoción Social, A.C.

Davis, Charles L. 1994. "Neoliberal Economic Policies and the Potential for Electoral Change in Mexico." *Mexican Studies / Estudios Mexicanos* 10, no. 2: 341–56.

Davis, Charles, and Kenneth Coleman. 1989. "Structural Determinants of Working-Class Politicization: The Role of Independent Unions in Mexico." *Mexican Studies/Estudios Mexicanos* 5, no. 1: 89–112.

de la Garza Toledo, Enrique. 1990. "Reconversión industrial y cambio en el patrón de relaciones laborales en México." In Anguiano 1990a, 315–362.

———. 1991. "Independent Trade Unionism in Mexico: Past Developments and Future Perspectives." In Middlebrook 1991c, 153–184.

———. 1993. "Reestructuración del corporativismo en México: siete tesis." *El Cotidiano* 56 (July): 22–30.

———. 1994. "Los sindicatos en América Latina frente a la reestructuración productiva y los ajustes neoliberales." *El Cotidiano* no. 64 (September–October): 3–15.

de los Ángeles Pozas, María. 1993. *Industrial Restructuring in Mexico: Corporate Adaptation, Technological Innovation, and Changing Patterns of Industrial Relations in Monterrey.* San Diego: Center for U.S.-Mexican Studies, University of California, San Diego.

DESEP-CUT. 1994. *Perfil e opiniões dos delegados ao V CONCUT (Primeiro Relatório).* São Paulo, Brazil: CUT.

Deyo, Frederic C. 1996. "Introduction: Social Reconstructions of the World Automobile Industry." In *Social Reconstructions of the World Automobile Industry,* ed. F.C. Deyo. New York: St. Martin's Press.

*Diario Clarín* (Buenos Aires, Argentina). n.d. Various issues.

DIESSE. 1995a. "The Brazilian Metalworkers and the New Factory Challenge: A Negotiated Change at Mercedes-Benz." Paper presented at the Xth Congress of the Asociación International de Relaciones del Trabajo (AIRT), Washington, DC, May.

———. 1995b. *Indústria automobilística brasileira: Informações gerais.* São Paulo: DIEESE.

Dieter, D. 1995. "The New Mexican Voter." Paper presented to XIXth International Congress of the Latin American Studies Association, Washington, DC, September.

Dombois, Rainer. 1985/86. *La producción automotriz y el mercado del trabajo en un país en desarrollo. Un estudio sobre la industria automotriz mexicana.* Volumes I and II. Berlin, Germany: Wissenschaftzentrum, Berlin Für Sozial for Schung, Paper Nos. IIVG-dp85–206 (Vol. 1), and IIVG-dp86–216 (Vol. 2.).

Dombois, Rainer, and Ludger Pries. 1995. "¿Necesita America Latina su propia sociología del trabajo?" *Revista Latinoamericana Estudios del Trabajo* 1: 97–132.

Domínguez, Jorge, and James McCann. 1995. "Shaping Mexico's Electoral Arena: The

Construction of Partisan Cleavages in the 1988 and 1991 National Elections." *American Political Science Review* 89: 34–48.

Doner, Richard F. 1991. *Driving a Bargain: Automobile Industrialization and Japanese Firms in Southeast Asia.* Berkeley: University of California Press.

Durande Ponte, Victor Manuel. 1991. "The Confederation of Mexican Workers, the Labor Congress and the Crisis of Mexico's Labor Pact." In Middlebrook 1991c, 85–103.

Economic Commission on Latin America and the Caribbean. 1994. *Preliminary Overview of the Economy of Latin America and the Caribbean, 1994.* Santiago, Chile: United Nations, Economic Commission on Latin America and the Caribbean.

*Economia Hoy* (Caracas, Venezuela). n.d. Various issues.

Elger, Tony, and Chris Smith. 1992. "Introduction." In Tony Elger and Chris Smith, eds., *Global Japanization? The Transnational Transformation of the Labour Process,* 1–26. London: Routledge.

Elner, Steve. 1993. *Organized Labor in Venezuela, 1958–1991. Behavior and Concerns in a Democratic Setting.* Washington, DC: SR Books.

*El Espectador* (Bogotá). 1993. "Importados se toman las vias." 4 July: 12A.

*El Financiero* (Mexico City, Mexico), n.d. Various issues.

*El Monitor de la NAFTA y comercio Latinamericano.* 1994. 12 September 1994: 1.

*El Universal* (Caracas, Venezuela). n.d. Various issues.

Esser, Klaus. 1993. "America Latina: Industrialización sin visión." *Nueva Sociedad,* no. 125 (May–June 1993): 27–46.

*Excelsior* (Mexico City, Mexico). n.d. Various issues.

FAVENPA. 1989. "Documento reunión informativa de asociados." Valencia, Venezuela: FAVENPA, June.

———. 1993. "Directorio de empresas venezolanas fabricantes de autopartes." Valencia, Venezuela: FAVENPA.

*FRAGUA* (Venezuela). 1994. No. 183 (March).

Frieden, Jeffry A. 1991. *Debt, Development and Democracy: Modern Political Economy and Latin America, 1965–1985.* Princeton: Princeton University Press.

*Gaceta Oficial de la República de Venezuela.* 1994a. Decreto 3.303, "Normas para el desarrollo de la industria automotriz," no. 35.386, 21 January.

———. 1994b. Decreto 121, "Reforma Parcial del Decreto 3.303," no. 35.456, 9 May.

Garza, María Teresa, and Luis Méndez. 1987a. "El conflicto de la Ford Cuautitlán." *El Cotidiano* 20 (November–December): 384–385.

———. 1987b. "La huelga en Volkswagen." *El Cotidiano* 20 (November-December): 381–383.

———. 1987c. "Respuestas obreras ante los embates del capital: La industria automotriz." *El Cotidiano* 20 (November–December): 374–380.

Gilly, Adolfo. 1990. "El régimen mexicano en su dilema." In Anguiano 1990a, 432–453.

Gómez, Miguel A., and María Teresa Ruiz. 1989. "La democracia proletaria en el sindicalismo insurgente de la zona industria norponiente de la Ciudad de México." In *Democracia y sindicatos,* ed. Victoria Novelo, 165–212. México, DF: Ediciones El Caballito.

Gonçalves Jr., Carlos Augosto, and João Paulo Cândia Veiga. 1995. "A regionalizaçao da indústria automobilística no Mercosul." Paper presented at the XIXth International Congress of the Latin American Studies Association.

González Tiburcio, E., and A. de Alba. 1992. *Ajuste económico y política social en México.* México, DF: El Nacional.

Graham, Laurie. 1992. "How Does the Japanese Model Transfer to the United States? A View from the Line." In Elger and Smith 1992, 123–151.

Grayson, George W. 1989. *The Mexican Labor Machine: Power, Politics and Patronage.* Washington, DC: Center for Strategic and International Studies.

Grebe López, Horst. 1993. "La industrialización latinoamericana ¿Sólo un recuento de frustraciones?" *Nueva Sociedad,* no. 125 (May–June): 47–57.

Greer, Charles. "Trends in the Utilization of Human Resources in U.S. Companies and Their International Implications." Paper presented at the II Congreso Americano de Relaciones de Trabajo, September 1993.

Grupo Sivensa (Venezuela). 1994. *Sivensa Global* vol. 3, no. 20 (July–August).

Guillén López, T. 1989. "The Social Bases of the PRI." In *Mexico's Alternative Political Futures,* eds. Judith Gentleman and Peter Smith, 246–51. San Diego: Center for U.S.-Mexican Studies, UCSD.

Gutiérrez Garza, Esthela, ed. 1989a. *Reconversión industrial y lucha sindical.* Caracas, Venezuela: Editorial Nueva Sociedad.

———. 1989b. "El futuro del sindicalismo en México." In Gutiérrez Garza 1989a, 13–18.

———. 1989c. "La recomposición de la clase obrera y el futuro del mundo laboral." In Gutiérrez Garza 1989a, 21–36.

———, ed. 1990. *La ocupación del futuro: Flexibilización del trabajo y desreglamentación laboral.* Caracas, Venezuela: Editorial Nueva Sociedad.

Guzmán, José. 1993. "Implicaciones del cambio tecnológico y organizacional sobre la fuerza de trabajo en General Motors (Planta Distrito Federal)." In Arteaga 1993a, 111–138.

Hammond, Frances R. 1993. "The Labor Impact of NAFTA." In *Sectoral Labor Effects of North American Free Trade,* ed. R. Fernádez, et al., 175–182. Austin, TX: Lyndon B. Johnson School of Public Affairs, University of Texas.

Hansen, Roger. 1971. *The Politics of Mexican Development.* Baltimore: Johns Hopkins University Press.

Harbour and Associates. 1994. *The Harbour Report 1994.* Flint, MI: Harbour and Associates.

———. 1996. *The Harbour Report 1996.* Flint, MI: Harbour and Associates.

Herrera Lima, Fernando. 1993. "DINA: Del enfrentamiento a la negociación." *El Cotidiano,* no. 56 (July).

Herrera Lima, Fernando Federico, and José Cruz Guzmán Sánchez. 1994. "Monografía sobre relaciones laborales y sindicalismo en la industria automotriz en México." Unpublished manuscript.

Hinojosa-Ojeda, Raúl, and Rebecca Morales. 1992. "International Restructuring and Labor Market Dependence: The Automobile Industry in Mexico and the United States." In *US-Mexico Relations: Labor Market Dependence,* eds. Jorge Bustamante, Clark Reynolds, and Raúl Hinojosa-Ojeda. Stanford: Stanford University Press.

Hoffman, Kurt, and Raphael Kaplinsky. 1988. *Driving Force: The Global Restructuring of Technology, Labour, and Investment in the Automobile and Components Industries.* Boulder, CO: Westview Press.

Humphrey, John. 1982. *Capitalist Control and Worker's Struggle in the Brazilian Auto Industry.* Princeton: Princeton University Press.

———. 1992. "'Japanese' Methods and the Changing Position of Direct Production Workers in Brazil." In Elger and Smith 1992, 327–47.

Hunter, L., J. Markusen, and T. Rutherford. 1992. "U.S.-Mexico Free Trade and the North American Auto Industry." *The World Economy* 15: 65–82.

IESA, CAVENZ, and FAVENPA. 1989. "Demanda de divisas de la industria automotriz." Caracas: IESA-CAVENZ-FAVENPA.

INCE. 1993. *Proceedings of the First Meeting of Workers and Managers of the Venezuelan Automotive Sector.* Caracas, Venezuela: INCE, in cooperation with CAVENZ, CTV, FAVENPA, FETRAMETAL, and FITIM.

Instituto Nacional de Estadística, Geografía e Informática (INEGI). 1990. *La industria automotriz en México (edición 1990)*. Aguascaleintes, México: INEGI.
———. 1992. *La industria automotriz en México (edición 1992)*. Aguascalientes, México: INEGI.
———. 1994. *La industria automotriz en México (edición 1994)*. Aguascalientes, México: INEGI.
———. 1995. *La industria automotriz en México (edición 1995)*. Mexico: INEGI.
International Labor Organization. 1995. "Relaciones de trabajo en Venezuela," Serie Relaciones de Trabajo, no. 79. Geneva: International Labor Organization.
———. n.d. "El trabajo en el mundo," no. 2. Geneva: International Labor Office.
International Metalworkers' Federation. 1995. *North American Integration: A Trade Union Perspective*. Geneva, Switzerland: International Metalworkers' Federation.
——— 1996. *The Purchasing Power of Working Time: An International Comparison, 1994–1995*. Geneva, Switzerland: International Metalworkers' Federation.
Iranzo, C., L. Betencourt, H. Lucena, and F. Sandoval. 1995. *La industria automotriz en Venezuela*. Unpublished study, Venezuela.
Jabbaz, Marcela. 1992. "Gestión social de las innovaciones tecnológicas en la industria argentina de procesos contínuos." Buenos Aires, Argentina: Centro de Estudios e Investigaciones Laborales.
Jauregui, R., ed. 1984. *Hechos y protagonistas de las luchas obreras argentinas*. Buenos Aires, Argentina: Editorial Experiencia.
Jenkins, Rhys. 1977. *Dependent Industrialization in Latin America: The Automotive Industry in Argentina, Chile, and Mexico*. New York: Praeger.
———. 1987. *Transnational Corporations and the Latin American Automobile Industry*. Hampshire, U.K.: Macmillan.
Jessop, Bob. 1990. "Regulation Theories in Retrospect and Prospect." *Economy and Society* 19, no. 2: 153–171.
*La Jornada* (Mexico City, Mexico). n.d. Various issues.
Juárez Núñez, Herberto. 1994. "Productividad en la industria automotriz: El caso de VW de México." *El Cotidiano*, no. 64 (September–October): 65–76.
Kantis, Hugo, and A. Quierolo. 1990. "Bloque metalmecánico y construcción. Reorganización industrial y eslabonamientos productivos en el sector automotriz: De la integración productiva autocentrada a la internacionalizacion pasiva." Programa de Asistencia Técnica para la Gestión del Sector Público Argentino, Proyecto de Análisis Sectorial en Base a las Técnicas de Insumo-Producto, SICE-PNUD-Arg 86-R01.
Katz, Jorge M., and Eduardo R. Albin. 1978. "From Infant Industry to Technology Exports: The Argentine Experience in the International Sale of Industrial Plants and Engineering Works." Buenos Aires, Argentina: United Nations Economic Commission for Latin America and Inter-American Development Bank, Research Programme in Science and Technology, Working Paper No. 14.
Katz, Jorge M., and M. Lengyel. 1991. "Reestructuración industrial e inserción internacional: El caso de la industria automotriz." Unpublished manuscript, Buenos Aires, Argentina.
Klesner, Joseph L. 1994. "Realignment or Dealignment? Consequences of Economic Crisis and Restructuring for the Mexican Party System." In Cook, Middlebrook, and Horcasitas 1994, 159–194.
Kornblith, Miriam. 1994. "La crisis del sistema político venezolano." *Nueva Sociedad*, no. 132 (November–December): 142–157.
Kosacoff, B., J. Todesca, and A. Vispo. 1991. "La transformación de la industria automotriz argentina. Su integración con Brasil." Document No. 40, CEPAL. Buenos Aires, Argentina: CEPAL.

Kronish, R., and K.S. Mericle, eds. 1984a. *The Political Economy of the Latin American Motor Vehicle Industry.* Cambridge: MIT Press.

————. 1984b. "The Latin American Motor Industry, 1900–1980." In Kronish and Mericle 1984a, 261–306.

La Botz, Dan. 1988. *The Crisis of Mexican Labor.* New York: Praeger.

————. 1992. *Mask of Democracy: Labor Suppression in Mexico Today.* Boston: South End Press/International Labor Rights Education and Research Fund.

Laurell, Asa Cristina. 1992. "Democracy in Mexico: Will the First be the Last?" *New Left Review* 194 (July/August): 33–53.

Lee, Naeyoung, and Jeffrey Cason. 1994. "Automobile Commodity Chains in the NICs: A Comparison of South Korea, Mexico, and Brazil." In *Commodity Chains and Global Capitalism,* eds. Gary Gereffi and Miguel Korzeniewicz. Westport, CT: Greenwood Press.

León, Samuel. 1990. "Modernización económica, proyecto político y consenso obrero." In Wilkie and Heroles 1990, 263–274.

Levaggi, Virgilio. 1994. "Las organizaciones empresariales." *RELASUR* (Venezuela), no. 4: 105–119.

Lienert, Paul. 1997. "The Road to Rio." *Automobile* 11, no. 12: 17.

Lima, Roberto Rocha. 1989. "Implementing the 'Just In Time' Production Systems in the Brazilian Car Components Industry." *IDS Bulletin* 20, no. 4: 14–17.

Lipietz, Alain. 1982. "Towards Global Fordism?" *New Left Review* no. 132 (March–April).

————. 1987. *Mirages and Miracles: The Crisis of Global Fordism.* London: Verso Press.

López, Carlos. 1989. "La recalificación de obra sin compensación salarial en General Motors." In Gutiérrez Garza 1989a, 97–100.

Lucena, Héctor. 1992. *Las relaciones laborales en Venezuela.* Caracas: Editorial Centauro, 2nd edition.

Luna, Roberto. 1991. "De obreros a cooperativistas: Los despedidos de la Ford." In *Testimonios de solidaridad 1,* ed. Instituto Nacional de Solidaridad, 17–27. México, DF: SEDESOL.

Martin, Scott B. 1997. "Beyond Corporatism: New Patterns of Representation in the Brazilian Auto Industry." In *The New Politics of Inequality in Latin America,* eds. Douglas A. Chalmers, Scott B. Martin, et al., 45–71. Oxford: Oxford University Press.

Martíns Rodrigues, Leôncio. 1991. *O declinio do sindicalismo corporativo.* Rio de Janeiro, Brazil: IBASE.

Marx, Roberto. 1993. "Quality and Productivity in Small- and Medium-Sized Firms in the Brazilian Automobile Industry." *IDS Bulletin* 24, no. 2: 65–71.

Maxfield, Sylvia. 1989. "National Business, Debt-Led Growth, and Political Transition in Latin America." In *Debt and Democracy in Latin America,* eds. Barbara Stallings and Robert Kaufman, 75–90. Boulder, CO: Westview Press.

Melgoza, Javier. 1993. "Estrategias sindicales, negociación y productividad: La experiencia del Sindicato Mexicano de Electricistas. 1984–1992." Paper presented at the Primer Congreso Latinoamericano de Sociología del Trabajo, Mexico City, November.

Méndez, Luis, and José Antonio Soto. 1990. "La UOI: una experiencia de lucha proletaria." *El Cotidiano* 37 (September–October): 29–35.

Middlebrook, Kevin. 1989a. "Union Democratization in the Mexican Automobile Industry: A Reappraisal." *Latin American Research Review* 24, no. 2: 69–93.

————. 1989b. "The Sounds of Silence: Organised Labour's Response to Economic Crisis in Mexico." *Journal of Latin American Studies* 21, no. 2: 195–220.

————. 1991a. "The Politics of Industrial Restructuring: Transnational Firms' Search for Flexible Production in the Mexican Automobile Industry." *Comparative Politics* 23, no. 3: 275–297.

————. 1991b. "State Structures and the Politics of Union Registration in Postrevolutionary Mexico." *Comparative Politics* 23, no. 4: 459–478.

————, ed. 1991c. *Unions, Workers, and the State in Mexico.* San Diego: Center for U.S.-Mexican Studies, UCSD.

————. 1995. *The Paradox of Revolution: Labor, the State, and Authoritarianism in Mexico.* Baltimore: Johns Hopkins University Press.

Montiel, Yolanda. 1987. *Industria automotriz y automatización: El caso de VW de México.* México: Centro de Investigaciones y Estudios Superiores en Antropología Social. (Cuadernos de la Casa Chata, 144).

————. 1990. "Trabajadores y reestructuración en Volkswagen de México." In Carrillo V. 1990a, 228–255.

————. 1991. *Proceso de trabajo, acción sindical y nuevas tecnologías en Volkswagen de México.* México, DF: Centro de Investigaciones y Estudios Superiores en Antropología Social. (Cuadernos de la Casa Chata, 167).

Moori-Koenig, Virginia, and Gabriel Yoguel. 1992. "Competitividad de las Pymes autopartistas en el nuevo escenario de apertura e integración subregional." Buenos Aires, Argentina: CEPAL, Documento de Trabajo CFI-CEPAL, No. 30.

Morales, R., and Jorge M. Katz. 1995. "Industrial Responses to Liberalization and Increased Competitiveness in the Latin American Automobile Industry." Paper presented to the joint ECLAC, IDRC, INTECH Conference, August.

Moreno, Omar. 1991. *La nueva negociación: La negociación colectiva en la Argentina.* Buenos Aires, Argentina: Fundación Friedrich Ebert.

Moreno Brid, Juan Carlos. 1992. "Structural Change in Mexico's Motor Vehicle Industry, 1977–1989." In *Industry on the Move: Causes and Consequences of International Relocation in the Manufacturing Industry,* ed. G. van Liemt. Geneva, Switzerland: International Labor Office.

Morris, John T. 1994. "Perspectives on Labor Conflict in Mexico." Paper presented at the Annual Meeting of the American Political Science Association, New York, NY, September.

————. 1995. "Industrial Restructuring and Labor Conflict in Mexico: The Automobile Industry in National Perspective." Paper presented at the XIXth International Congress of the Latin American Studies Association, Washington, DC, September.

Mortimore, Michael. 1995. *Transforming Sitting Ducks into Flying Geese: The Mexican Automobile Industry.* Santiago, Chile: United Nations, Division of Production, Productivity, and Management.

Navarrete, Jorge Eduardo. 1990. "Mexico's Stabilization Policy." *CEPAL Review* 41 (August): 31–44.

Navarro Delgado, Eduardo. 1989. "La defensa del reglamento interior del trabajo frente a la ofensiva de los círculos de calidad." In Gutiérrez Garza 1989a, 85–87.

Nelson, Joan. 1992. "Poverty, Equity, and the Politics of Adjustment." In *The Politics of Economic Adjustment: International Constraints, Distributive Conflicts, and the State,* eds. Stephen Haggard and Robert Kaufman, 245–49. Princeton: Princeton University Press.

Nofal, M.B. 1994. "Diagnóstico de competetividad industrial. Sintesis regional. Sector automotriz y autopartes." Project BID-MERCOSUR, June.

*NotiSofsa.* 1989. No. 36 (March): 2–4.

Novick, Marta. 1991. "Nuevas tecnologías de gestión y acción sindical. Los métodos japoneses de producción en la industria argentina." *Estudios del Trabajo* 1, no. 1.

Novick, Marta, Maria Bartolomé, and Maria Buceta. 1995. *Nuevas formas de relaciones interfirmas y calificaciones emergentes en el escenario de la reconversión del complejo automotriz argentino, en educación, eslabonamientos productivos y formación profesional.* Buenos Aires: Convenio, Ministerio de Cultura y Educación, Confederación General del Trabajo.

OCEI (Venezuela). 1993. *Principales indicadores de la industria fabril, 1988–1991.* Venezuela: OCEI, September.

———. n.d. *Encuestas industriales.* Various issues, 1988–1992. Venezuela: OCEI.

Ortiz, Luis. 1996. "Union Response to Teamwork: The Case of Opel Spain." Paper presented at the Fourteenth Annual International Labour Process Conference, Birmingham, UK, March.

Othón Quiroz, José, and Luis Méndez. 1992. "El conflicto de la Volkswagen: Crónica de una muerte inesperada." *El Cotidiano* 51 (November–December): 81–91.

Pacheco Méndez, Guadalupe. 1991. "Los sectores del PRI en las elecciones de 1988." *Mexican Studies/Estudios Mexicanos* 7, no. 2: 253–282.

Palafox, Rogelio. 1989. "La estrategia empresarial en Volkswagen." In Gutiérrez Garza 1989a, 89–95.

Pérez, Carlota. 1989. *Cambio técnico, reestructuración competitiva y reforma institucional en los países en desarrollo.* Discussion Paper No. 4, World Bank, Washington, DC.

*Philadelphia Inquirer.* 1994. "After 8 Months of NAFTA: The Borders Have Blurred." 11 September: D1–2, D7.

Piore, Michael J., and Charles F. Sabel. 1984. *The Second Industrial Divide: Possibilities for Prosperity.* New York: Basic Books.

Ponce, Armando Meza. 1984. *Fábrica y poder, mecanismos de control empresarial: El caso de la ensambladora de automóviles Ford Villa.* México: Centro de Investigaciones y Estudios Superiores en Antropología Social.

Przeworski, Adam. 1985. *Capitalism and Social Democracy.* Cambridge: Cambridge University Press.

———. 1987. "Capitalism, Democracy, Pacts," Unpublished manuscript, Department of Political Science, University of Chicago.

Ramírez, José Carlos. 1993. "Recent Transformations in the Mexican Automobile Industry." *IDS Bulletin* 24, no. 2: 58–64.

Ramírez, José Ernesto. 1994. *Innovaciones en la empresa dinámica de negociación: Conflictos y perspectiva.* Bogotá, Colombia: FESCOL, Debate Sindical, No. 9.

*La República* (Bogotá, Colombia). 1989. "Inversión extranjera a Sofasa por 9.450 millones de pesos." 25 November 1989: 2A.

———. 1990. "En Sofasa-Renault reportaron perdidas por $3.137 millones." 31 March: 1A–2A.

Rinehart, James, David Robertson, Christopher Huxley, and Jeff Wareham. 1992. "Reunifying Conception and Execution of Work under Japanese Production Management? A Canadian Case Study." In Elger and Smith 1992, 152–75.

Rodrigues, Iram Jácome. 1993. *Trabalhadores, sindicalismo e democracia: A trajetória da CUT.* Unpublished Ph.D. thesis, Department of Sociology, Universidade de São Paulo.

Rodríguez L., Javier. 1993. "Transformación productiva y relaciones laborales en Nissan Mexicana." In Arteaga 1993a, 57–111.

Rojas, Eduardo. 1993. "La relación ciencia-sindicatos. Temas prácticos, técnicos y críticos." *Nueva Sociedad,* no. 124 (March–April): 146–157.

Roxborough, Ian. 1981. "The Analysis of Labour Movements in Latin America: Typologies and Theories." *Bulletin of Latin American Research* 1, no. 1: 81–95.

———. 1984. *Unions and Politics in Mexico: The Case of the Automobile Industry.* New York: Cambridge University Press.

———. 1992. "Inflation and Social Pacts in Brazil and Mexico." *Journal of Latin American Studies* 24, no. 3: 639–664.

Roxborough, Ian, and Ilán Bizberg. 1983. "Union Locals in Mexico: The 'New Unionism' in Steel and Automobiles." *Journal of Latin American Studies* 15, no. 1: 117–135.

Roxborough, Ian, and Mark Thompson. 1982. "Union Elections and Democracy in Mexico: A Comparative Perspective." *British Journal of Industrial Relations* 20, no. 2: 201–217.

Ruigkrok, W., R. Van Tulder, and G. Baven. 1991. "Cars and Complexes: Globalisation versus Global Localization in the World Car Industry." Brussels: Monitor-Fast Programme.

Russell, James W. 1993. "Free Trade and Economic Displacement in Mexico." In *Sectoral Labor Effects of North American Free Trade,* ed. R. Fernández, et al., 43–50. Austin, TX: Lyndon B. Johnson School of Public Affairs, University of Texas, Austin.

Sáenz, José Enrique. 1986. "Biografía de un sindicato: El caso de Sintrasofa." Graduation Project submitted to School of Economics, Universidad Nacional, Bogotá, Colombia.

Samstad, James G., and Ruth Berins Collier. 1995. "Mexican Labor and Structural Reform: New Unionism or Old Stalemate?" In *The Challenges of Institutional Reform in Mexico,* ed. Riordan Roett, 1–31. New York: Lynne Rienner.

Sánchez, Rómulo. 1993. "Industria Automotriz." Caracas, Venezuela: Ediciones IESA, Documento de base no. 9, Proyecto Competitivo.

Sandoval, Sergio A. 1990. "Conflictos laborales y relaciones capital–trabajo en la Ford de Hermosillo 1986–1989." *Revista Estudios Sociales* 1, no. 1: 123–150.

Sandoval Godoy, Sergio A., and Cristina Taddei Bringas. 1993. "Límites en la implementación del modelo japonés de organización del trabajo. Los casos de la Ford y las maquiladoras japonesas." In Covarrubias V. and Solís 1993, 126–134.

Scheinman, M. 1993. "Corporate Strategy, Globalization, and NAFTA: Mexico's New Role." In *Driving Continentally: National Policies and the North American Auto Industry,* ed. M.A. Molot. Ottawa: Carleton University Press.

Secretaría de Hacienda y Crédito Público. 1992. *El proceso de enajenación de entidades paraestatales.* México, DF: SHCP.

———. 1993. *Mexico: A New Economic Profile.* Mexico, DF: SHCP.

Secretaría del Trabajo y Previsión Social (STPS). 1995. *Encuesta nacional de empleo, salarios, tecnología, y capacitación en el sector manufacturero, 1992.* México, DF: Secretaría del Trabajo y Previsión Social.

———. n.d. *Prontuario Laboral.* Various issues, 1985–1989. México, DF: Secretaría del Trabajo y Previsión Social.

———. n.d. *Estadísticas Laborales.* Various issues, 1991–1994. México, DF: Secretaría del Trabajo y Previsión Social.

Secretaría del Trabajo y Previsión Social (STPS), Dirección General de Registro de Asociaciones. 1993. *Directorio de secretarios generales de organizaciones obreras, 2a edición.* México, DF: Secretaría del Trabajo y Previsió Social, Subsecretaría "A."

Sengenberger, Werner. 1992. "Intensificación de la competencia, reestructuración industrial y relaciones de trabajo." *Revista Internacional del Trabajo* 111, no. 3: 221–289.

Shaiken, Harley. 1990. *Mexico in the Global Economy: High Technology and Work Organization in Export Industries.* San Diego: Center for U.S.-Mexican Studies, UCSD.

———. 1991. "The 'Universal Motors' Assembly and Stamping Plant: Transferring High-Tech Production to Mexico." *Columbia Journal of World Business* 26, no. 2: 125–137.

———. 1994. "Advanced Manufacturing and Mexico: A New International Division of Labor?" *Latin American Research Review* 29, no. 2: 39–71.

———. 1995. "Technology and Work Organization in Latin American Motor Vehicle

Industries," Santiago, Chile: Economic Commission for Latin America and the Caribbean.

Shaiken, Harley, and Harry Browne. 1991. "Japanese Work Organization in Mexico." In Székely 1991a, 25–50.

Shaiken, Harley, and Stephen Herzenberg. 1987. *Automation and Global Production: Automobile Engine Production in Mexico, the United States and Canada.* San Diego: Center for U.S.-Mexican Studies, UCSD.

Shaiken, Harley, Stephen Herzenberg, and Sarah Kuhn. 1986. "The Work Process under More Flexible Production." *Industrial Relations* 25, no. 2: 167–183.

Shapiro, Helen. 1991. "Determinants of Firm Entry in the Brazilian Automobile Manufacturing Industry, 1956–1968." *Business History Review* 65, no. 4: 876–947.

———. 1994. *Engines of Growth: The State and Transnational Auto Companies in Brazil.* Cambridge: Cambridge University Press.

———. 1996. "The Mechanics of Brazil's Auto Industry." *NACLA Report on the Americas* 29, no. 4: 28–33.

Sindicato dos Metalúrgicos de São Bernardo do Campo e Diadema. 1992. *Reestruturação do complexo automotivo brasileiro.* Unpublished Report, Brazil, March.

Sindicato de Obreros y Empleados de la Planta de Montaje de la General Motors de México, S.A. 1990. *Estatutos.* México, DF: CROC.

Sindicato de Trabajadores de Ford Motor Company-C.T.M. 1977. *Estatutos.* México, DF: SITRAFORD.

SMATA (Argentina) 1992/93. *Memoria y balance.* Unpublished records.

Spalding, Hobart. 1977. *Organized Labor in Latin America.* New York: New York University Press.

Spangeneberg, Ricardo. 1995. "La conflictividad sindical." Thesis, Universidad de Buenos Aires, Argentina.

Spyropoulos, George. 1994. "El sindicalismo frente a la crisis: Situación actual y perspectivas futuras." *RELASUR* (Venezuela), no. 4: 81–104.

Storper, Michael, and Richard Walker. 1989. *The Capitalist Imperative: Territory, Technology and Industrial Growth.* Oxford: Basil Blackwell.

Székely, Gabriel, ed. 1991a. *Manufacturing across Borders and Oceans: Japan, the United States, and Mexico.* San Diego: Center for U.S.-Mexican Studies, UCSD.

———. 1991b. "In Search of Globalization: Japanese Manufacturing in Mexico and the United States." In Székely 1991a, 1–25.

Tagliabue, John. 1997. "New Economics of Economy Cars." *New York Times,* 25 January: D1, D20.

Talavera, Fernando, and Francisco Muñoz. 1991. *El movimiento democrático de los trabajadores de la Ford (1987–1991).* México, DF: Taller de Economía del Trabajo (TADET), UNAM.

*El Tiempo* (Bogotá). 1993. "Sofasa dice que no habrá paro laboral," 13 November: 3B.

Trejo Delarbre, Raúl. 1990. *Crónica del sindicalismo en México (1976–1988).* México, DF: Siglo Veintiuno Editores.

Tuman, John. 1994a. "Organized Labor under Military Rule: The Nigerian Labor Movement, 1985–1992." *Studies in Comparative International Development* 29, no. 3: 26–44.

———. 1994b. "The Politics of Labor Quiescence and Confrontation in the Mexican Automobile Industry, 1980–1992." Unpublished Ph.D. thesis, Department of Political Science, University of California, Los Angeles.

———. 1996a. "Unions and Restructuring in the Mexican Automobile Industry: A Comparative Assessment." *Industrial Relations Journal* 27, no. 4: 317–30.

———. 1996b. "Japanese Transplants, the Mexican State, and Industrial Transformation(s): The Case of Nissan Mexicana." Paper presented at the Fourteenth Annual International Labour Process Conference, Birmingham, UK, March.

———. 1996c. "Corporatism, Government Labor Policy, and Wage Bargaining in Contemporary Mexico: A Reappraisal." Paper presented at the Annual Meeting of the American Political Science Association, San Francisco, CA, September.

———. 1997. "Explaining Union Responses to Privatization: Organized Labor in the Mexican and Argentine Telecommunications Sectors." Working Paper, Department of Political Science, Texas Tech University.

Tuman, John, and Gregory Greenway. 1997. "Recons..ucting State–Labor Relations in Contemporary Mexico: Foundations and Implications of a New Bargain." Paper presented at the Annual Meeting of the American Political Science Association, Washington, DC, August.

*Unomásuno* (Mexico City, Mexico). n.d. Various issues.

Van Liemt, Gijsbert. 1993. "La mundialización de la economía: Posibilidades al alcance de los trabajadores y estrategias de empresas en los países de costos laborales altos." *Revista Internacional del Trabajo* 112, no. 1: 55–74.

Veneconsultores. 1995. "Una política industrial para el Estado Carabobo." Carabobo, Venezuela: Veneconsultores, March.

Viana, H. Avalos I., A. Balaguer, M.A. Cervilla, and C. Suárez. 1993. "Estudio de la capacidad tecnológica de la industria manufacturera venezolana." Valencia, Venezuela: Editorial Iesa, Centro de Producción e Innovación Tecnológica, July.

von Bülow, Marisa. 1995. "Reestructuración productiva y respuestas sindicales: El caso de la Ford Motor Company." Paper presented at the XIXth International Congress of the Latin American Studies Association, Washington, DC, September.

Ward's Communications. 1994. *Ward's Automotive Yearbook, 56th Edition*. New York: Ward's Communications.

Wehmhorner, Arnold. 1993. "Rasgos estructurales y tendencias regionales de los sindicatos asiáticos." *Nueva Sociedad,* no. 124 (March–April): 158–167.

Weiss, Dimitri. 1992. "La nueva gerencia." *Revista Personal* (Buenos Aires), no. 37.

Wilkie, James W., and Jesús Reyes Heroles G.G., eds. 1990. *Industria y trabajo en México*. México, DF: UNAM.

Williams, Edward, and John T. Passé-Smith. 1992. *The Unionization of the Maquiladora Industry: The Tamaulipan Case in National Context*. San Diego: Institute for Regional Study of the Californias, San Diego State University.

Womack, James P., Daniel T. Jones, and Daniel Roos. 1990. *The Machine that Changed the World: The Story of Lean Production*. New York: Harper Perennial.

Zapata, Francisco. 1986. *El conflicto sindical en América Latina*. México, DF: El Colegio de México.

———. 1990. "Towards a Latin American Sociology of Labor." *Journal of Latin American Studies* 22, no. 2: 375–402.

———. 1992. "Social Concertation in Mexico." In *Participation in Public Policy Making: The Role of Trade Unions and Employers' Associations,* ed. Tiziano Treu, 146–58. New York and Berlin: Walter de Gruyter.

———. 1995. *El sindicalismo mexicano frente a la reestructuración*. México, DF: El Colegio de México.

———. 1996. "Labor Relations, Economic Development and Democracy in the 21st Century." *Industrial Relations Journal* 27, no. 1: 65–73.

Zazueta, César, and Ricardo de la Peña. 1984. *La estructura del Congreso del Trabajo: Estado, trabajo y capital en México*. México, D.F.: Fondo de Cultura Económica.

# About the Editors and Contributors

**Glauco Arbix** is Professor of Political Science, University of Campinas (Brazil), and researcher with the Engineering Production Department, Polytechnical School of the University of São Paulo, Brazil.

**Mauricio Cárdenas P.** is Director of the Organization Studies Area in the School of Business at the Universidad de los Andes, Bogotá, Colombia.

**Ana María Catalano** is Adjunct Professor of Sociology and Labor Relations at the Universidad de Buenos Aires, Buenos Aires, Argentina.

**Héctor Lucena** is Profesor Titular in the Escuela de Relaciones Industriales, Universidad de Carabobo, Carabobo, Venezuela.

**John T. Morris** earned his Ph.D. in Government from the University of Texas at Austin in 1994. His research focuses on the politics of economic restructuring and labor relations in Latin America.

**Marta S. Novick** is Profesora Titular in Sociología del Trabajo, Facultad de Ciencias Sociales, Universidad de Buenos Aires, Buenos Aires, Argentina.

**Iram Jácome Rodrigues** is Professor of Economics, University of São Paulo, Brazil.

**John P. Tuman** is Assistant Professor of Political Science, Texas Tech University, Lubbock, Texas.

# Index

## I

Imports. *See* Trade
Import-substitution industrialization
    (ISI), 5, 6–8, 24*n.2,* 115–116, 128,
    154, 155
International Metalworkers' Federation,
    17
Italy, 125, 126, 127, 141

## J

Japanese automobile industry
    automation in, 38
    production in, 124, 125, 126, 127
    wages in, 17, 141
Jenkins, Rhys, 5, 6, 7, 155
Jessop, Bob, 7
Job rotation, 15
Job training, 145
Just-in-time (JIT) production, 8, 19,
    23*n.1,* 39, 74*n.16,* 108

## K

Kantis, Hugo, 34, 36
Katz, Jorge M., 31, 32, 35, 37, 38
Kosacoff, B., 31
Kronish, R., 5, 7

## L

Labor force
    in Argentina, 26, 28, 31, 34, 35, 45
    in Brazil, 77, 80, 81
    in Colombia, 98–99
    in Mexico, 142
    in Venezuela, 182–184
Labor productivity
    in Argentina, 41–42, 71
        collective bargaining agreements
            and, 63–64
        evaluating, 65–67, 69
    in Mexico, 142–143, 171
    in Venezuela, 185
    wages and, 75*n.29,* 170–171
Labor unions, 4, 15–16
    in Argentina, 19, 23, 46–69
        collective agreements of, 40, 51,
            53–54, 60–69, 72
        conflict levels of, 56–60

Labor unions *(continued)*
        development of, 46–47
        Fordist system, 29–30, 32–33
        strategies of, 47–56, 72
    in Brazil
        and flexibilization, 90–91, 92
        and negotiated restructuring, 81–87,
            89, 91–92
        new unionism movement, 79–80
        obstacles to negotiation, 93
        plant-level, 19–20, 85–86, 93*n.3*
        political reaction against
            concertation, 88–90
        state role in, 90
        in tripartite organization, 20, 78
    in Colombia, 20, 95–96
        collective agreements of, 96, 97,
            107–108
        conflict relations of, 98–100,
            101–105
        development of, 96–98
        hunger strike of, 103–104
        restructuring response of, 95,
            109–110
        strikes of, 96–97, 99, 100, 101, 102,
            104
    in Fordist systems, 7, 29–30, 32–33, 90
    in Mexico
        collective agreements of, 139, 144,
            145, 163, 175–176*n.25*
        conflict relations of, 144–145
        democratization movements in, 21,
            153, 155–159
        official organizations, 115, 150, 151
        PRI and, 150, 151–152, 173–174*n.13*
        restructuring response of, 21, 23,
            149–150, 152, 159–171, 175*n.24*
        state controls over, 151
        strikes of, 150, 155, 159–161,
            175*n.21*
    state-corporatist, 7, 19, 22, 23, 24*n.3,*
        151–153, 187
    in Venezuela, 22
        accommodation of, 196–199
        in assembly plants, 189–190
        in auto parts plants, 190–191
        collective bargaining of, 189,
            191–196
        confederations of, 186–187
        development of, 185–186
        membership in, 188–189